EXILED HOME

GLOBAL INSECURITIES

A series edited by Catherine Besteman and Daniel M. Goldstein

EXILED HOME

SALVADORAN
TRANSNATIONAL
YOUTH *in the*
AFTERMATH *of*
VIOLENCE

SUSAN BIBLER COUTIN

Duke University Press   Durham and London   2016

Library of Congress Cataloging-in-Publication Data
Names: Coutin, Susan Bibler, author.
Title: Exiled home : Salvadoran transnational youth in the
aftermath of violence / Susan Bibler Coutin.
Other titles: Global insecurities.
Description: Durham : Duke University Press, 2016.
Series: Global insecurities | Includes bibliographical references
and index.
Identifiers: LCCN 2015040909|
ISBN 9780822361442 (hardcover : alk. paper) |
ISBN 9780822361633 (pbk. : alk. paper) |
ISBN 9780822374176 (e-book)
Subjects: LCSH: Salvadorans—United States. | Salvadoran
Americans—United States. | United States—Emigration and
immigration. | El Salvador—Emigration and immigration.
| Salvadorans—Legal status, laws, etc.—United States. |
Refugees—United States. | Unaccompanied immigrant
children—United States.
Classification: LCC E184.S15 c688 2016 | DDC
973/.004687284—dc23
LC record available at http://lccn.loc.gov/2015040909

Cover art: "Cementerio de zapatos," homenaje a Mons.
Romero, de la serie *Mis pies son mis alas*, de Walterio Iraheta.
("Cemetery of Shoes," an homage to Archbishop Romero,
from the series *My Feet Are My Wings*, by Walterio Iraheta.)

— to Casey

CONTENTS

ACKNOWLEDGMENTS

My deepest debt of gratitude is to the many individuals who agreed to participate in interviews but who remain nameless here for reasons of confidentiality. I feel extremely privileged, inspired, and humbled to have had the opportunity to speak with all of you, to document some key moments in your lives, and to reflect with you on the significance of U.S. and Salvadoran immigration policies and histories. I have been changed as a result, and I now view the world differently. I hope that this book in some way does justice to the many accounts that were entrusted to me and that it serves to re/member.

I am also indebted to the many individuals and organizations that facilitated the research for this book by inviting me to events, referring me to others, allowing me to make announcements about the project, and brainstorming with me. I thank Henry Aguilar, Jesus Aguilar, Kay Andrade-Eekhoff, Tony Azúcar, Beth Baker-Cristales, Norma Chinchilla, Grace Delgado, Ester Hernández, Luis Perdomo, Alex Sanchez, Daniel Sharp, Samuel Uribe, and Kristine Zentgraf for their help. I am also grateful to the Central American Resource Center (CARECEN), Los Angeles; CARECEN Internacional in San Salvador; the Centro de Intercambio y Solidaridad, El Salvador; El Rescate, Los Angeles; and Homies Unidos, El Salvador, for their assistance. In particular, I could not have done interviews with individuals who had been deported to El Salvador were it not for the incredibly valuable assistance of Luis Perdomo, to whom I owe a tremendous debt. There are other individuals who also assisted but who are not named here for reasons of confidentiality: I am extremely grateful to you as well.

This material is based on work supported by the National Science Foundation under Grant No. #SES-0518011. Any opinions, findings, and conclusions or recommendations expressed in this material are those of the author and do not necessarily reflect the views of the National Science Foundation.

I thank William Flores for sharing his copy of the script to *De la locura a la esperanza* and for permission to reproduce his photo of actress Rocio Enriquez performing in the play; Carlos Henriquez Consalvi for permission to reproduce a photo from the collection held by the Museo de la Palabra y la Imagen; Beatriz Cortez for permission to reproduce one of the stills from *Pasaje Los Ángeles* and for her corrections to my description of the commemoration of the 1992 peace accords; Maya Chinchilla for permission to reprint the poem "Central American-American"; and GusTavo Adolfo Guerra Vásquez for permission to reprint the poem "hybrideities/hibrideidades."

I had the benefit of numerous graduate student research assistants, who lent their expertise to the project, including Joshua Clark, Katie Dingeman-Cerda, Véronique Fortin, Danny Gascon, Tim Goddard, Glenn Trager, and Sylvia Valenzuela. I am fortunate to have worked with such skilled, sensitive, and smart assistants.

I also am grateful to the members of the 2015 University of California, Irvine (UCI) "Ethnography Lab Group"—Alyse Bertenthal, Josh Clark, Véronique Fortin, Justin Perez, and Daina Sanchez—for stimulating conversations and moral support.

Some of the material in this book draws on ideas and material presented in earlier publications and has been substantially revised here. Portions of chapter 1 draw on sections of my 2013 paper, "In the Breach: Citizenship and Its Approximations," published in the *Indiana Journal of Global Legal Studies* 20(1): 109–140. My analysis of deportation, presented in chapter 4, was worked out in several of my earlier publications, including "Deportation Studies: Origins, Themes, and Directions," which appeared in 2014 in *Journal of Ethnic and Migration Studies* 41(4): 671–681; "Place and Presence within Salvadoran Deportees' Narratives of Removal," published in 2013 in *Childhood* 20(3): 323–336; "Falling Outside: Excavating the History of Central American Asylum Seekers," published in 2011 in *Law and Social Inquiry* 36(3): 569–596; and "Confined Within: National Territories as Zones of Confinement," which appeared in 2010 in *Political Geography* 29(4): 200–208. Some of the ideas that inform chapter 5 were first developed in "Re/Membering the Nation," which appeared in 2011 in *Anthropological Quarterly* 84(4): 809–834.

This book manuscript has been long in the making and has benefited from conversations with and comments by numerous colleagues, including Leisy Abrego, Allison Alexy, Kay Andrade-Eekhoff, Sameer Ashar, Beth Baker-Cristales, Ulla Berg, Victoria Bernal, Jacqueline Bhabha, Tom Boellstorff, Sergio Bran, Don Brenneis, Noelle Brigden, Kitty Calavita, John Campbell, Jennifer Chacón, Leo Chavez, Maya Chinchilla, Norma Chinchilla, Michael Collyer, Marianne Constable, Maria Lorena Cook, Beatriz Cortez, Catherine Dauvergne, Alexandra Délano, Robin DeLugan, Katie Dingeman-Cerda, Heike Drotbohm, Ingrid Eagly, Antje Ellerman, Julia Elychar, David Engel, Mario Escobar, Allison Fish, Danny Gascon, Ilana Gershon, Ruth Gomberg-Muñoz, Roberto Gonzales, Carol Greenhouse, Dirk Hartog, Ines Hasselberg, Ester Hernandez, Josiah Heyman, Nancy Hiemstra, Alexandra Innes, Carolina Kobelinsky, Louise Lamphere, Stephen Lee, Hester Lessard, Randy Lippert, Cecelia Lynch, Mona Lynch, Dora Magaña, Cetta Mainwaring, Chowra Makaremi, Lynn Mather, Bill Maurer, Connie McGuire, Cecilia Menjívar, Julie Mitchell, Michael Montoya, Ellen Moodie, Hiroshi Motomura, Alison Mountz, Michael Musheno, Benjamin Nienass, Karina Oliva Alvarado, Rachel O'Toole, David Pedersen, Héctor Perla, Nathalie Peutz, Keramet Reiter, Justin Richland, Gaspar Rivera-Salgado, Horacio Roque Ramirez, Ana Patricia Rodríguez, Rubén Rumbaut, Kim Scheppele, Daniel Sharp, Jonathan Simon, Rachel Stryker, Susan Terrio, Monica Varsanyi, Erica Vogel, Wendy Vogt, Leti Volpp, Roger Waldinger, William Walters, Joe Wiltberger, Peter Wissoker, Barbara Yngvesson, and Elana Zilberg. This list is necessarily incomplete, as I have been fortunate to participate in a rich, intellectual environment, in which stimulating conversations and exchanges abound. Thank you to everyone, not only those listed here but others who would be named if somehow this rich, intellectual environment could materialize within these acknowledgments. I especially thank two key segments of this environment: my UCI colleagues in the departments of Criminology, Law and Society, and Anthropology.

Earlier versions of portions of this manuscript were presented at meetings of the American Association of Law Schools, American Anthropological Association, American Ethnological Society, American Sociological Association's Historical/Comparative mini-conference, International Studies Association, Law and Society Association, Society for Cultural Anthropology, and Western Society of Criminology; and at Arizona State University; California State

University, Los Angeles; California State University, Northridge; UCLA; the Center for the Study of Law and Society and the Townsend Center at the University of California, Berkeley; the International Center for Migration, Ethnicity, and Citizenship at the New School, New York; the International Institute for the Sociology of Law; Northwestern University; Ohio State University; Radcliffe Institute for Advanced Study, Harvard University; Princeton University; School of Oriental and African Studies at the University of London; the University of British Columbia; UCI; the University of California, San Diego; and the University of Colorado, Boulder. I am grateful to the conference and panel organizers for giving me these opportunities and to all of the discussants and audience members for their comments and questions.

I also would like to thank Alyse Bertenthal, Michelle Lipinski, Alison Mountz, and Caitlin Patler for providing written comments on portions of the manuscript, and Keramet Reiter for reading and commenting on the entire manuscript before I sent it out for review. I am also grateful to the anonymous reviewers, and especially Daniel Goldstein, Catherine Besteman, Don Brenneis, and Susan Terrio. Of course, any remaining errors are my own.

I wrote this book while serving as associate dean for academic affairs of the Graduate Division at UCI, so I also would like to thank the Graduate Division dean, Frances Leslie, for providing a model of how to continue to do research while also doing administrative work. I thank her as well for granting me an administrative leave in the final stretch of writing. My colleagues in the Graduate Division have also been an inspiration.

I am honored to have my book appear in the Global Insecurities series edited by Daniel Goldstein and Catherine Besteman, and I thank them both for their interest in my work. It has been a pleasure to work with Gisela Fosado at Duke University Press. I am grateful to her for believing in the project and for her editorial support and guidance. I also appreciate the work of her assistant, Lydia Rose Rappoport-Hankins, and of all of the Duke University Press staff that are helping the book come to fruition.

Several friends and colleagues have been a source of moral support throughout the writing process. Lynn Mather and Tom Boellstorff provided publishing advice. Barbara Yngvesson is always a source of inspiration and my work has been in dialogue with hers for many years. Véronique Fortin became an ethnographic collaborator, which created countless opportunities for conversation about writing and research. Cecelia Lynch listened to me talk through dilemmas. Victoria Bernal was always a sounding board for ideas. Julie Mitchell and I traveled to new places. Jennifer Chacón let me audit her immigration law course. The Central American Resource Center in Los Angeles became a home-away-from-home for me during the years that I was writing, and the CARECEN legal staff deepened my understanding of immigration law.

Lastly, I am grateful to my family. My parents first taught me how to write, and they have always believed in me. My husband accompanied me throughout this journey. My children keep me sane and remind me to walk away from the computer (though now, I have to tell them the same thing!). I thank my son Jordy for letting me write about his experience at the commemoration of the Salvadoran peace accords. I was pregnant with my son Casey when I did the first interview for this project, so he was with me in more ways than one throughout. This book is dedicated to him.

INTRODUCTION

MARCH 19, 1987. On the front lawn of a church in Santa Rosa, California, several dozen people — including me — gathered to welcome the Northwest Coast section of a national caravan of Central American refugees and solidarity workers. The refugees were undocumented immigrants who were at risk of being deported from the United States to face violence in their home countries and, by traveling with them, the solidarity workers sought to provide a measure of protection. The refugees were undocumented because they were part of a mass displacement of civilians that had been generated by civil wars between left-leaning insurgents and right-wing governments in El Salvador and Guatemala. Victims who fled to the United States were rarely able to get visas to enter legally and so were undocumented. Although they could apply for asylum after they came to the United States, such petitions were generally denied due to U.S. military and economic support for the very governments the refugees had fled. So, to raise public consciousness about the violence being perpetrated in Central America, U.S. involvement in that violence, and Central Americans' need for refuge, Central American and U.S. solidarity workers had resorted to such tactics as organizing caravans and establishing sanctuaries for Central American asylum seekers. Participants in such activities ran legal risks. Undocumented Central Americans could be detected and deported, while U.S. citizens could be prosecuted on migrant-smuggling charges, as had occurred the previous year in Tucson, Arizona. Nonetheless, the mood that March day was defiant. As the caravan arrived, honking loudly, its hosts clapped and chanted, "Stop the war in El Salvador!"

A doctoral student in anthropology at Stanford University, I had come to join the caravan on its last leg, as it returned to San Francisco after having departed almost a month earlier. I was doing dissertation research regarding the U.S. sanctuary movement, a grass-roots network of congregations that had declared themselves "sanctuaries" for Salvadoran and Guatemalan refugees. I had chosen this research topic because of both my academic interests in social change and my own commitment to human rights. I had come that day to understand and document the caravan's efforts to overcome divisions between those directly affected by wartime violence and those living in U.S. communities seemingly distant from the conflict. I also was available to assist by translating at events.

After caravan participants and hosts filed into the church, one of the Central Americans presented a *testimonio*, or "testimony," a firsthand account of persecution and violence, "in which speaking subjects who present themselves as somehow 'ordinary' represent a personal experience of injustice ... with the goal of inducing readers [or listeners] to participate in a project of social justice" (Nance 2006:7; see also Padilla 2012). Speaking in Spanish, a Salvadoran caravan participant told a harrowing story. He had been in his ninth-grade classroom when the Salvadoran army entered his school and took away five of his classmates. He stopped going to school and moved to the countryside for greater safety. When three of his uncles were killed, he decided to leave El Salvador. Despite the life-threatening situation he faced in El Salvador, he was deported several times by U.S. officials. After his mother and siblings received death threats, he also took the risk of making one return trip to El Salvador of his own volition, to help them escape to the United States. The speaker concluded by emphasizing the importance of ending U.S. military aid to El Salvador.

Though the *caravanistas* dispersed, first to sleep in the homes of local hosts and then to continue on to their next destination, the *testimonio* that was recounted at this reception lingered. Across time and space, this testimony invoked young students who had been abducted, uncles who had been assassinated, the terror of death threats, and the urgency of the young man who spoke. His words posed a challenge: Would social justice be achieved in Central America? Would the violence that led him and others to leave El Salvador be acknowledged? And would those affected by civil war and human rights violations be able to secure refuge in the United States? These questions are still with us today.

Re/membering and Dismemberment

The political and legal dynamics that shaped the caravan that long-ago March day also affected a generation, as Salvadorans who fled the devastation of the 1980–1992 Salvadoran civil war faced legal and other challenges in the United States. During the 1980s, Salvadorans who entered the United States were regarded by U.S. officials as economic migrants, despite the war in their homeland. By the 1990s, a decade of advocacy resulted in legal remedies for these asylum seekers, yet the 1992 peace accords jeopardized their abilities to qualify for these remedies. Many were not able to obtain residency until the early 2000s, while others remained undocumented or had only temporary status. For young people, who immigrated to the United States as children and grew up there, the circumstances were particularly stark. Those who were able to become U.S. citizens resolved their immigration situation but often were left with questions about the civil war, the relationship between national events and their family's history, and their places in both the United States and El Salvador. Those who were noncitizens remained vulnerable to deportation, as even lawful permanent residents could be removed if convicted of crimes. And those who were undocumented or had only temporary legal status faced uncertain futures in the United States and often had only dim memories of El Salvador, their country of legal citizenship. This book examines the experiences of such young people, focusing on the power and limitation of the nation-based categories of membership that they encountered, embraced, or rejected. In particular, I explore young people's efforts to *re/member*, that is, to negotiate their *membership* within the United States and El Salvador, while also deepening *memory* of Salvadoran social history, political violence, and immigrant experiences. Public accounts of individual life histories, such as the testimony recounted during the 1987 caravan described above, were key to such forms of re/membering as individuals experienced being exiled, whether physically, legally, or socially, from the multiple homes they had occupied.

Re/membering is made necessary by the *dismemberment* associated with civil war, displacement, emigration, the denial of legal status, and removal. By deploying the term *dismemberment*, I bring together two meanings of *dismember*: (1) not remembering or erasing, and (2) the breaking apart of bodies, polities, and nations. Dismembering thus refers to the separation of persons from history, the literal injury or destruction of bodies,[1] the embodied nature of structural violence (Farmer 1996), and the denial of membership, either by forcing people to flee their country of citizenship or by preventing them from being granted membership in the country where they reside. As individuals are dismembered, so too are nations whose citizens go elsewhere or that are made up of people who officially do not belong (Coutin 2007). It is sometimes hard to discern the violence of such processes, as the very state practices that define individuals as outsiders—practices such as surveillance and requests for identity documents—can become so common that they are taken for granted (Coddington 2011). Such erasures of dismemberment obscure the histories through which people become deportable or crime becomes rampant or police adopt authoritarian measures.

Thus, through dismemberment, histories are repressed or distorted.[2] Examples of such erasures of knowledge abound.[3] Regarding South Africa, Martha Minow (1999) and other scholars (e.g., Wilson 2001) have examined how the extent of atrocities committed by the apartheid regime was publicly denied. Regarding Argentina, Diana Taylor (1997) developed the notion of percepticide to describe the ways that, during the 1976–1983 dirty war, Argentine military rulers "disappeared" people in broad daylight, while also discouraging the general populace from "knowing" about or acknowledging the reality of the disappearances. Taylor writes that the military repression was "a performance that 'disappears' its audience" (61). Even as instances of state repression were erased from public knowledge, accounts of the dangers that alleged "subversives" posed to the Argentine nation circulated widely and were cited to justify the role that the Argentine military assumed in public life. "Not knowing" is therefore made possible through a public performance of a void, the knowledge that cannot be permitted to circulate. And regarding responses to state terrorism, the movement to make truth commissions and international criminal courts key components of democratization derives in part from the need to set the record straight about human rights violations (Hayner 1994; Kaye 1997; Roche 2005).

In the United States, the scapegoating of immigrants for crime, terrorism, cultural change, and the nation's economic woes is another example of historical erasure.[4] Leo Chavez has identified the popular myth that there is a "Latino threat" that jeopardizes the United States through illegality, overpopulation, pollution, and disease (2008; see also Inda 2006). This myth ignores the fact that "illegal aliens" were produced historically, as changes in U.S. immigration law and policy forbade the presence of certain people, while creating opportunities for others to legalize (Ngai 2004). Even noncitizens who are in this country legally are on "probation," so to speak, in that their legal status can be revoked if they are convicted of certain crimes or if they fail to meet paperwork deadlines and presence requirements (Kanstroom 2007; Motomura 2006). Border enforcement has given rise to a burgeoning detention-center industry (Welch 2002), pushed border crossers into terrain where they face increased risks (Nevins 2002), and made the journey for undocumented migrants both more expensive and more deadly (Andreas 2012). These enforcement practices *naturalize* borders, citizens, and aliens, that is, they treat them as naturally existing, rather than socially and historically constructed phenomena.[5]

In contrast to dismemberment, re/membering not only reveals these histories but also makes it possible to draw connections between them. Children who immigrated during the 1980–1992 Salvadoran civil war experienced multiple forms of violence, including bombings, battles, the assassination of family members, displacement, separation from loved ones, and immigration policies that forced many to hide their presence while living in the United States as unauthorized immigrants. Emigration exiled young people from the lives and places they had occupied before, creating profound disjunctures that they subsequently sought to understand, overcome, or, in some cases, reinforce.[6] At the same time, emigration transformed nations, dispersing the Salvadoran citizenry, altering neighborhoods in the United States and elsewhere, creating new understandings of ethnicity and nationality, and reconfiguring the spaces that young people left behind and joined. For youths, such rapid reconfigurations entailed erasures—of knowledge, memory, history, and being. Indeed, some of the most profound erasures occurred in the 1990s and 2000s, when youths who grew up in the United States were deported to El Salvador, thus reproducing (but in the reverse direction) the family separations that they had experienced as children (Dingeman-Cerda and Coutin 2012). Such displacements, erasures, and traumas have been both countered and exacerbated through various forms of re/membering (Schwab 2010). Youths revisit their own pasts, students organize on behalf of the undocumented, activists forge new relationships with the Salvadoran state, Central American writers record their communities' histories, and state officials seek to incorporate diasporic citizenries. These strategies, with their complex effects and gaps, reshape nations, citizens, and membership.

As an analytical concept and a social practice, re/membering makes at least four contributions to understanding migration and social violence. First, by

providing access to subjective experiences, re/membering reveals commonalities in the violence of war, poverty, crime, exile, emigration, criminalization,
and deportation. Both in the United States and under international law, political asylum has been reserved for individuals with a well-founded fear of being
persecuted due to their race, religion, nationality, social-group membership, or
political opinion (Bohmer and Shuman 2008; Smith 1989). In contrast, individuals who are fleeing dire economic circumstances or criminal violence have
been subjected to deportation if apprehended (Harris 1993). Such distinctions
depoliticize economic deprivation and citizen insecurity, while also creating
the potential for explicitly political violence to be turned into something else,
at least discursively.[7] Importantly, re/membered accounts highlight not only
the indirect impacts of violence on those who are exposed to its effects, but
also the violence that is intrinsic to securitization and border control (Mountz
2010). Individuals are not intrinsically "illegal" or deportable; rather, they have
to be made to be so (Dauvergne 2008; Ngai 2004). This redefinition is accomplished through a series of actions and omissions, such as bureaucratic
delays, denying asylum to alleged "economic immigrants," and distinguishing
between generalized and direct violence. Violence thus takes both mundane
and dramatic forms (Arias and Goldstein 2010), a theme that is further developed in chapter 1.

Second, in that they address both membership and memory, re/membered
accounts reconnect subjects to national communities. Personal stories stand in
for those of a broader community (Cho 2008) and thus potentially can overcome "gaps between certain official versions of the past (history) and underrepresented understandings of the past (memory)" (DeLugan 2012:107; see
also Darian-Smith 2007; DeLugan 2010). Even though history has been seen
as objective and memory as subjective, the two are linked in that "memory is
what establishes the relationship of the individual to history" (Visweswaran
1994:68). In fact, because numerous legal processes require individuals to produce personal narratives, biographies are both the substance of testimonies
and products of law, though they take different forms in different contexts.
Asylum applicants produce affidavits recounting their experiences of persecution, individuals seeking a suspension of deportation detail the extreme hardship that a potential removal would cause them, and naturalization applicants
must demonstrate their "good moral character" over the five years (three in
the case of those who are spouses of U.S. citizens) that they have been legal
permanent residents. "Biographies" in the form of criminal records or arrest
histories can also be used to disqualify individuals for particular statuses. In

the case of deported 1.5-generation youths—that is, those who immigrated as young children and who therefore share characteristics of both first-generation immigrants who are born outside of the country and second-generation immigrants who are raised in the United States (Abrego 2011; Kim et al. 2003)—the securitization of immigration law has made de facto membership both salient and elusive. This theme is explored further in chapters 4 and 5.

Third, re/membering is temporally complex in that it entails revisiting the past with an eye toward achieving a more just future. Re/membering suggests that far from being inert, the past haunts the present. Avery Gordon defines haunting as "an animated state in which a repressed or unresolved social violence is making itself known" (1997:xvi). Re/membering such unresolved social violence is a creative process, one that involves "putting life back in where only a vague memory or a bare trace was visible" (22). Re/membering is thus akin to *archaeology* in that it excavates the historical layers that underlie current realities, making it possible to reconnect historical conditions (such as violence that provokes emigration) to what might otherwise appear to be intrinsic individual characteristics (such as illegality). Chapter 4 explores this process further by detailing the uncanny repetitions through which denials of asylum during the 1980s left some Salvadoran youths vulnerable to deportation in the 2000s. Re/membering such historical conditions is also generative in that revisiting "the conditions under which a memory was produced in the first place" makes it possible to produce "a countermemory, for the future" (22). Thus, alongside historical repetitions are differences that appear through attention to *generation*, a theme taken up in chapter 2, which examines the lives of 1.5-generation and second-generation migrants growing up in the United States, and chapter 3, which analyzes youth activism.

Fourth, re/membering highlights ways that both memory and membership are spatialized through presence, absence, and return. By fixing origin and nationality, law has the power to pull individuals to particular territories, to make them disappear from others, and even to place them outside of nations altogether, thus exiling them from "homes" in multiple senses (McGuire and Coutin 2013). Temporal calculations of presence and absence are therefore also spatializations. Additionally, to the degree that Salvadoranness in the United States has been defined in relation to an origin elsewhere, youths who strive to find and/or produce their own identities often *return*, whether literally or figuratively, to their countries of origin.[8] Whether legally present or unauthorized, noncitizens occupy an ambiguous zone between societal membership and legal exclusion,[9] with the result that those who are removed through deportation are key members of U.S. families and communities. In fact, Kanstroom (2007) writes of the de facto deportation of U.S.-citizen children and spouses who accompany deportees. Re/membering engages such spatialization in that it both seeks legal recognition of the de facto forms of membership that youths who are not (or not yet) citizens already practice *and* challenges racializing exclusions to which even citizens are subjected (de Genova and Ramos-Zayas 2003), themes developed in chapters 3 and 4. Thus, young people's accounts of their own lives compete with more dominant interpretations, in which, for example, the violence that compelled them to emigrate is defined as poverty or in which the marginalization they experienced in the United States is defined as a likelihood that they will become criminals. These competing interpretations of origins and trajectories make the space and time "before" emigration one of flux and conditionality. Exploring this alternative understanding of origin as one of movement rather than stasis gestures toward futures in which multiple memberships might be acknowledged.

Youth Migration between the United States and El Salvador

The idea for doing the research for this book was inspired by interviews that I conducted in 2000–2001 with 1.5-generation Salvadoran migrants. At the time, I was conducting interviews with Salvadorans who had pending applications for U.S. residency. Although most of these interviewees had migrated as adults, I had occasion to interview young people who had immigrated as children and grown up in the United States. I was immediately struck by the differences between their experiences and those of other interviewees. For example, in contrast to accounts of adult migrants who described El Salvador as the place in which they had lived, worked, or studied, a recently naturalized 1.5-generation Salvadoran woman who had never returned to her homeland described El Salvador as "this fabled place. It's like enchanted. It's like, it's like a fantasy to me. . . . There's a large part of me that is still there . . . living." Another 1.5-generation Salvadoran woman, who had a pending application for U.S. residency, felt that her lack of permanent legal status in the United States and her lack of memory of El Salvador made her unreal: "It's like—there is nothing. There is nothing here, there is nothing there. . . . You're just walking around, and you're just, you're like invisible to everything else. Everybody else is solid but you're not." These interviewees' descriptions of El Salvador, a place to which they felt tied by birth and perhaps also (in the case of the second speaker) by potential future deportation, highlighted both the power and inaccessibility of origin. The first speaker imagined El Salvador as "enchanted," whereas the second speaker thought of it as a void. What did El Salvador mean to youths who were Salvadoran citizens but who primarily knew the United States? And how were these meanings produced?

These questions about origin, status, and belonging resonate with the experiences of other immigrant communities in the United States. It is not uncommon for 1.5-generation youths to be pulled between nations, feeling that they are both here *and* in their country of origin, while also fearing that they belong in neither place (Boehm 2012; Hondagneu-Sotelo and Ávila 1997; Zavella 2011). Immigrant families from multiple nations have experienced marginalization and social exclusion, particularly due to their legal status, with even U.S.-citizen children of migrant parents worrying about the deportation of family members (Dreby 2012, 2015; Gurrola, Ayón, and Salas 2013; Jefferies 2014). Many migrant children have had to endure separations from family members, violence in their country of origin, or trauma while en route to the United States (Abrego 2014b; Boehm 2012; Foner and Dreby 2011; Jaycox et al. 2002; Ong 2003). As well, Salvadorans who have migrated to other countries, such as Canada or Costa Rica, have encountered discrimination, have struggled with the ambiguity of their identities and social locations, and have sometimes turned to historic examples of resistance—such as the 1932 peasant uprising that gave rise to mass killings of indigenous people in El Salvador, or even the Salvadoran civil war—for inspiration in overcoming such challenges (Carranza 2007; Hayden 2003). These commonalities suggest that the material recounted in this book speaks to the circumstances of other immigrant groups as well.

At the same time, across these commonalities, the experiences of 1.5-generation and second-generation Salvadoran youths who came to the United States during the 1980s and 1990s are also unique in several key ways. First, as detailed further in chapter 1, there is a historical specificity to the events that led them and their families to emigrate. Young people were particularly affected due to forced recruitment, frequent university closures, bombings that drove civilians out of rural communities, and death-squad activity against suspected dissidents. The pages that follow will recount numerous instances of social violence, including those of a Salvadoran college student who saw photographs of the Salvadoran civil war and came to understand these images as part of his own history, a boy who found a hand in a garbage dump in his hometown and did not consider that out of the ordinary, a woman who only learned from her cousin that her mother had almost been killed during the war, a child who witnessed an execution and then played with the corpse, and young people who want to understand the relationships among such events, their lives in the United States, and their connections to El Salvador.

Second, the unique legal history of Salvadoran immigrants to the United States poses in a particularly stark fashion what are wider dilemmas surrounding memory and membership. During the 1980s, Salvadorans who fled to the United States without authorization were told that the violence that they had experienced was not political, that they had not been "singled out" for persecution, and that they could return safely to their homeland. Many remained in the United States anyway, avoiding apprehension if possible. In 1990, Salvadorans were allowed to apply for Temporary Protected Status (TPS), which had been newly created by the Immigration Act of 1990. Additionally, in 1991, a class-action suit that was settled out of court gave Salvadorans and Guatemalans the right to de novo asylum hearings.[10] These two remedies resulted in temporary statuses that did not authorize Salvadorans to petition for their relatives to join them in the United States or to travel to El Salvador to visit family members but did allow recipients to remain in the country. Then, in 1997, passage of the Nicaraguan Adjustment and Central American Relief Act (NACARA) enabled Salvadorans and Guatemalan TPS recipients and asylum applicants to seek legal permanent residency on the basis of the lives that they had created in the United States instead of on their need for refuge. This was an important development, given that peace accords were signed in El Salvador in 1992 and in Guatemala in 1996, thus largely placing asylum out of reach. Yet interim NACARA regulations were not issued until 1999, with the result that most applicants could not obtain residency until the 2000s. This long legal struggle denied membership to Salvadorans for many years while also denying legal recognition of the conditions that had caused them to migrate in the first place.

Third, immigration enforcement, which escalated in the mid-1990s, had a particularly strong impact on Latino youths in the United States, including Salvadorans. Restrictive federal legislation that was passed in 1996 stiffened the immigration consequences of criminal convictions and foreclosed many other avenues of legalization, with devastating consequences for Salvadorans and other migrants. Deportations to El Salvador, a country of approximately six million, skyrocketed from 3,928 in 2001 to 37,049 in 2013, making El Salvador the fourth most common destination for removals from the United States (U.S. Department of Homeland Security 2011; U.S. Immigration and Customs Enforcement 2013). With these escalated deportations, once again, family members were being separated, as deportees left behind parents, siblings, and children. Once again, deportees were subjected to violence, in this case, by gang members, security guards, and sometimes the police. And once again, this violence was largely considered apolitical in nature and therefore not grounds for asylum in the United States.

Fourth, while immigration from El Salvador to the United States had existed previously, dramatic increases when the war began in the 1980s meant that Salvadoran children who immigrated then were the first large-scale generation of Salvadorans to be raised in the United States. The 1.5-generation migrants and their U.S.-born counterparts were socialized in U.S. schools, formed part of the fabric of U.S. neighborhoods, and sought to create new definitions of Salvadoranness in the United States (Baker-Cristals 2004a). Theirs is a story neither of straight assimilation nor of a transnational identity, though it shares features of each (Menjívar 2002; Portes and Rumbaut 2001; Rumbaut and Portes 2001). Rather, the 1.5-generation and second-generation Salvadoran and Central American activists, organizers, writers, artists, and students whom I interviewed described an effort to create a new space and public presence for members of their generation, one distinct from their parents' generation and from that occupied by other ethnic and racial groups in the United States. Youths emphasized the need to move away from the issues of refugee rights that defined earlier Central American struggles (including the 1987 caravan) to instead focus on such concerns as access to higher education, media imagery associating Salvadoranness with gangs, and the quality of inner-city schools. In this sense, Salvadoran youths were like other immigrant children, who found it important to establish political and social agendas that differed from those of their parents' generation (Kasinitz, Mollenk, and Waters 2004). At the same time, youths sought to distinguish themselves as Salvadorans and Central Americans from Chicanos or Latin Americans more generally. Thus, Salvadoran youths sought to generate their own identities, create new institutions, and secure public recognition in a specifically U.S. context.

I should note that, in examining the experiences of 1.5- and second-generation Salvadorans, I use the term *youth* to convey both a particular life point (the formative stage in which one anticipates or has recently gone through the transition to adulthood) and a loosely bounded generation (individuals who were children during the Salvadoran civil war and its immediate aftermath). In this sense, I am attempting to consider both "the effects of historical period" (that is, immigrating during the civil war) and "generation-since-immigration" (that is, being part of the 1.5 and second generation of Salvadoran immigrants) (Telles and Ortiz 2008:283). At the same time, I do not want to overemphasize homogeneity, given that "'generation' can perhaps be more accurately conceived of as a spectrum of different life experiences" than as a clearly bounded category (Boehm 2012:115). I suppose I also use *youth* to signal the fact, generally speaking, that I am from the same generation as their parents, the cohort who immigrated as adults during the civil war. Indeed, as I interacted with interviewees, I found myself thinking that many were in the same age range as my undergraduates and were just a bit older than my own children. At the same time, *youth* has analytical significance for this project, because it was the potential discrepancy between being born in El Salvador but raised in the United States that created the conundrum that is the focus of this study. As Sharika Thiranagama explains, "Youth as an 'age span' has a particular charged valence within . . . the shuttling back and forth between experience, relations, structures and selves" (2011:45). Likewise, Cal Morrill and colleagues define youth as "a socially constructed category located in liminal social spaces, at the blurred boundaries between 'childhood' and 'adulthood'" (2000:526, citations omitted). Salvadoran immigrant youths' accounts of shuttling across such blurred boundaries reveal how nations, persons, and histories are remembered and reassembled in the aftermath of violence.

Ethnography

My analysis of the relationships that 1.5-generation and second-generation youths have forged with the United States and El Salvador relies on ethnography, which I see less as a "research method" than as a way of knowing. As such, ethnography has much in common with the re/membering practices in which Salvadoran youths are engaged. For one, although anthropological approaches to ethnography have in the past assumed that individuals were part of clearly bounded cultural groups, this view has come into question. Writing in the late 1980s and early 1990s, the anthropologist Marilyn Strathern (2004) described the anthropological problem of enumerating cultures and representing them. Now it is not clear what "a" culture is—a particular village? a region? a kin group? a nation?—nor is it clear how to bound the categories "Salvadoran," "Central American," or "youth." For another, drawing on the work of Stephen Tyler, Strathern suggested that ethnographies produced knowledge by evoking certain responses in readers and therefore were evocative rather than representational. Likewise, testimonies disseminate knowledge by making listeners witnesses to the events that are narrated (Hirsch 1998) and thus to the collective realities that individual accounts convey (Arias 2001; Behar

1996; Beverley 2004; Nance 2006). Both testimonies and ethnography enable individuals to enter realities that are imagined as simultaneously whole and partial, representative of a collectivity and yet narrated from particular experience. Ethnographies therefore put forward truth claims by assembling the documentary record that makes them evident.[11]

The documentary record on which this book relies was assembled through interviews with migrants in Southern California and in El Salvador, discussions with officials and advocates who work with such migrants, and my own prior involvement in and research about legal and political advocacy on behalf of Central Americans. I met interviewees in various ways. I made announcements in Central American studies classes taught by my friends, as well as in large lecture courses. I met leaders of Central American student groups, who then referred me to their co-organizers. I consulted with Salvadoran youths who worked in community organizations. The legal staff at the Central American Resource Center (CARECEN) in Los Angeles helped me to locate TPS registrants who were 1.5-generation migrants. Some interviewees gave me names of relatives or coworkers. I sent out email announcements to list-servs for students who participated in the California Dream Network. And in El Salvador, I worked with the San Salvador offices of CARECEN Internacional and Homies Unidos to locate 1.5-generation migrants who had been deported.

Between 2006 and 2010, I interviewed 106 individuals, consisting of forty 1.5-generation and second-generation youths in Southern California; forty-one youths who had been deported and who were interviewed in El Salvador; and twenty-five nongovernmental organization members or immigrant rights organizers who worked with youths in California or in El Salvador. The age of the 1.5-generation and second-generation youths interviewed in the United States ranged from eighteen to thirty-seven, with an average age of twenty-five (most were in their twenties). Interviewees who had been deported were somewhat older, from twenty-two to sixty-nine with an average age of thirty-three. But when a couple of outliers (the sixty-nine-year-old and a fifty-two-year-old) are removed, all but two of the remaining deportee sample were in their twenties and thirties, and the average age of deportees interviewed drops to thirty-one. Interviewees included undocumented college students in the United States, deportees struggling to find their place within El Salvador, immigrant rights activists, poets, writers, student organizers, TPS recipients, gang violence prevention workers, newly naturalized U.S. citizens, Salvadoran officials who worked with deportees, and some Salvadoran youths born in the United States to immigrant parents. Interviews, which each lasted one to two hours in duration, examined migrant youths' legal histories, that is, youths' lives in El Salvador, emigration to the United States, future plans, and returns to El Salvador (in some instances, as deportees). Interviewees' legal statuses varied and included U.S. citizenship, lawful permanent residency, TPS, asylum seekers, and undocumented. Approximately half of the U.S. interviewees were women, whereas, due to the difficulty of recruiting female participants, all of the deportees who were interviewed were men.[12] Follow-up interviews were conducted with about half of the U.S. participants at one to two years after the original interviews. These made it possible to track changes in interviewees' attitudes and circumstances. I also draw on interviews with ten 1.5-generation Salvadorans that I conducted in 2000–2001 as part of my earlier research, for a total "sample" of 116. Unless otherwise noted, throughout this book, pseudonyms are used for all interviewees.

Clearly, this sample is not representative of Salvadoran youths in the United States or of the broader population of deportees. Given that I accessed individuals through universities and community organizations, the U.S. sample is probably better educated, on average, than the broader population of Salvadoran youth. Nonetheless, this potential skewing has the advantage of including individuals who had already assumed leadership positions and who, through their own activism, scholarship, and, in some cases, business activities, were directly or indirectly helping to define what it meant to be Salvadoran or Central American within the United States. It is important to recognize, though, that there are many Salvadoran immigrant youths who were not able to attend college and who were working at low-income jobs. The experiences of several such individuals are discussed at some length in the pages that follow. Furthermore, those who were interviewed in El Salvador included numerous individuals who had not made it through high school and who faced such challenges as drug addiction, gang membership, and criminal convictions. While many deportees were also taking on leadership positions in their own workplaces and communities, others continued to be challenged in seeking employment and other opportunities. Interviewees' occupations varied widely and included professional positions (for instance, in universities or corporations), self-employment, blue-collar work (in construction or transportation), studying, and being unemployed. Each interviewee received a $35 gift certificate or (in El Salvador) cash as compensation for participating.

Interviews coincided with and therefore described events of national and international importance, including the 2006 mass mobilization in the

United States on behalf of immigrants' rights, efforts to secure comprehensive immigration-reform legislation, the election of the first Frente Farabundo Martí para la Liberación Nacional (Farabundo Martí National Liberation Front, or FMLN, the coalition that made up the guerrilla forces in El Salvador and that has since become a political party) Salvadoran president in 2009, advocacy surrounding the California and federal Dream acts (addressing the legal status and financial aid eligibility of undocumented college students), the passage of Arizona Senate Bill 1070 (which required noncitizens to carry identification and authorized Arizona police to question individuals regarding their immigration status), and the impact of the 2008–2009 recession and its sluggish recovery on immigrant communities. Interviews also discussed deeply personal issues, such as postponing marriage in order to maintain eligibility for a family-based visa, reunions with parents following lengthy separations, and the psychological impacts of being deported. When possible, I also participated in conferences, meetings, festivals, and other events organized by or about youths.

It is important to note that the biographical accounts that I elicited during interviews were not unlike those produced as part of broader efforts to re/member the histories of Salvadoran youths in the United States. It was common for students and community organizations to deploy individual testimonies as part of advocacy work. For instance, the Students United to Reach Goals in Education (SURGE), a student group at California State University, Los Angeles, occasionally put out calls for "testimonies" over its list-serv, and, during an act of political theater at the L.A. city hall in December 2007, it featured the personal stories of three students who were either undocumented or who supported educational access for undocumented students (see chapter 3). Such stories are more examples of *testimonio*. Other interviewees collected oral histories themselves, as part of a *memoria histórica* (historic memory) project designed to document the history and cultural life of Central Americans (see also Silber 2011). Although they were elicited during interviews, the narratives that I analyze here—and, indeed, the decision to participate in an interview—were linked to this advocacy work. For example, one interviewee, an electrician who had never attended college, likened being interviewed to marching for TPS renewal. For him, telling me of his experiences was a form of collaboration. Therefore, my own ethnographic activities cannot be set apart from the forms of re/membering that I analyze in this book. The narratives generated during interviews were also acts of re/membering.

I analyze interview material against the backdrop of other work that I have done, some of which—such as my short caravan experience—I bring forward here.[13] I became involved in Central American issues through the work of Salvadorans and Guatemalans who sought to publicize human rights abuses and mobilize U.S. solidarity workers (Perla and Coutin 2010). When the Salvadoran civil war began, I was an undergraduate student at the University of California, Berkeley, and, though aware of the conflict, was not particularly involved in solidarity work. I do recall participating in a dance marathon to raise funds for CISPES, the Committee in Solidarity with the People of El Salvador. The dance team that won the marathon's costume contest came as Ronald Reagan's domino theory, each dancer dressed as a domino with "Cuba," "Nicaragua," "El Salvador," or "Your backyard" written on his or her cap. Later, as a graduate student at Stanford, when I was homing in on Latin America as my area of research specialization, I attended meetings of the Stanford Central American Action Network (SCAAN), a group that, before my time, published an edited volume entitled *Revolution in Central America* (SCAAN 1983). I remember joining the Stanford contingent of a peace and freedom parade in San Francisco and chanting as participants marched through the streets. In 1984, I spent the summer in Colombia studying Spanish, and in 1985, I spent three months in Argentina, studying at a university in Buenos Aires and interviewing members of the Madres de Plaza de Mayo, an organization made up of mothers who demanded justice for young people who had been disappeared during the dirty war in Argentina. My experience in Argentina deepened my interest in and commitment to human rights issues. When the 1985 Tucson sanctuary trial made national news, I realized that the sorts of concerns being addressed by the Madres were playing out in my own community, where Central Americans who were fleeing violence and persecution were not being granted refuge. I therefore decided to make the sanctuary movement the subject of my doctoral dissertation.

For me, the sanctuary research that took me to the 1987 caravan initiated over two decades of research focused on political and legal advocacy by and on behalf of Central Americans. In 1987–1988, I lived first in Oakland, California, and then in Tucson, Arizona, while doing fieldwork within the sanctuary movement. As part of my fieldwork, I participated in sanctuary coalitions, answered phones at the East Bay Sanctuary Covenant office, collected clothing and food donations, scheduled speakers, interpreted for doctors who offered free services to Central American refugees, documented asylum applications, attended church services and vigils, translated during public testimonies, observed asylum hearings, and interviewed more than one hundred movement participants. My 1993 book about the U.S. sanctuary movement detailed how movement participants drew on and reinterpreted law, culture, and their faiths as they created a means and a language of protesting violence in Central America. By the mid-1990s, I lived in Los Angeles, home to approximately half of the Salvadoran population in the United States, and I embarked on my second major research project: a study of the ways that Salvadorans and Guatemalans who had spent the 1980s seeking asylum devised new legal strategies in the 1990s, after the civil wars in El Salvador and Guatemala came to an end. For that project, I also did fieldwork, which consisted of volunteering with the legal services programs of three Los Angeles–based Central American community organizations, observing immigration court hearings, attending protests and marches on behalf of immigrants' rights, and interviewing activists, attorneys, and Central Americans with pending asylum applications (Coutin 2000). In 2000–2002, I turned to my third major project: a study of the significance of the Salvadoran population for El Salvador and for the United States. Through interviews with government officials, advocates, and migrants in Los Angeles, Washington, DC, and San Salvador, I analyzed how it was that, in a time of heightened immigration restriction, exceptions were carved out for Salvadoran migrants who, in the 1980s, had been regarded as undeserving of a legal status (Coutin 2007). For me, research was always a way to advance both knowledge and justice, in that I sought to document and make visible the experiences of groups (refugees, the undocumented) that have been marginalized in the United States.[14]

Throughout this book, I interweave snippets of such material both as a way to situate myself in the accounts and histories presented here and as part of the documentary process entailed in re/membering. Like youths who seek (or, in a few cases, want to leave behind) their own histories, I include prior moments of community history that I have experienced and that can contribute in some sense to the "record." I also draw on literary and cultural sources (novels, performances) where appropriate. Such forms of knowledge or explication are part of the cultural production of Central American youths (Rodríguez 2009), and I employ them (but in abbreviated form) neither to further analyze nor to buttress my own claims, but rather to evoke. I therefore conclude this introduction with an account of one such experience, a dramatic production that exhorted audience members to explore and recount their own histories, in short, to re/member.

FIGURE I.1 Dress left behind at El Mozote. Reprinted with permission of the Museo de la Palabra y la Imagen in San Salvador, El Salvador.

FIGURE I.2 Actress Rocio Enriquez in *De la locura a la esperanza.* Reprinted with permission from William Flores. Photo from the play, *De la locura a la esperanza.*

¿Y la Suya? (and Yours?)

OCTOBER 24, 2009. With great excitement, I approached the Los Angeles Theatre Center to see a performance of the play *De la locura a la esperanza*, written and directed by William Flores. The play's title was the same as a 1993 truth commission report on El Salvador. Central American advocates had pointed out to me that it was hugely significant that this play, dedicated to recounting Salvadoran history, was being performed in such a key Los Angeles venue.

The play was accompanied by an exhibit from the Museo de la Palabra y la Imagen in San Salvador. The exhibit featured photographs of the civil war and artifacts from El Mozote, the site of one of the most infamous massacres in which, in December 1981, residents of an entire village had been killed, with the exception of a single survivor. I was particularly sobered by a delicate child's dress and toy on display in a case.

In the theater, I stood in line with Salvadorans speaking English and Spanish, and I saw people I knew from my work with community organizations. I took a seat inside and watched as the curtain rose to reveal a dress that resembled a shroud. The form took life as a woman—seemingly a ghost, evoking Rufina Amaya, the lone survivor of the massacre at El Mozote—recounted the history of her community:

> Siento un poco de temor al hablar de todo esto, pero al mismo tiempo reflexiono que mis hijos murieron inocentemente. ¿Porque voy a sentir miedo de decir la verdad? Ha sido una realidad lo que han hecho y tenemos que ser fuertes para decirlo. [I am a little afraid to speak of all this, but at the same time, I reflect that my children died innocently. Why am I going to be afraid to tell the truth? What they have done is a reality, and we have to be strong to tell it.][15]

Folk dancers performed scenes of courtship and village life. Then the army arrived, and a voice-over reminded audience members that the United States had supplied the Salvadoran government with more than $4 billion in military aid during the war. In a chilling scene, soldiers destroyed the corn that village women had gathered, throwing stones and brutally stomping as the name of each child killed in El Mozote was read. After this destruction, the ghostlike woman lamented the loss, with great anguish. But the play concluded with a message of hope. A children's chorus sang:

Que canten los niños que alcen la voz, que hagan al mundo escuchar,
que unan sus voces y lleguen al sol en ellos está la verdad
Que canten los niños que viven en paz y aquellos que sufren dolor,
que canten por esos que no cantarán porque han apagado su voz

[Let the children sing, let them raise their voice, let the world be made to
   listen
let their voices unite and reach the sun, in them is the truth,
May the children who live in peace and those who suffer sing,
let them sing for those who will not sing because their voice has been
   silenced.][16]

The woman concluded by emphasizing the importance of preserving history.
She repeated, "Esta es mi historia. ¿Y la suya? ¿Y la suya? ¿Y la suya?" (This is
my story. And yours? And yours? And yours?)[17] Once again, she froze at center
stage, as though her moment to come to life had run out, and, behind a screen,
her body disappeared, to be replaced once more by a shroudlike dress.

And, reader, what is *your* story?

JUNE 29, 2007. In her apartment in Pico Union, Milda Escobar, a recent college graduate and youth organizer, nursed a recently injured ankle and told me of the multiple forms of violence that, at the age of twenty-seven, she had already experienced. In 1985, as a five-year-old, Milda had traveled from El Salvador to the United States with the help of a *coyote*. She described this departure as akin to an abduction, saying, "As children, we were taken out." In the United States, she reunited with her parents who had immigrated earlier and whom she scarcely remembered: "And I had to go to an apartment to live, with five other people, and I was supposed to call these two people my parents? When I didn't know them?" Milda did not leave behind violence, however. At her new home in Los Angeles, one of her cousins shot and killed another cousin, and, as an eight-year-old, in approximately 1988, she had to translate when the police arrived to investigate this incident. The same year, her family gained the opportunity to become legal citizens through the amnesty program that had been created through the 1986 Immigration Reform and Control Act (IRCA), and Milda, her mother, and her U.S.-born sister returned to El Salvador to pick up her mother's green card at the U.S. embassy. Although the country was at war, Milda experienced this trip as a vacation. Her family traveled around, visiting relatives and participating in hometown festivals. When it came time to return to the United States, however, Milda discovered that her mother had made a serious error. Though Milda was not eligible for a green card, her mother had assumed that she could reenter the United States by showing her elementary school records. Milda recalled,

> We went to the airport to go back to the United States. And my mother had brought her green card, and for my sister she brought her U.S. passport, and for me, she brought my report card! The guy at the airport just laughed at us. He said, "You're not going back into the U.S. with this!" . . . And she had to go back [to the United States] right then, because of the dates on the visa that she had. So she said, "You're going to go back home with Grandma, and your father is going to come and get you!"

In 1988 or 1989, while she waited for her parents to bring her back to the United States, Milda experienced the Salvadoran civil war firsthand.[1] Once, when she was away, her grandmother and a cousin were beaten and their door was macheted. Her family had to flee. Milda also had direct contact with the combatants: "We would be called to meetings with the Frente [Frente Farabundo Martí para la Liberación Nacional (Farabundo Martí National Liberation Front, or FMLN), the guerrilla forces]. And I know they weren't going to hurt us or anything, but it was scary seeing people with weapons. I developed a defense mechanism. I used to cross my eyes, so then they would think that I couldn't see very well, and they wouldn't take me."

Eventually, Milda's parents arranged for her aunt to bring her to the United States, again with the services of a *coyote*. Milda had harrowing experiences during this trip. In Mexico, immigration agents chased and shot at her and her fellow travelers. She was held in a safe house with sixty other migrants, without food, for several days. There, a male smuggler came after one of his female colleagues with a gun. Later, on a bus en route to Mexico City, a girl began to cry and a woman slapped her to make her be quiet. The driver—also affiliated with the smugglers—"grabbed [this woman] by the hair, and threw her off the truck. And she was just left there. The truck drove off and left her there." Milda and other migrants were captured by the Mexican Federal police, but the smugglers paid a bribe in exchange for the group's release. Then, when Milda and her aunt finally arrived in Mexico City, the smuggler demanded additional money from her family. Alerted by phone, Milda's father arrived and arranged for Milda and her aunt to enter the United States. Holding a Mickey Mouse doll as though she were a tourist who had gone to Tijuana for the day, Milda entered the country.

These experiences, Milda related, left psychological scars on both her and others. Milda had nightmares and got into fights at school. To escape such conflicts, Milda returned to El Salvador in 1994, which turned out to be a trans-formative experience: "That was when I became Salvadoran again. Prior to that time, I didn't want to be Salvadoran; I was embarrassed. But when I went back to live there, I made peace with the country."

After again returning to the United States, Milda sought to overcome what she described as a silence about the impact of the Salvadoran civil war on her generation. She explained, "The older generation denies our existence. They are in denial. To them, we don't seem Salvadoran. 'We were in the war,' they say. And the implication is, 'How Salvadoran are *you*, really?'" In college, Milda had the opportunity to ask a guest speaker from El Salvador, "How do young people there deal with the war?" Incredulously, she related, "And do you know what he said? He said, 'They don't deal with it, I think. Because they don't re-member it.' Can you believe it? An academic stated, 'They don't remember it.'"

What permits experiences such as Milda's to be described as not memorable? How is the violence of civil war and emigration ignored or defined as some-thing *other than* violence? What accounts for such silences? To address these questions, this chapter analyzes 1.5-generation Salvadorans' accounts of the violence of civil war, emigration, and living in the United States as an undocu-mented person. To do so, I draw on understandings of violence developed by scholars and activists who have documented the not-always-visible violence of structural racism, entrenched poverty, and institutional policies.[2] Philippe Bourgois (2003), for example, strives to recount the racism and class subjuga-tion that have produced those whom he calls "social structural victim[s]" who deal crack in New York, while Farmer (2004) stresses that structural violence is systemic, indirect, and sometimes hard to discern, given that the victims often attribute their injuries to accident, their own behavior, or bad luck. In U.S. legal contexts, mental suffering carries less weight as evidence of harm than physical injuries do, a perspective that makes it hard for some forms of violence to be legally recognized (Jenkins 1996). Additionally, the state is deemed to possess a monopoly on the legitimate use of force, so apprehension, detention, incarceration, deportation, and even the death penalty tend to be distinguished from rather than construed as violence.[3] Asylum law is designed to protect indi-viduals who are singled out for persecution rather than those who are indirect targets of generalized violence or who are victims of common crime (Anker 1992; Coutin 2001; Godoy 2005).[4] Violent occurrences that are nonagentive, such as enforcement policies that push border crossers into terrains where they perish (Magaña forthcoming; Nevins 2002), or the injuries and worse caused by microbus crashes where traffic laws are not enforced (Moodie 2006), tend to be seen as mere accidents. Similarly, social suffering that has become normalized may appear to be disconnected from the broader economic, political, and historical structures that produce it (Menjívar 2011a; Pine 2008). When such suffering is ignored or unacknowledged, then, individuals' experiences of violence are denied, making it difficult for them to pursue justice (see also Hume 2008).

Alongside the widespread public silence about the violence behind Salvadoran migration to the United States has been a corresponding silence in U.S. schools and reportedly even within many Salvadoran immigrant families about the Salvadoran civil war.[5] Perhaps familial silence is not altogether surprising, given that, during the war years, admitting to political involvement or speaking of abuses placed one at risk (Hume 2008; see also Lauria-Santiago and Binford 2004). Additionally, for Salvadoran parents, who may have viewed childhood "as a special stage of life to be protected and cherished" (Horton 2008:929), it may have seemed inappropriate to speak of such traumatic experiences. For immigrant youths, such silence has nonetheless given rise to a project of recuperating historical memory by locating their own early memories within broader historical processes. Youths seek to discover, as one interviewee stated, "What are we? We're Salvadoran, but why? Why are we here?" In Salvadoran youths' project of historical recuperation, memory is larger than the individual, as events associated with war and emigration take on "extraordinary salience" (Halbwachs 1992:223), producing in some cases a desire to visit, study, or serve El Salvador, while also staking justice claims that reconnect youths as deserving members of the U.S. polity. Such an effort to recuperate memory is evident in Milda's question, "How do young people there [in El Salvador] deal with the war?"

It is particularly important to analyze the forms of *violence* and *silence* experienced by children such as Milda, because dichotomies between politics and crime, structure and agency, and direct violence and indirect violence are particularly pronounced in their cases and contribute to silencing their experiences (J. Bhabha 2014). As the social psychologist and Jesuit Ignacio Martín-Baró, who was murdered in El Salvador in 1989 by Salvadoran security forces, noted, instead of protecting children, silence can exacerbate trauma by failing to provide children with constructive and creative ways to confront painful experiences (1990:244–245). Although some children were combatants in the civil war (Dickson-Gómez 2003, 2009) and some noncombatant children were directly targeted or abducted during the conflict (Amnesty International 2008; Binford 1996), many (but not all) interviewees described experiencing the war as part of the environment in which they grew up rather than as an event in which they were directly involved. They saw bodies, heard battles, hid from soldiers or guerrillas, and knew family and community members who were killed. As Milda described, such encounters left scars, disrupted lives, and shaped migration experiences, while children, due to their youth, were shielded from receiving explanations about what they had seen.

The violence of the war then was transformed into the violence of emigrating without authorization (Zúñiga Núñez 2010), given that the United States was reluctant to grant travel visas to Salvadorans or to award them asylum. The violence of emigration is hard to discern in that family separations, trips through dangerous terrain, and exposure to smugglers and others who profit from the undocumented appear to result from choices made by migrants rather than from structural forces or from policy makers' decisions. The experiences of children, who, in the scholarly literature, are defined "in effect, as luggage, as in phrases like 'the immigrant sent for his wife and children'" (Orellana, Thorne, Chee, and Lam 2001:578), are obscured in such accounts. Furthermore, in immigration cases in the United States, children are frequently included as dependents or derivatives, rather than as the primary applicants for a particular status, and therefore were rarely fully informed about the legal processes within which they participated. Nonetheless, children, like other migrants, are affected by the immigration laws that award status to some while denying it to others, as well as by criminal justice policies that target youths, especially those from low-income and minority communities (Farrell 1995). These policies, in turn, rechannel the violence of the emigration of the 1980s and 1990s into the deportations of the 2000s (Coutin 2011), and they potentially reproduce trauma across generations (Cho 2008; Dickson-Gómez 2002; Schwab 2006).

By retracing these interconnections, this chapter recounts how violence produced dismemberment through war, emigration, and immigration laws that prohibited movement and presence. Collectively, these forms of violence dismembered in multiple senses: (1) part of the population of El Salvador was dispersed and driven out of national territory, thus "dismembering" the nation of El Salvador; (2) individuals' ability to cross international borders in search of safety was not recognized and unauthorized migrants were not able to enjoy state protection, so the Salvadoran citizenry was broken apart; (3) families were dismembered as relatives were geographically separated; (4) some suffered physical injury on their journeys and were dismembered literally; and (5), in the United States, immigration law dismembered by distinguishing between residents based on their legal status, thus also defining many as outside of the U.S. nation. In recounting and reconnecting these forms of dismemberment, I also seek to overcome silences, in short, to re/member.

War

The separation between persons and history that I take up in this book can be traced to the Salvadoran civil war,[6] which dismembered physically, in that some were injured or killed, their bodies discarded as refuse or as warnings to others. It also dismembered civically in that those who were targeted for state violence were defined as *outside* of the nation, as the enemy, and as unworthy of human rights. The 1.5-generation youths who eventually migrated to the United States were caught up in both of these processes. Some lost family members or were injured during the war. Others saw bodies and body parts or knew that they and their own relatives were at risk. A few actually became combatants or were at risk of forced recruitment. Collectively, these children experienced an insecurity that made their own status in El Salvador unclear (Silber 2011).[7] For many interviewees, insecurity made their family's circumstances unstable, leading some or all family members to move, either within or outside of the country (Menjívar 2000). The sources of this instability, its grounding in wartime violence, and its linkages to family separations or economic difficulties were not always made clear to youths themselves, perhaps out of the desire to shield youths from painful knowledge (Ostrow 2002). In contrast to the suffering inflicted by combat or by death-squad activity, youths' experiences of wartime violence often seemingly appeared either insignificant or better forgotten.

The Salvadoran civil war that provoked these experiences erupted in 1980 due to a history of stark social inequality, a shrinking space for political opposition, and a rise in repression (Wood 2003). Elsewhere, Hector Perla and I (2010:9) summarized this history as follows:

> From 1932 until the late 1970s El Salvador was ruled by a series of military dictators who came into office either through uncompetitive elections or coups. Starting in the late 1960s this system of governance began to be challenged by a growing collection of social movements. By 1972 this challenge

had evolved to include a coalition of political parties of the centre and left (National Opposition Union, or UNO) with the support of many important civil society actors, which fielded a strong presidential candidate, José Napoleón Duarte. While it is widely believed that the UNO coalition won these elections, its candidates were not allowed to take office. In fact its presidential candidate was arrested and tortured, and had to go into exile. This electoral challenge was repeated in 1977 with similar results, anointing another high-ranking military officer, Carlos Romero, winner of the presidential race.

As a result of government intransigence, these institutional political challenges were accompanied by an upswing in social movement mobilization among unions and student, peasant, and religious organizations. The Salvadoran government responded to this contentious political challenge in much the same way that it met the formal political challenges to its authority—with violence; but it went after the social movement with even greater and ever-increasing levels of brutality. This brutality fed support for the incipient but rapidly growing armed revolutionary organizations that began forming in the early 1970s and would come together in 1980 to form the FMLN.[8]

The civil war lasted from 1980 to 1992 and was characterized by surveillance, roadblocks, forced recruitment, bombings, battles, abductions, torture, and massacres. Among the most notorious government assassinations during this period were those of the liberationist priest Father Rutilio Grande in 1977; the Salvadoran archbishop Oscar Romero, a critic of the military repression, in 1980; and four Maryknoll sisters in the same year. From 1981 to 1984, the guerrilla forces sought an immediate military victory and fought accordingly. When a victory was not forthcoming, the insurgents devised an alternative strategy of wearing away at the Salvadoran armed forces through prolonged war. To counter this effort, the Salvadoran military strafed areas that were deemed zones of guerrilla support, causing high levels of civilian casualties (Byrne 1996; Montgomery 1995). The U.S. government viewed the civil war as a battle between Western democracy and international Communism. Discounting the indigenous causes of the conflict, the Reagan administration insisted that if the guerrillas gained power in El Salvador, then Communism could spread throughout the region, thus threatening the security of the United States. During the 1980s, the U.S. government sent $6 billion in military and other aid to El Salvador (Schwarz 1991). By the end of the 1980s, it became clear that a military stalemate had been reached, and in 1989, as efforts to negotiate a peace agreement faltered (Aguilera Peralta, Macías, and Rodríguez, 1988; Córdova Macías 1993), the guerrilla forces launched a final offensive designed to demonstrate their military strength. During this offensive, an armed forces unit assassinated six Jesuit priests, their housekeeper, and her daughter, provoking international condemnation. In 1992, peace accords officially ended the Salvadoran civil war. Key elements of the accords included a cessation of hostilities; the reconstitution of the FMLN as a political party; a purging of officers responsible for human rights violations; the replacement of existing security forces with the Policía Nacional Civil (National Civilian Police), 20 percent of whom were to be former guerrilla combatants; the establishment of a Human Rights Ombudsry to guard against future abuses; the formation of a truth commission; and a plan for national reconstruction (Popkin 2000). Seventeen years later, in 2009, the FMLN candidate Mauricio Funes won the Salvadoran presidential elections and became the first FMLN president in Salvadoran history.

Like Milda Escobar, most of the 1.5-generation youths whom I interviewed lived through at least some portion of the Salvadoran civil war, though their memories of the conflict differed. Some related that they did not remember the war, either because they were too young or they lived in an area that was not affected. Some knew that someone in their family was killed or that there was a problem but did not know the details, describing the war as something that had happened to others. For example, Araceli Muñoz, who was nineteen at the time of our interview and who had immigrated to the United States at the age of three, told me, "My mom . . . said that they were in a city where they would always see—I guess—I guess it would be the armies. They would be walking by and they would always, you know, have that—they would be wondering if whether that night maybe they could—there would be some attack there or something." Likewise, David Zavala, a twenty-nine-year-old Temporary Protected Status (TPS) recipient who came to the United States at the age of seven, related, "One of my, that I know, let me see—one of my—he's kind of my cousin—I think cousin or uncle, his brother got killed by the war." Araceli's repetition of "I guess" and David's uncertainty about his relationship to the family member who was killed indicate that they were unclear about the details of their family's experiences. In contrast, other interviewees who did not remember the war themselves had learned detailed accounts that they narrated as part of family histories. Juan José Olvera Saldivar, an engineering student who was minoring in Central American studies, recounted the following:

From conversations that I've had with my father, I know that he was a construction laborer, and he used to be in a union, and they used to travel to different *departamentos* in El Salvador. And they used to have conferences to talk about how they weren't getting paid enough, the right amount of money. So I guess they [the union] got really big, and they started threatening the whole union, so he had to leave. . . . My Dad had to flee here because of political [issues], and he just sometimes talks to me about how he would see casualties, like beheaded, a lot of beheaded people.

Other interviewees remembered the war themselves, instead of having to rely on stories others had told them, but did so in the shadowy, only partially explicable fashion typical of childhood memories generally. Marta Dominguez, who came to the United States in 1986 at the age of eight, recalled "one time that we were living with my aunt, and it was late at night, and we were already sleeping and then we heard like gunshots. And, my aunt just said, you know, to throw ourselves on the ground—and then she said, you know, don't worry about it, it's just like drunk men outside." Only in retrospect, Marta said, did she realize that this incident was probably part of wartime violence. Veronica Reina, who was born in the United States, had traveled to El Salvador in 1992 at the age of four. She said, "I seriously remember driving in the car and seeing like the military people like in stations underneath these like canopy kind of things and with their guns. And I was so intimidated. I was like holding on to my grandpa because I was like . . . I was scared. I saw guns." Rafael Espinoza, who came to the United States at the age of ten, said he was unaffected by the war: "But I did see holes in the walls of our house, and I didn't know what they were, until later, I learned that they were bullet holes. Because we had, you know how the houses over there are made with cement? So the bullets left a big patch in the wall." Marisa Salgado, an eighteen-year-old who had immigrated at the age of nine, said that she was only a baby during the war and therefore she had no memories of her own. But, she related, "My mom says that when I was born like, um, there would be shooting and stuff and she would have to [put] pillows on my ears . . . because I was so little then." Drunken men, "canopy things," mysterious holes in the walls, and pillows over a baby's ears marked wartime childhoods.

Additionally, among interviewees, there were some who were older during the war, whose families were directly involved or who lived in areas of combat, and who recounted vivid, detailed memories of particular incidents or experiences. Adelmo Ariel Umanzor was only five or six years old when he saw his

FIGURE 1.1 Bullet holes in wall at El Mozote. Photo by author.

father, a mayor, carry dead bodies to the town square for identification. He also remembered "the soldiers . . . walking people with their hands tied with their thumbs—tied behind their back. Because you didn't see people tied by their hands, you saw them tied, you know, tied by their thumbs—with nylon I think it was." Adelmo's uncle drove a bus and let Adelmo sit in the last seat in the back.

> Then one time we were driving to San Salvador and outside the town . . . the guerrillas stopped us. And they stopped us and to ask for donation, you know. . . . They would . . . inform us what they were fighting for; what they were doing. . . . From the opposite side there was a bus coming, right. And it was full of people. And I noticed that there were sticks coming out of the bus. And there were soldiers on top of that bus too—in the bus, on the top of the bus. . . . And what they did they just fumigated our bus with bullets. You know they didn't care who was in there. They didn't care like what we were doing there. They just shattered all the windows. And most of the bullets that hit the bus hit the back of the bus and that's where me and my brother were sitting. And I just remember that—that I hit the ground and then my brother just froze, you know. And then I was trying to pull

him down. They were screaming and screaming and the glasses were, you know, hitting the floor and everything. And that's what I remember. And I said, why?

Bayardo Morazan had lived in San Salvador until 1980, and he was actually present at Archbishop Oscar Romero's wake, a historic event. He described what happened:

> We went to the wake where they, you know, they started shooting into the crowd and that was really scary. . . . Being in the crowd, you know, you felt like—we were not in the church because you couldn't fit in the church anymore, but being in the plaza and all of a sudden these shots, you know, from buildings—someone's shooting from the buildings. And people panic. And people started running. And, you know, people got trampled. And, you know, you see all this, you know, older ladies getting just, you know, just—they were not shot, they were trampled on, you know. That was, you know, that was something.

Whether shadowy or vivid, direct or learned, memories of wartime experiences were potentially traumatic (Martín-Baró 1990; Zúñiga Núñez 2010). One interviewee, who had been a child soldier during the war, suggested that an entire generation had been marked by the violence. He asked, "Why are we looking at the gang problem as a social disease instead of taking a historical and cultural approach to it? These gangsters, as people call them and tie them to terrorist links, are the kids that were traumatized during the civil war."

Although some youths' parents spoke openly to them about the civil war, many interviewees complained of adults' unwillingness to talk about the conflict (Hamilton and Chinchilla 2001). Some learned about their families' experiences when relatives reacted to documentaries of the civil war. Rafael said that his parents "must have been affected. Because recently, there have been lots of films about the civil war, and they have all of them, and when we watch them, my parents comment, like, 'Oh, remember that?'" Marilyn Funes was unaware that her mother had almost been killed by a death squad until, during a visit to El Salvador when she was a teenager, her cousins revealed this information. Marilyn related, "And after that I tried to approach her on that and she just says, 'Be quiet. Don't say nothing. I don't want to hear it. This didn't happen.'" Some interviewees stated that their family members were too traumatized to speak about the war, not wanting to relive painful memories. Saul Henriquez said that his parents felt he benefited by not knowing about the violence, adopting the attitude, "It's good that you don't remember what happened over there. Just forget about that stuff." Cesar Quintanilla complained that when his mother did answer his questions, she simply repeated the accounts of the war that are prevalent in the media, accounts that Cesar viewed with suspicion.

Traumatic knowledge coupled with silences about the war led to varied reactions. Many sought to uncover the truth about their families' and countries' histories. In the absence of concrete knowledge, Rosa Hernández sought to fill in missing details through speculation: "Maybe my mom was a rebel. I know my mom's family, two of my grandma's brothers were guerrillas, and then my mom's aunt, the one I interviewed, two of her sons were guerrillas. And then on my dad's side, all I know is that there's my grandpa and my grandma, and a couple of sisters of my grandma and a couple of sisters of my grandpa, and like my dad never really talks about his family or anything. So I don't know. Maybe there's something there too, you know? They don't talk about it." Such quests for deeper knowledge are likely furthered by the unfathomable nature of war, depths of suffering and experience that can most likely never be fully known (Scarry 1985). Other interviewees reported, in contrast, a reluctance to know more. Graciela Nuñez was "kind of scared" to visit the country "because of all those creepy stories of El Salvador," while Moises Quintero thought that if he spoke his mind in El Salvador, he could be shot. And to still other youths, the violence of the war became normalized. For instance, Manuel Cañas remarked, "I do remember that once when I went to a garbage dump that was near where we used to live, I found a hand of a guy sticking out. I didn't make a big deal out of that." For Manuel, a hand (and presumably a body) in a garbage dump was something to be ignored, though clearly, because he remembered this experience years later, it *was* a big deal.

Clearly, youths were involved in the civil war in multiple capacities, including as bystanders, potential recruits, relatives of combatants, and (more rarely) combatants themselves. In short, the range of experiences that "dismembered" youths was not unlike that of the Salvadoran population more generally. Collectively, such experiences form what Zúñiga Núñez (2010:67; my translation), drawing on Martín-Baró (1990), terms as a psychosocial trauma, defined as "wounds created at a specific historic moment, where social relations have crystalized in a determined form" (see also Kleinman, Das, and Lock 1997).[9] Unlike for adults, however, many youths' knowledge of the war derived either from others' accounts or from hazy recollections, and the effects of such knowledge were not always fully recognized or acknowledged.

As youths and their families fled the country, the violence of civil war was transformed into the violence of emigration.

Emigration

I characterize emigration, like civil war, as a form of violent dismembering. This characterization may appear strange, because migrants, even those who are subject to brutal persecution, make a conscious decision to leave, make their own arrangements, and find their own means of paying for the costs of the trip. Nonetheless, emigration, particularly when it is unauthorized, exposes individuals to physical danger and even death, the mode of travel (for instance, hidden in the trunk of a car) is dehumanizing (Coutin 2005a), and the decision to leave is made within a context of diminished alternatives (Spener 2009). The agents of emigration violence may be diffuse, including the former Salvadoran officials who authorized war and human rights violations, the U.S. officials who failed to offer refuge, Mexican officials who denied safe passage through Mexican territory, border enforcement agents in multiple nations, and smugglers and others who prey on the undocumented.[10] Indeed, in the case of El Salvador, depopulating areas of guerrilla support was a key counterinsurgency strategy, as the government sought to drain the civilian "sea" that nurtured the guerrillas (Schwarz 1991).

Children experienced this dismemberment in unique ways. Some children accompanied their parents when they first emigrated, others (particularly teenagers) emigrated without their families, and still others were initially left behind and then rejoined parents later on. Children were not just "brought," like luggage; rather, they were active participants in the emigration process (Orellana et al. 2001) and therefore have their own experiences and interpretations of traveling, being smuggled, separating from or rejoining caregivers, or making lives for themselves in their parents' absences. Some youths have vivid memories of their journeys, others have heard accounts of why and how their families emigrated, and others have had to contend with subterfuge or silence about their parents' plans for their lives. The violence of having to emigrate without authorization played out in the silences, separations, and uprootings that marked children's lives.

Although emigration from El Salvador to the United States, Mexico, and other Central American countries had existed for some time (Hamilton and Chinchilla 1991, 2001; Menjívar 2000), the violence of the civil war, coupled with human rights violations, caused a mass exodus. According to Byrne (1996:115; see also M. García 2006), by 1984, "within El Salvador there were 468,000 displaced people (9.75 percent of the population), 244,000 in Mexico and elsewhere in Central America, and 500,000 more in the United States, for a total of more than 1.2 million displaced and refugees (25 percent of the population)." In addition to going to the United States, Salvadorans fleeing the war traveled to Costa Rica, Canada, Australia, or Europe (Hayden 2003; Gilad 1990). The war was not the sole cause of emigration. Additionally, people migrated for personal reasons (such as conflicts with parents), to rejoin relatives who had already left, and to obtain better economic opportunities. However, these motives were often interrelated, given heightened tensions associated with violence and the disruptions that the war wrought on the Salvadoran economy. Furthermore, it was common for families to try to send or bring adolescent children to the United States due to the increased risk of being forcibly recruited, faced by young people in that age group. Due to U.S. immigration controls and U.S. support for Salvadoran authorities, most Salvadorans who traveled to the United States did so without authorization.

Some interviewees told me that the silence that surrounded their families' experiences of the Salvadoran civil war also enveloped their own journeys to the United States. Those who emigrated at very young ages often did not have their own memories of the trip, and others who were born in the United States did not know how their parents had traveled there. Ernesto Duran, who was born in the United States, said of his parents' trip, "My parents, okay, so they didn't talk about it. I don't know the details. . . . They never told me what years [they came]." Saul Henriquez, who was a college student at the time of our interview, suspected that his young age and the trauma of emigrating had erased any memories that he had of the journey and whatever preceded it. He said, "I was born in '81 and this [emigration] happened in like '85, mid-'85, so I was about four and a half. . . . I don't have any recollection of my—of El Salvador and, even worse, coming over here I don't remember anything. Nothing at all. . . . I'm thinking it was maybe just, you know, traumatic; I'm thinking it was, you know, that something happened."

Some interviewees were able to fill in the details of their journeys by obtaining stories from others. Rosa Hernández interviewed her mother for a class paper and only then learned that she had crossed the border separately from her mother, while Juana Rocio overheard the story of her family's immigration experiences when her parents were being interviewed by an attorney who was preparing their asylum claim. For some, the lack of knowledge about their own pasts was deeply troubling. Nelson Almendrez, who was half-Mexican and half-Salvadoran, had been unable to learn how his father came to the United States. He told me, "It feels like I'm missing a part of my history. You know, I know I'm Salvadoran, but I don't know that part of it."

Many interviewees who did remember their own journeys described common practices that are used to bring children into the United States without authorization, namely, passing through an official checkpoint using false papers, acting as the son or daughter of someone who had the legal right to cross the border, pretending to be asleep in the backseat of a vehicle, learning a few English words, and carrying items that suggested that they were from the United States. Because the documentary standards to which young children were held were less stringent than those applied to adults, it was easier for children to use false papers. Due to their age, authorities were also less likely to question children about their status. One interviewee, who entered the United States at age four or five, along with her older brother, provided a typical account: "So for me and my brother back then it was easy because we only use some people's birth certificates to get us from—to over here. And it wasn't as before—like now it's really hard to get in. So back then I remember we were passing the borderline and when the people that was bringing us they were like, 'Oh, fall asleep, fall asleep. Pretend you're asleep.' And we did. And that's how we came here." Some interviewees even used false papers to enter the United States by plane.

Many interviewees stressed that their own entries into the country were relatively easy, because they were able to travel as though they were legal residents. A few, though, reflected on the terrifying possibility of becoming permanently separated from their parents, who had had to be smuggled in. Rosa Hernández, who was only a year old when she entered the United States, said that her mother had been hidden under the carpeting in a motor home, while Rosa was in another vehicle, passing as someone else's daughter. Rosa's mother told her "that the lady just took me from her and said, 'Okay, she's going to go in with me in the other car.' And now she realizes, with everything that goes on on television, that they could've taken me away and never have given me back to her." These relatively easy entries could have turned into terrible losses.

Other interviewees who were slightly older while traveling or whose families did not have the resources or connections to arrange for their children to enter the country through a checkpoint described undergoing severe deprivation. Milda Escobar, whose narrative is quoted at length at the beginning of this chapter, was shot at by Mexican authorities, housed by smugglers in violent and crowded conditions, and exposed to insect bites, thirst, and hunger. Bayardo Morazan and his family were repeatedly robbed, until they ran out of money and had to wait for relatives to send more. Manuel Cañas, who had emigrated at the age of eight, was brought from El Salvador to Mexico by his father and then was handed over to a smuggler for the rest of the way. He recalled, "The guy that my dad handed me over to . . . handed me over to another guy. And that guy used to get drunk. He was always drinking. Once we went to the beach, and I was crying for my father, because I didn't know this guy." Juana Rocio traveled with her own parents, but, as they later told her, she still was almost stolen:

> Once . . . there was this big fence, right? And . . . my mom she—she basically jumped over the fence, right? It was like along Guatemala or somewhere around there. And my dad he was holding me. There was another lady behind, right? She—like she was part of like the group or something. And then, um, like he told her, you know, "Hold my daughter for like a little bit," right? I was three years old, so imagine. And so he jumped and then the lady she did hold for like a little bit, and, um, but then while my dad was on the other side, it was a huge fence too—the lady, she started running away with me. So she was basically gonna steal me. . . . And my dad saw that and, you know, he rushed behind her. . . . So that was one of the risks. I was actually going to be, you know, stolen, abducted. . . . I was three, so I mean I couldn't even, you know, save myself. I was so little.

In contrast to Juana, who marveled at the frightening possibility that she could have been abducted at the age of three, some interviewees stressed that their ages made them oblivious to the terrors of the trip. Jessica Morales described trying to feign sleep in the backseat of a car as "like a big game," while Bayardo Morazan recalled,

> I was so young and, you know, I didn't really understand it. I mean part of me, you know—I mean part of me wanted to get caught so I could be sent back and be with my siblings. But the other part of me looked at it as an adventure, you know. You know, it was—it was a trip, you know. So, I never really—I mean there were times when it was scary, you know, well every time that we came in contact with the authorities it was scary, but every-

thing else was really exciting. And then the places where we stayed at people were really nice and, um, you know, they usually have kids, so I, you know, have friends to talk to, you know, constantly from places where we stopped.

In addition to the travails of the trip itself, interviewees' experiences involved separations, deceptions, and family reconfigurations that sometimes resulted in lifelong wounds. Chief among these was the painful absence of parents who emigrated first, leaving children in the sometimes inadequate care of other relatives. After her parents left her behind in El Salvador, Marta Dominguez and her brother traveled back and forth between the home of an aunt who was "kind of like physically abusive" and a grandmother who "wouldn't take care of us the way she should." Marta described moments when her aunt would visit her cousins as "bittersweet," because she "always thought like, 'Oh, you know, one day my mom is gonna like come, to visit us.'" Sandra Mejillas was separated from her parents for two to three years, when she was a toddler. She felt abandoned and found the explanation that they had gone to the United States mystifying: "I have memories about being confused about not having my parents with me. The general feeling of being orphaned. . . . The children my age would also taunt me because of that. You know, 'Your parents are not here.' . . . And there was this general confusion of where *is* the United States? Like, 'They're in the U.S.' Well, where *is* that?" Some children were not even forewarned that their parents were leaving. Walter Olivar, who was seven when his mother left, recalled:

My [mother] didn't tell us that she was coming to the U.S. because she knew that it would be a big impact for us. So I remember her the day that she left. She left on April 28th, I believe. I don't know the exact date, but, oh, in April it was—in April of 1989. And I was—I remember her saying, "I'm going to go to my dad's house in Guatemala." So, to my grandpa's house—to visit him and everything. And it was just a little bit awkward because, you know, when she left, you know, she usually when she would go she would come back right away, maybe three days at the most or something like that. But then she never came—she didn't come—she didn't come back right away. It was like more than a week already. And I remember at this time I started, you know, telling myself, "Where's my mom?" Like, "Why isn't she here?" And at that point I remember like, you know, myself, every single night I would wake up crying because I would have dreams of her being eaten by this big, like, legs or some big ol' monster.

Walter speculates that his initially poor performance in school—he did not pass first grade—was due to his sorrow over his mother's departure. His nightmares of his mother being devoured by legs (which made her leave?) or a monster are telling, as is Sandra's confusion over the location of the place to which her parents had gone. Both of these examples demonstrate the traumatic impacts of family separation on children. The ambiguity of such losses, in which "a loved one is physically absent but psychologically present" can delay grieving and prolong trauma (Suárez-Orozco, Suárez-Orozco, and Todorova 2008:58).

In addition to being separated from parents who emigrated first, interviewees also often had to cope with their own eventual separation from the person or persons who cared for them in El Salvador during parents' absences. These departures were made more poignant by the advanced ages of some caregivers, who might not be expected to survive many more years, as well as by the uncertainty of an eventual reunion. Adelmo Umanzor was emotional describing his last encounter with his grandfather:

> I remember the day that we were leaving my grandpa was still alive. And he was an old man, very old-fashioned. He smoked tobacco, chewed tobacco every single day, so his smell I won't never forget. And I won't forget the day that he went to my house, the day before we were coming to the U.S., and he—and he cried to my mom, why we were leaving him, right? And, um, I remember I was in the—in the—not in the shower because there was no showers there, right, but I was taking a shower. And I remember hearing him crying and my mom was crying too. And I couldn't get out of the bathroom. That was the hardest thing to do, leaving my grandpa. The thing was I couldn't get out of the bathroom. So I was crying, he was crying the whole time. And I never said bye to him. A year later he died.

Walter Olivar's grandmother had to take a tranquilizer the day that he and his siblings left to join his mother in the United States. He recalled, "You know, people were crying and everything and saying that they're going to miss us; and to go back; and my grandma, same thing; all my family; my aunts and everything, crying that we're leaving. 'We don't know when we'll see you again. I don't know what's going to happen and everything.'" His grandmother, who had predicted that their departure would cause her death, passed away two years later. Manuel Cañas lived in El Salvador with his father after his mother went to the United States. When his mother sent for him, his father told him only that they were going on a trip. It was not until they reached Mexico that his father revealed that Manuel would be continuing on alone. Manuel said, "I didn't know. Not until we got there. Then he said, 'You're going to see your mom, but I'm going to stay behind.' It was hard, very hard. I was always close to my dad."

Though family separations were difficult, reunions could also be fraught, as children sometimes found that the parents they rejoined in the United States were like strangers, who in some cases had acquired other partners and children (see also chapter 2). Marisol Sanabria was separated from her mother from the age of one month to six years. When Marisol's mother returned to El Salvador to get her, Marisol did not recognize her: "For me it was really hard to like I don't know, get used to her—I was like 'Take me home, take me home.'" When Pedro Marroquín arrived in the United States after a six-year separation, he said, "I didn't recognize my mom anymore, because I was going to be—I was eleven, I was going to be twelve. And then—because she was pregnant also. And so it was kind of like kind of shocking." After Jessica Morales's father fled to the United States following threats from death squads when she was three years old, Jessica invented a myth that the singer Julio Iglesias was her father: "My dad resembles him and I really thought growing up that Julio Iglesias was my dad. So when I would see him on TV I would say, 'Oh, that's my dad.'" Two years later, when she rejoined her father in the United States, she did not recognize him: "I did not think that that was my dad because as I told you I thought Julio Iglesias was my father. So at first I would hug him, but it was— I really in my heart I felt this is not really my dad—this is not how I remember my dad. So he was really—he was really hurt because I wouldn't really hug him. I wouldn't really spend too much time with just him. I didn't trust him. I really didn't trust him. And my brother and my sister would say, 'You're so dumb, that's Dad.' But I just—in my five-year-old mind that wasn't my dad."

One more theme emerges in interviewees' accounts of emigration, and perhaps provides some protection against the pain of separation: namely, that as children, they were desired. Children repeatedly describe the risks that their parents took for their sakes: returning to El Salvador to bring them to the United States and thus risking a legal case that was in process, almost being left behind by a smuggler but then gathering the strength and courage to go forward for the sake of their children, and enduring danger along the way. Araceli Muñoz's comment, "My mom was, you know, really persistent. She said she wanted me here," and Manuel Cañas's statement, "I guess my mom wanted me to be there, because she wanted a better life for me," were echoed by other interviewees who described the lengths to which parents went to bring children to the United States. Many interviewees thus tempered their recollections of childhood pain with their knowledge, as adults, that they were valued.

Clearly, for interviewees, fictional and real families took multiple forms and became intertwined, as they in some cases suffered parental absences, created alternative families, pretended to be someone else's child in order to cross the border, and then rejoined parents who seemed to them to be strangers. It is important to remember that even in Salvadoran families in which no one has immigrated to the United States, children may temporarily be cared for by relatives other than their parents, and family members may move between households for economic or other reasons. In El Salvador, it is common for extended family members—aunts, grandparents, cousins—to live together and share resources, including childcare. A key difference between such arrangements and those associated with immigration, though, is that the unauthorized nature of immigration makes such flexible arrangements indefinite, due to the difficulty of crossing the border legally coupled with the need to remain outside of the country for safety or to earn the remittances that can sustain family members left behind (Abrego 2009; Glick Schiller, Basch, and Szanton Blanc 1995; Menjívar and Abrego 2012). At times children were deceived, as when relatives did not tell them of impending trips, perhaps because parents either could not bear to tell children they were leaving or wanted to protect children for as long as possible. And at times children themselves participated in a deception, as when trying to enter the United States using false papers. In so doing, they were following parents' or other agents' (e.g., smugglers, relatives) instructions, placing these above those of the more distant authority of government officials.

These two earlier forms of violence—war and emigration—in turn also ran through the legal regime that immigrant youths encountered in the United States. The Salvadoran civil war dismembered through death, injury, and displacement. Emigration dismembered by breaking apart families, removing individuals from their countries, and exposing emigrants to violence en route. And the U.S. immigration regime in turn dismembered by failing to recognize Salvadoran refugees' needs for safety and families' needs for unity. This legal order, with its prohibitions on travel without authorization, has shaped youths' lives in complex ways.

Law

The dismemberment of wartime violence and of emigration also assumed legal form in the denial of legal status to Salvadoran refugees who came to the United States in search of safety. Thus, denying violence also denies membership. Due to restrictive immigration policies in the United States and the emergency conditions in which many left, the majority of Salvadorans who emigrated during the war years did so without status, as undocumented immigrants. They therefore began their stay in the United States as nonmembers. Living within U.S. territory nonetheless confers limited legal personhood in the form of legal rights that can be exercised (Motomura 2006), including the right to defend oneself against deportation if apprehended. Initially, Salvadorans sought to remain in the United States on the grounds that they could not safely return to their country due to the war. Instead of claiming membership in the United States, they therefore stressed the ways that they were endangered by their own government. After peace accords were signed in 1992, however, Salvadorans' rationale for seeking to remain in the United States shifted to the roots that they had set down and the degree to which they had already become de facto members of the U.S. nation. Salvadorans' abilities to make this argument were adversely affected by the 1996 immigration reforms that eliminated or restricted multiple avenues through which the undocumented could gain status. Salvadorans were able to obtain some exemptions from these restrictions, but they also had to stake their membership claims during a period when immigrants increasingly were criminalized. The statuses and life opportunities available to 1.5-generation youths were shaped by these histories.

During the 1980s, the primary defense available to Salvadorans within deportation proceedings was to request asylum on the grounds that they had a well-founded fear of being persecuted in their country of origin on the basis of their race, religion, nationality, social-group membership, or political opinion. Due to U.S. support for Salvadoran authorities, however, few Salvadorans' asylum applications were granted: only 528 out of 19,735 cases decided between June 1983 and September 1986, a grant rate of 2.6 percent (Silk 1986). Generally, to be awarded asylum, individuals had to prove that they had been singled out for persecution, that their persecution was based on one of five grounds (race, religion, nationality, political opinion, or social-group membership) and that they had a well-founded fear of persecution if they had to return. In denying Salvadorans' asylum claims, U.S. authorities argued that these applicants were victims of generalized violence, that this violence did not fall under one of the grounds for granting asylum, and that they were emigrating primarily for economic reasons—to get a job—rather than in search of safety (Anker 1992; Coutin 2001). Denials of asylum therefore also denied individuals' experiences of persecution, and thus furthered a silence about human rights abuses being committed in Central American countries.

To counter silence regarding human rights abuses, Central Americans mo-

bilized a solidarity movement made up of religious groups, refugee commit-
tees, and community organizations (Coutin 1993; Perla 2008; C. Smith 1996).
Among other goals, solidarity workers sought to secure legal recognition of
Central American asylum seekers' claims. At the beginning of the 1990s, they
achieved two victories: (1) a class-action suit that was known as *American
Baptist Churches v. Thornburgh* and that accused the U.S. government of dis-
criminating against Salvadoran and Guatemalan asylum seekers was settled
out of court, giving these migrants the right to apply (or reapply) for asylum
under special rules designed to ensure fair consideration of their claims; and
(2) the Immigration Act of 1990 created TPS and designated Salvadorans as the
first group to receive this status (Blum 1991). When TPS expired after eighteen
months, President George H. W. Bush granted Salvadoran TPS recipients the
right to extend their stays by applying for DED, or Deferred Enforced Departure status, which was then extended until 1996. Both TPS and DED, like asylum, focused on Salvadorans' need to remain outside of their country due to
emergency conditions there, rather than on the ties that they had established in
the United States. Yet, unlike asylum, neither TPS nor DED enabled recipients
to become legal permanent residents and eventually citizens. TPS and DED recipients were therefore in a legal limbo, not removable but also not regarded as
members of the United States (Hallett 2014; Menjívar 2006; Mountz, Wright,
Miyares, and Bailey 2002).

Alongside these measures that focused on Salvadorans' needs to remain
outside of El Salvador were initiatives to gain legalization based on the lives
that they had lived in the United States. In 1986 IRCA created a legalization
program for special agricultural workers (SAWs) and immigrants who had been
continuously and illegally present since January 1, 1982. Salvadorans who had
migrated prior to this date or who were agricultural workers were able to qualify and then to submit family visa petitions for other family members. When
the 1996 reforms eliminated an immigration remedy known as "suspension of
deportation" on which many Salvadorans had pinned their hopes, advocates
sought to restore Salvadorans' suspension eligibility. Prior to 1996, suspension
of deportation had been available to immigrants who could demonstrate good
moral character, seven years of continuous presence, and that deportation
would cause an extreme hardship. By joining forces with Nicaraguans (who
had fled the leftist Sandinistas), Salvadorans and Guatemalans (who had fled
right-wing governments) were able to achieve bipartisan support for passage
of the Nicaraguan Adjustment and Central American Relief Act (NACARA),
which allowed Nicaraguans to adjust their status to legal permanent residency

and Salvadorans and Guatemalans to apply for the equivalent of suspension of deportation, a much slower and less secure process. To address this disparity in remedy made available to similarly situated Central Americans, the Clinton administration granted Salvadoran and Guatemalan NACARA applicants a rebuttable presumption of hardship, which ensured that the vast majority of NACARA applications would be approved. By the early 2000s, Salvadoran NACARA applicants and their families were becoming lawful permanent residents (LPRs), and by the late 2000s, these new LPRs were undergoing naturalization.

Then, in 2001, the legal scenario for Salvadoran immigrants shifted once more, due to the devastating Salvadoran earthquakes that occurred in January and February 2001. As a humanitarian gesture, the United States made Salvadorans who had been in the United States since February 13, 2001, eligible for TPS. As a result, Salvadorans who had not qualified for earlier remedies were able to secure temporary status, and they have been eligible to renew it repeatedly, most recently, until September 9, 2016.[11] Those who have done so have been in legal limbo for approximately fourteen years, as of this writing.

As these remedies were created and implemented, immigration enforcement tactics increasingly defined noncitizens—whether lawfully present or not—as outsiders and potential criminals. The Illegal Immigration Reform and Immigrant Responsibility Act (IIRIRA) and the Anti-terrorism and Effective Death Penalty Act, both passed in 1996, expanded the range of criminal convictions that made even LPRs deportable, eliminated waivers (known as 212-C) through which "criminal aliens" had been able to ask immigration judges to allow them to remain in the United States, made detention mandatory for many immigrants who were placed in removal proceedings, and provided additional funding for removal and border enforcement. Additional measures brought criminal and immigration policies together. These measures include efforts to criminally prosecute undocumented immigrants for illegal entry or reentry, and Secure Communities (www.ice.gov/secure_communities/), a program through which immigration and criminal law enforcement authorities share information in order to identify noncitizens who have come into contact with the criminal justice system (Chacón 2007; Eagly 2010; Stumpf 2006). Salvadorans who entered the country too late to qualify for earlier remedies or who fell out of status (for example, due to failing to attend a court hearing or to submit a TPS renewal application) were potentially subject to removal.

Salvadorans who immigrated to the United States as children had to navigate these legal developments, and did so with varying degrees of success.

Because of their age at the time of their immigration, many depended on their parents to take legal steps on their behalf. Not all interviewees understood their own status or the means through which it had been achieved. Additionally, many youths were part of mixed-status families. Their parents, siblings, aunts, uncles, cousins, and grandparents might be U.S. citizens, LPRs, TPS recipients, or undocumented, due to immigrating earlier or later, failing to apply for status when it became available, or being born in the United States (particularly in the case of younger siblings). Regardless of their own success in securing status, therefore, many remained concerned about the ways that U.S. immigration law would impact their relatives (Dreby 2012).

Rosa Hernández's experience illustrates the ways in which Salvadoran youths were "dismembered" by U.S. immigration law, even when they succeeded in naturalizing. Rosa had emigrated in 1984 at the age of one and a half, along with her mother. Her father had entered the country earlier, fearing that he would be forcibly recruited by either the Salvadoran army or the guerrilla forces. Rosa was carried through a checkpoint in the arms of a woman who pretended to be her mother, while her own mother was smuggled in under the carpeting of a motor home. Her father was able to secure papers that permitted him to gain status, but her mother could not. Rosa stated, "My dad filed for, um, for I don't know through what it was in 1986, I believe. And he filed for his papers in '86. And my mom was afraid to do all that, because I guess they had like a date? It was like if you had been here from '81 and before? And so she was afraid to lie?" In 1989, her parents formally married and her father petitioned for Rosa and her mother. In 1993, after the war ended, Rosa and her mother returned to El Salvador, but only one month later, the petition for Rosa came through and she and her mother had to return to the United States. Rosa was able to fly into the country, but her mother had to travel by land once again, as an undocumented immigrant. In 1997, her family returned to El Salvador to live. Rosa's mother still did not have legal status, but Rosa, who was now an LPR, became concerned that her family planned to be outside of the United States for so long that she would lose her permanent residency. She explained,

I knew, "Okay. If we leave and I stay over there, that means I can't come back. Because if I don't come back within six months, I lose my residency." . . . And I would always tell my mom, "Look! You don't have papers, but that doesn't mean I don't want to have papers." Because at that—she still didn't have papers. And I would tell her, "That's not fair! Because if I want to come back, you guys are going to take that from me!" And I would tell my dad, and he would say, "Oh, don't worry about it! I'm a U.S. citizen. I could always ask for you!"

Even though Rosa stayed outside of the United States for more than a year, she was able to successfully reenter the country as she had been issued a new Salvadoran passport in which her original departure date did not appear.[12] The official who inspected her advised Rosa that she might be eligible to naturalize. So, at the age of fifteen, after returning to maintain her LPR status, she investigated that possibility:

> I went to ask, and they said, "Oh, no, you're not eligible for that." I don't remember the reason they gave me, but they said, "You're not eligible for that." . . . And at the time I was only fifteen. I went to Immigration and around. And you know, fifteen-year-old girl, who's gonna pay attention to her? And my dad wasn't here, and he was the U.S. citizen. I guess maybe if he had gone, "Here's my passport, I'm a U.S. citizen, this is my daughter, blah blah blah," maybe it would have been different. But when they saw my green card, and it had a little thing on the back, they said, "Oh, you need a new green card. That's what you need to do."

Several years later, in 2003, Rosa successfully naturalized. She explained that she did so for two reasons: (1) she learned that El Salvador permitted dual citizenship, so she would not lose her Salvadoran citizenship, which she had come to value deeply; and (2) she had married and an attorney advised her that if she naturalized, she would improve her husband's chances of gaining status.

Several things are significant about Rosa's narrative. First, as a child, her knowledge of immigration law was limited. From the details that she provided, I inferred that Rosa's father had qualified for amnesty through IRCA, but Rosa did not know the name of the program through which her father had obtained residency. Likewise, Rosa did not understand the reason that she was not eligible to naturalize when she first sought to do so. Furthermore, Rosa's ability to maintain her status depended on her parents. Believing that she would lose her LPR status if she was outside of the country for more than six months (in fact, LPR status is lost if a person is outside of the country for more than one year, not for six months),[13] Rosa tried to return to the United States in a timely fashion; however, her father did not permit her to do so. Even with this limited knowledge, Rosa herself took initiative, approaching U.S. immigration authorities when she was only fifteen years old in an effort to naturalize. This combination of initiative and lack of full legal knowledge is not unusual among the children of immigrants (Menjívar 2002; Orellana et al. 2001).

Second, Rosa's successful efforts to legalize involve a mixture of legal and quasi-legal activities. Her original entry into the United States was unauthorized—though, at the age of one, she certainly cannot be held responsible for that decision.

Third, family dynamics and legalization initiatives are intertwined. It is not uncommon for men to take risks that women are unwilling to take, such as submitting fraudulent paperwork or even applying for TPS, which can be considered risky as it reveals one's presence to authorities. Rosa's father became a citizen while her mother—who eventually acquired residency—remained undocumented. Her family's decision to leave the United States in 1997, just as the 1996 immigration reforms were being implemented, could have been an attempt to prevent Rosa's mother from acquiring six months or more of unlawful presence, which would have disqualified her from reentering the United States legally. Rosa's family relationships were impacted by their statuses. Rosa's younger brother, born in the United States, was a U.S. citizen while Rosa was still attempting to secure residency. Rosa had to risk separation from her mother when her mother was still undocumented. Even though she became a U.S. citizen, she had relatives who were at risk of deportation. Her family was transnational, partly through choice and partly through necessity, an outcome that, depending on her relatives' circumstances, might be repeated within her own generation.

Fourth, and perhaps most significantly, even though Rosa's father left El Salvador due to the civil war, it was IRCA, rather than TPS, DED, NACARA, or asylum, that provided an immigration remedy for Rosa and her family. That is, her father immigrated through a general legalization program rather than through programs that had been devised to aid victims of persecution. The political circumstances that led her family to the United States in the first place are not officially acknowledged in her own legal history.

David Zavala's experiences provide a contrasting account. David emigrated in 1986, at the age of seven. His mother had left El Salvador two years earlier, due to both the war and personal reasons. David remained behind with his father, with whom he had a close relationship. When he left for the United States, he was told that his father would eventually follow, something that never happened. Growing up in the United States, David was undocumented. In California, he attended a protest of Proposition 187 and recalled being strongly encouraged by a high school teacher to whom he revealed his legal status: "And he kept on telling me, 'You know what, it doesn't matter, you know, just get good grades and then—and you know, let me give you some numbers to call.'" But David did not call the numbers, which presumably were for agencies or attorneys who could help with immigration status.

Unlike Rosa's father, David's mother did not secure legal status. David recalled, "I guess my mom . . . wasn't on the ball with immigration stuff because I guess there was an amnesty and she could have hustled more and tried to get that, but she didn't. But that's okay, you know. I'm over it. I was—I got upset. I was upset for a while that she didn't."

David explained that his mother had applied for amnesty, but her application had been denied. When I asked for more details, suggesting that perhaps she had applied for asylum rather than for amnesty, David concurred, "Yeah, it was asylum. When she came she somehow went to the—she had a court [hearing] and the judge ordered deportation, but she never left. And she's been here. She could have fixed her papers because she was under the NACARA. She was doing all that, but that came up—the ordered deportation—so it was denied. It said residency denied."

David seemed somewhat confused about his mother's circumstances. He told me,

> She didn't get good advice because she somehow—she was getting the work permit and somehow . . . it was not TPS. I think it was asylum or something. They got a work permit through that. And then she went to different kind of people and then this one person sent stuff to, ah—tried to get the work permit—she sent it to the government and I guess the packet wasn't enough. The government was actually more—they wanted more, um, documentation that she was here before.

Depressed over his legal situation, David fell into drug use: "I didn't have much opportunities. It's just like, 'I'm here, and I don't want to go back, but I'm stuck.'" When David tried to go to college, he found that he was charged out-of-state tuition that he could not afford. He briefly obtained a work permit through his mother's NACARA case, but because his mother was ordered to be deported, he was advised to simply let it expire and not reapply. Unable to study, David began to work in construction, digging ditches for pipes for swimming pools. Finally, in 2001, fifteen years after he originally entered the United States, David was able to obtain temporary status due to a natural disaster (the earthquakes) that inspired the U.S. government to make TPS available to Salvadorans who were already in the country. He explained: "I kind of tried to stay informed like in newswise and, yeah, sometimes you know, Spanish news. My mom used to always watch that. And, um, they'd announce the former president of El Salvador and George Bush in [the] 2001 hurricane over there. Thank God for the hurricane. So, tragedy for some, benefit to others."

After obtaining TPS, David learned that the law in California had changed and that he could attend community college without paying out-of-state tuition. At the time of our interview, he was completing an associate's degree in psychology while working at a public library. His long-term goal was to complete a four-year degree at a California State University campus and become a writer. David continued to be affected by immigration law, however. As a TPS holder, he was unable to travel internationally, including to El Salvador to see his father, from whom he had been separated for more than two decades. Additionally, his girlfriend was undocumented and was unable to legalize, despite having U.S.-citizen relatives, because she had accrued more than one year of unlawful presence. David commented, "I can't see [being an] American citizen yet, but I'm a Salvadoran citizen, so. It feels weird though 'cause it's like you're, um, I'm here and there. It's like I'm half here and half there and in between two worlds."

Again, multiple aspects of this narrative are significant. Like Rosa, David had lived in the United States for most of his life. Yet, while Rosa had been able to naturalize, David was in what he described as a limbo, holding only TPS. The key difference in their immigration histories appears to be actions taken by their parents: Rosa's father was able to secure residency and to petition for her, whereas David's mother remained in an insecure status. Seemingly, David's mother bypassed the opportunity to qualify for amnesty fraudulently, and she received poor legal advice regarding asylum, TPS, and NACARA, thus failing to qualify for those remedies as well. When he was a child, David had to rely on his mother for his own immigration opportunities. He had a temporary work permit through his mother's NACARA case, but then he fell out of status until the opportunity to apply for TPS on his own arose. Although David qualified for TPS, his narrative demonstrates that he did not fully understand his own immigration history. He attributed the 2001 TPS award to a hurricane rather than the earthquakes, and he seemed confused about how and why his mother remained without status. These experiences left emotional scars. David felt "stuck" and had fallen into both drug use and depression for a period of his life. Even after he acquired TPS, he was unable to travel internationally, as Rosa had done, and he therefore was unable to reunite with his father in El Salvador. He could not live a transnational family life even though he had a parent outside of the United States. Although his circumstances had improved after the award of TPS, he remained vulnerable to changes in immigration law and to the possibility that his girlfriend could be deported. Finally, the violence that had first forced his mother to leave El Salvador was never legally acknowledged, despite his mother's NACARA application.

These two accounts demonstrate the degree to which child migrants' legal status can depend on the actions and knowledge of parents, as well as the ways that the violence of civil war and of emigration is both denied and reproduced in these young people's immigration histories. Rosa, David, and other young people had to flee El Salvador at a time when their rights as citizens, including the right to be secure from violence and persecution, were not protected. In the United States, the circumstances that had led them to leave were not acknowledged, and they were not welcomed with a grant of membership rights. Over time, some, such as Rosa, were able to gain residency and even citizenship while others, such as David, remained undocumented or only temporarily authorized. This lack of membership (legal status) and of memory (recognition of wartime violence and persecution) were interconnected and in turn affected their abilities to be members of families and to forge their own relationships with spouses or significant others who might themselves be undocumented or legally vulnerable. Law itself exacts a violence, including family separation, social exclusion, psychological damage, and confinement within national territory (Menjívar and Abrego 2012). Yet youths were not necessarily overcome by this legal violence, as Rosa's and David's experiences demonstrate. Despite challenges, they moved forward with their lives, forming relationships, having children of their own, and attempting to study, work, and pursue their own life goals. In so doing, they countered dismemberment with re/membering.

Conclusion

This chapter has interwoven accounts of the Salvadoran civil war, emigration, and law in order to re/member people, histories, nations, and relationships that were broken apart or denied through violence. In legal contexts, immigration status is often depicted as an aspect of a person rather than as a product of policies and histories (Peutz and de Genova 2010), emigration is seen as an action that a person takes rather than as a form of violence to which he or she is subjected, and denials of Salvadoran asylum seekers' claims defined the violence of the Salvadoran civil war as something other than persecution. A set of dichotomies underlies these distinctions. "Real" violence—for example, violence that can be legally cognizable in an asylum claim—is presumed to be physical in nature, direct in application, and with an identifiable agent or perpetrator (Coutin 2001; Jenkins 1996; Kleinman, Das, and Lock 1997). Violence that is perpetrated by social structures and legal regimes, that is manifested psychologically and socially as well as physically, and that appears to be indirect rather than targeted is more difficult to discern. These dichotomies obscure the histories that this chapter has tried to elucidate. Thus, the violence that interviewees experienced included seeing dead bodies in the streets, having to hide under beds, enduring the absence of a parent who fled death-squad threats, being handed over to a smuggler, assuming a false identity in order to cross the U.S.-Mexico border, and living in the United States as an undocumented immigrant. The denial of membership and of memory runs through each of these events. By reproducing interviewees' accounts of their own lives, I have sought to re/member, and thus reconnect, emigration to the violence of the war and legal histories to the reasons that people left. Thus, the accounts reproduced here are not only *about* re/membering; in addition, they are *instances of* re/membering. By eliciting and reproducing these accounts, ethnography too can integrate past and present, historic events and individual lives, violent ruptures and the social conditions that engendered them. In forging such connections, ethnography can contribute to challenging dismemberment.

While dismembering may occur in multiple immigration contexts, these processes take unique forms in the lives of Salvadoran child migrants. Although adults may believe that children were largely passive victims, who, due to their ages, may be able to repress memories of the conflict, interviewees suggest that they in some cases participated actively (as child soldiers or potential recruits) and certainly either remembered or had heard about the war. Rather than protecting children, silences—about the conflict, parental departures, or even children's own legal status—may instead fuel nightmares, such as about mothers being eaten by monsters. Emigration also takes unique forms in the lives of children. Very young children who emigrated without authorization were able to pass as the offspring of other individuals when they went through a checkpoint. Many pretended to be asleep in a car and thus avoided being questioned by immigration officials. Older children who emigrated illicitly often depended on parents or parental substitutes—aunts or uncles who accompanied children—or even smugglers themselves. While some children experienced emigration as an adventure in which they were treated kindly, others suffered traumatizing deprivations or witnessed violent incidents, such as the abandonment of fellow travelers along the way. For children, emigration created a complex set of relationships—to caregivers while parents were absent, to pseudoparents who helped them across the border, and to their own parents who might at the moment of reunion seem to be strangers. Emigration also entailed separations from parents and caregivers, sometimes permanently. Children who did not emigrate may also have experienced shifting family relationships, as family members move between households as work opportunities, economic circumstances, and intimate relationships change. In the case of emigration, however, the distances between family members may have been greater and more difficult to traverse, due to prohibitions on travel. Children's abilities to overcome such prohibitions, by gaining legal status, also depended to some degree on parents. This dependency is a direct result of laws that enable adults to include children in their own immigration cases, and also of children's ages at the time that particular remedies became available. Children, particularly teenagers and young adults, often also have had to serve as brokers, approaching immigration officials for information, translating for parents, and, when possible, taking charge of their own immigration cases. In the process, they seek to re/member, to gain membership in multiple countries, to enable their own family members to acquire status, and to understand their own histories. War, emigration, and il/legalization thus set the stage for childhoods that the interviewees lived in the United States, where they were, as David noted, "in between two worlds."

Commemoration

JANUARY 15, 2012. My sixteen-year-old son Jordy and I attended an event at the Central American Resource Center (CARECEN) in Los Angeles: an artistic exhibit in commemoration of the twentieth anniversary of the signing of the Salvadoran peace accords. Jordy was interested in going because he got extra credit in his Spanish class if he attended a cultural event and wrote a short essay about it. On the drive over, I asked him what he knew about the Salvadoran civil war and whether he wanted to learn more. The answers were "not much" and "yes," so I spent the whole drive lecturing him about the causes of the war, the formation of the FMLN, Archbishop Romero's assassination, the phases of the conflict, human rights abuses, U.S. involvement, refugee issues, the final offensive, and the peace accords and their aftermath. Because I was talking and not paying attention to where I was going, I turned on the wrong street, so we had to drive a couple of blocks out of our way. I have an uncanny ability to get lost even when I know exactly where I'm going.

We walked in and went upstairs, where we saw about fifteen to twenty-five people walking around and talking to each other. The first person I saw was Joaquín Romero (not a pseudonym), a Salvadoran photographer and activist whom I hadn't seen in years. He recognized me as well and came over to chat. As we shook hands, he pointed to Jordy and asked, "¿Es el pequeñito?" ("Is he the little one?") Joaquín remembered Jordy as a baby, when I used to bring him with me to Central American events. I said that he was. For me, this was sort of an amazing moment. Jordy was born in 1995, only three months after I began the research for my book *Legalizing Moves*, which is dedicated to Jordy. Joaquín was one of the founders of CCCA, the Centro Comunitario Centroamericano, which was involved in refugee and solidarity work during the 1980s. Joaquín used to take photos of marches and other events, and when it came time for me to choose a cover for *Legalizing Moves*, he allowed me to reproduce a photo that he had taken of one of the NACARA marches.

After chatting with Joaquín for a bit, Jordy and I walked around the room to look at the exhibit. Works by the artists Beatriz Cortez and Carolina Rivera were featured. Both were available to talk about the exhibit. Along one wall were photographs of a room. Beatriz explained to us that she lived in El Salvador until 1989, when, during the final offensive, she was given two hours' notice that she was going to leave the country. She didn't have time to pack all her things, and afterward she had no photographs of the room that she had lived in as a child. So she re-created the room in miniature from memory and then took photographs of the replica. These were the photos that appeared on the wall of the room. The series of photos was entitled *Pasaje Los Ángeles*, her home's address in San Salvador. I was struck by the sense of sharp loss that would lead someone to re-create and then photograph their childhood room.

In the back of the room was a small glass case containing some bones. It was entitled "XX," which is the label that designated the remnants of unidentified bodies of the disappeared. I don't know what kind of bones they were. Beatriz told us that she had found them in her garden and had brought them back. I thought that she meant the garden of her childhood home, which, I assumed, she had visited as an adult. Actually, she told me later, she found them at her home in San Fernando, California.

We then viewed an installation called *Árbol de la memoria/Tree of Memory*. A card explained that the installation was made out of an orange tree and moss. The "tree" basically looked like a thick branch leaning upright with moss growing on top of it. There were no leaves. Jordy asked Beatriz about the significance of the moss and the fact that it was from an orange tree. Beatriz said

FIGURE 1.2 Still from Beatriz Cortez's series *Pasaje Los Ángeles*. Reprinted with permission from Beatriz Cortez.

that she found the pieces of this orange tree in her yard, so this was something that she brought back, and that when she found it, it was broken into pieces, so she had to put it back together, even though it now appears to be one piece. She placed it upright, but with the roots facing upward instead of downward. It was basically dead, so she added the moss, which is growing out of the trunk or branch, as a symbol of hope. The name of this type of moss is "baby's tears."

For me, the most powerful element of the exhibit was a ball of grass, about two feet in diameter. Accompanying this ball of grass was a soundtrack that, according to a sign, consisted of the names of the victims of the massacre at El Mozote, but I couldn't make out anything. It just sounded like static. After a while, it stopped, and then when it started again, I could make out the names very clearly. It was sad to hear them continue to be read. One of the artists explained that the soundtrack had the same number of tracks as victims. Each track added one more name. So, first, you heard a single name and it was clear. Then you heard two names simultaneously. Then three names simultaneously. And so on, until, the artist explained, you couldn't make out the names and it sounded like rain.

In a corner in the back of the hall was a small room, and in it a video loop played. The video showed a room. A card explained that this was the room of a disappeared person and that the film depicted the way that the memory of a disappeared son was kept alive by a mother who was now aging. In the video, the room gradually became full of tropical plants, which covered over the furnishings. Suddenly, the pristine room would appear again. These clear representations were meant to symbolize the memory of the disappeared when someone was looking at the room and bringing the memory alive once more.

In another part of the room a sheet hung between two poles, and projected onto the sheet from behind was a life-sized sketch of a bed that had a thin mattress. This bed represented visually a story that Carolina had written about a disappeared person. At 6:00 PM, Carolina performed her story. She turned on a recording of someone (herself, I presume) reading the story "La Cama," as she lay in a fetal position as though she were hiding under the bed. She also caressed the bed, appeared to jump on the bed, and shook a large board to make sudden banging, shooting, or stomping sounds. As she moved around, we heard the story, which was about how the bed served as a hiding place, the fact that the bed gave a backache but that the person who slept there was too proud to have a mattress and bed to complain, childhood memories of the bed as a place to play, and the violence of the bed being thrown against the wall when the military entered the home in search of someone.

After the performance ended, Jordy and I prepared to go. We said goodbye to Joaquín and to Beatriz. She told Jordy, "Tuviste suerte porque te perdiste la guerra." ("You were lucky because you missed the war.")

Later, Jordy let me read the essay that he wrote about his experience visiting this exhibit. To my surprise, I read, "I did not know that this had happened." How could my own son not know about the Salvadoran civil war when I had devoted much of my adult life to working with immigrants who fled this conflict? I realized suddenly that, just like the parents of the young people I had interviewed, I too had attempted to shelter my own son from knowledge of the many accounts of violence, human rights abuses, and immigration histories that I have heard. Despite my publications, I had perpetuated a silence. But the exhibit countered this silence. The conclusion to Jordy's essay stated, "This was something I had never experienced before, despite disaster and pain, there was still vitality and vibrancy in the eyes of the survivors. It made me think that it is important to defend one's beliefs. I also realized that I did not know that this had happened. The purpose of this event was accomplished because I never will forget the hope or the whispering sound of the names of the victims of the massacre at El Mozote."

Central American migrants who are children often find themselves inhabiting multiple worlds. In the following passage from his novel, *The Tattooed Soldier*, Héctor Tobar conveys examples of the rich hybridities developed by such children who grow up in Los Angeles, as well as uncanny juxtapositions of childhood playfulness with crowded living conditions and neighborhood dangers:

> Longoria studied his books for hours, the damp air of his austere room filled only by the Sunday afternoon sounds of the Westlake Arms. At night the sounds of lovemaking were sharpest, but during the day the noise of children dominated the apartment building's acoustic universe: eager, treble-toned voices of boys and girls, balls bouncing down the narrow corridors, tricycles squeaking across the floor in the apartment above him, boys opening windows and calling to their playmates across the inner courtyard. They were American-born children, and their talk was like no language Longoria had heard before, a crazy mixture of schoolyard English, the Central American Spanish of their parents, and the strange, Mexican-influenced argot of the neighborhood.
>
> "Fijate, vos, que ese vato from La Mara got in a fight with that dude from la Eighteenth Street who lives down the block. Yeah, right there in the class. Real chingazos. El de la Salvatrucha estaba bleeding y todo."

The children argued with their siblings and pleaded with their mothers. The mothers did not allow their sons and daughters to play outside, in the free-fire zone of the street, or on the front steps, where a platoon of gang members held sway. (Tobar 1998:59)

These images that Tobar conveys in his novel resonate with interviewees' accounts of their own childhoods growing up in the United States where many of them also developed their own versions of Spanish, encountered gangs, lived in cramped apartments, and struggled to make sense of where they fit in this new location that they had come to occupy. To many, the nature of this location was not particularly clear, as the dismemberment brought about through the violence of the Salvadoran civil war, of emigrating, and of being denied full membership in the United States placed them in gaps or "everyday ruptures" (Coe et al. 2011) between El Salvador and the United States, law and illegality, protection and vulnerability, belonging and exclusion, and the many ethnic and racial categories that they encountered. They were Latino but were not members of the dominant Latino groups (usually Mexican and Mexican Americans in Los Angeles or Dominicans or Puerto Ricans in New York). Many entered the country without authorization but then were able to participate in school activities just like other children did (Gonzales 2011). Their families often came to the United States in search of a better life but found themselves in neighborhoods ridden by poverty and crime. And youths over time began to feel part of the country but were often reminded of the ways that they were different. Recall David Zavala's comment in chapter 1: "It's like I'm half here and half there and in between two worlds" (see also Boehm 2012; Zavella 2011).

In this chapter, I draw on interviewees' accounts of these experiences in order to detail the lives that Salvadoran child migrants and their families created for themselves within these gaps. In so doing, I pursue three goals. First, I seek to present a social history both of Salvadoran immigrant youths and of the institutions in which they were located.[1] Producing this social history counters silences surrounding youths' arrivals in the United States and details how youths became part of the fabric and history of communities and institutions. Countering silences and recognizing immigrant families' participation in local communities are forms of re/membering. Second, I seek to highlight young people's creative responses to the circumstances that they encountered (Boehm et al. 2011). Youths' narratives demonstrate that they were not merely passive subjects whose lives were determined by others; rather, where possible, they advocated for themselves, with teachers, parents, and peers (see also Gardner 2012). Attention to such creativity emphasizes the way that re/membering does not merely return to or bring forward the past but also generates new understandings and new social forms "as children appropriate, reinvent, reproduce, and contest features of adult society" (Dreby 2015:135). Third, by narrating this social history and highlighting youths' creativity, I also seek to throw into relief the structures and assumptions that youths encountered. Thus, piecing together Salvadoran immigrant youths' accounts of their own childhoods in the United States also sheds light on how belonging and exclusion are measured and produced. This history therefore has broad significance in that it reveals the ways that U.S. communities both welcome and exclude newcomers; and how both memory and membership are shaped in the process.

Examining the lives of Salvadoran immigrant youths challenges more common understandings of a "gap" as something that must be eliminated if justice is to be achieved. In law and society research, for example, there is a long tradition of "gap studies" (Seron and Silbey 2004; Trubek 1990), which highlight the ways in which law-in-action often falls far short of the promise of law-on-the-books. Closing the gap would be a means of bringing practice into alignment with policy or rule. Likewise, in academic circles, to say that there is a "gap in the literature" suggests that new research should fill this void. In the case at hand, in contrast, the gaps that youths occupy are both traumatizing and spaces out of which new possibility may emerge (see also Cho 2008). They are traumatizing because they are sites of violence: children suffer separations from family members, are exposed to crime, and live in impoverished conditions. At the same time, a gap can be an opening (Cabot 2013), a new dimension within which innovative forms of being can be devised, a place connecting that which lies beyond the gap. Thus, by living *in* the gap, Salvadoran youths do not eliminate disjuncture, rather they make something of it, they re/member, putting back together the families, nations, communities, and lives taken apart by trauma, war, the nation-state form, and global inequalities.

Institutions played key roles in setting the parameters that youths navigated as they forged lives in this country. Youths settled into homes and neighborhoods, navigated complex family relations, participated in schools, negotiated their connections to other youths, and prepared to transition into adulthood. Much of the literature on immigrant youths examines such experiences in order to determine what promotes youths' success or life chances. For example, Portes and Rumbaut (2005:986; see also Portes and Zhou 1993) describe three possible outcomes for the children of immigrants: (1) a transition to the "middle-class white mainstream," in which case "ethnicity will soon be a matter of personal choice"; (2) strong identification with ethnicity as a source of strength; and (3) identification with ethnicity as a "mark of permanent subordination." In contrast, my own focus is less on what predicts youths' success or failure but rather on identifying forms of citizenship, belonging, and exclusion that are manifested and created in the lives of children. Even though access to public schooling provides youths with some protection from the impact of their immigration status until they are in their late teens (Gonzales 2011), at earlier ages, children still live with fear that they or their relatives will be deported (Dreby 2012, 2015; Jefferies 2014), and they also have to find places for themselves within the structures that make up life in their communities. As they do so, they undergo formative experiences that teach them who they are and that create opportunities for them to challenge others' definitions. They learn about race, double standards within the educational system, socioeconomic inequality, and the depths or limitations of their own capabilities. As a relatively new immigrant group, they also encounter misunderstanding and stigmatization, even on the part of peers. Youths' varied responses to such experiences have helped to reshape the institutions within which encounters take place.

My account of youths' childhood experiences is therefore organized around key institutions in which they negotiated their status: families, neighborhoods, schools, peer groups, and transitions to college or the workplace. Youths' experiences of these institutions weave a new strand into the history of the particular U.S. communities where they came to reside, while also providing insight into the categories within which identity and presence are made meaningful.

Insertion and Reconfiguration: Family and Neighborhood

When they immigrated to the United States, Salvadoran children joined families and neighborhoods that were, in turn, transformed by their presence. Examining these histories makes it possible to tease out the multidirectional and multifaceted relationships between immigrants and the communities in which they have settled. Much of the literature on these relationships focuses on how the "context of reception" influences the trajectories of particular immigrant groups (DeWind and Kasinitz 1997; Portes and Rumbaut 2006; Portes and Zhou 1993). Thus, immigrants who experience a "negative context of reception" (Portes and Rumbaut 2001:277), that is, who move into neighborhoods characterized by violence, poverty, and poor schools and who are denied status, training, and job opportunities, may experience downward mobility (see also Waldinger and Feliciano 2004). This model of the incorporation process treats context as separate from immigrants who are arriving;[2] however, once they arrive, immigrants—including children—have to find or make a place for themselves, often in terms that did not exist before their arrival. Therefore, the story of their arrival is about not only assimilation, but also creativity, as children and their families forge new social relations, thus altering the community—the "context"—in which they come to reside (Espiritu and Tran 2002). The temporal relationship between "context" and "incorporation" is therefore complex: context can itself be produced through the insertion of immigrant children and families into preexisting neighborhoods.

Upon arriving in the United States, one of the earliest lessons that many interviewees recalled learning was that gangs and violence were prevalent in their neighborhoods. The danger posed by gangs and crime seemed different from the wartime violence to which they were accustomed. Marta Dominguez, who came to the United States in 1986 at the age of eight, recalled, "We weren't allowed to play outside because, I guess, of the neighborhood we lived in. Because we lived in South Central [Los Angeles]. And I was used to playing outside. You know, having that liberty? So I didn't like that. I felt like, kind of like, being in jail, you know. Because it's kind of like my freedom was taken from me." Children quickly developed strategies to minimize their own danger. Manuel Cañas avoided the kids who might beat him up and never wore neck chains, so that he would not be a target. When they were able to do so, families moved to areas perceived to be safer. Jessica Morales attended Virgil Middle School,[3] which she described as "probably the worst experience I've had in any of my schooling," and she was slated to continue on to Belmont High School, a similar environment, until she told her mother, "I don't want to go there, because if I go there I think I'm going to start getting into trouble again." Using a fake address, her parents were able to send her to a high school in Van Nuys. Jessica's father also befriended the drug dealers outside of the building where they lived: "They would say, 'Oh, no, those are Martin's kids, leave them alone.'" Despite such efforts, numerous interviewees were exposed to violence. Manuel Cañas described such incidents:

> I don't remember why we moved to South Central, but we moved to Slauson and Vermont. And within a week, it had been barely a week of moving in, and there was a drive-by. A guy had an automatic. And I remember shooting and shooting. And my dad was like "Get down!" . . . [And] I remember

once, they went into P.E. and they were shooting at everyone. I remember I heard the shots [and people were running].

For some, violence became such a part of life that it came to seem normal. Julian Becerra, for example, characterized his East Hollywood neighborhood as "a nice place. . . . It was just gangs, you know, and violence, but we didn't see that everyday. We saw it like once a year or something."

One reason that Salvadoran child migrants were concentrated in neighborhoods characterized by violence was the impoverished conditions in which their families lived (see also Van Hook, Brown, and Kewena 2004). Parents often worked long hours for low wages, sometimes holding down two jobs or bringing work home. Graciela Nuñez recalled that her mother had worked in "garment factories. And then she had my sister a year later, so by the time she was twenty she was undocumented, and couldn't speak English, and had two girls, and was working at sweatshops." Pedro Marroquín noted that his mother, who was a live-in nanny, was often away working for a week at a time. For Sandra Mejillas, it was common to see her mother doing piecework at home: "So I was used to having large bags of pieces, garment pieces, and Mother just going 'Zoom [on the sewing machine]!' All day, all night." Jessica Morales became distraught as she described her mother's first job: "She would go door-to-door and sell this sweet bread. And when she told me that I—I became really emotional because I could never imagine my mom going door-to-door to sell bread." For many, working in such positions meant downward mobility, compared to their lives in El Salvador. Saul Henríquez described his father's experience: "My dad had a good job in El Salvador. So my mom always said, 'Your dad had the cleanest hands in El Salvador.' And we come over here, and he worked, he used to make furniture. 'So your dad, his hands changed so much.'" Some child migrants felt deprived in comparison to other children, while others felt that the cast-off clothes and toys provided by the children for whom their mothers cared enabled them to appear well off. And some felt that their parents' labor paid off. Veronica Reina commented that her parents had given her "the perfect childhood experience."

Emblematic of the severe poverty experienced by some migrants is the fact that many had to share resources, including housing. Numerous interviewees remarked on the crowded living conditions they experienced when they first arrived. These conditions were a stark contrast to what they had expected prior to immigrating (Mahler 1995), as Marta Dominguez explained: "When I came I thought my parents were going to live like in this mansion because everybody would say, you know, like here everybody just lives well and everybody is rich and everybody has like all these like wonderful things. But when I came, my parents were living in a like a converted garage and like a small room where all like five or six of us lived there, um, with one bed." According to interviewees, it was not uncommon for as many as fifteen people to live in a one-bedroom apartment. Rosa Hernández had this experience and recalled sleeping with her mother on the kitchen floor, because the living room and bedroom were already full. Similarly, Jessica Morales was allowed to sleep on the sofa, along with her brother and grandmother, "while everybody else lined up like sardines on the floor in the living room. . . . And one of the problems we had was mice. So you can imagine what it was like for these people." Interviewees' accounts of such experiences, which were usually temporary (lasting from several months to a few years), until their parents' earnings permitted moving to another home or apartment, reflect both extreme poverty and also a strategy of relying on relatives for support, taking in new arrivals, and pooling scarce resources (Menjívar 2000). Indeed, Cecilia Molina's listing of the relatives with whom she lived when she first arrived is indicative of the abundance of close family relations that were available to some child migrants: "We all lived in the same house when we first moved there. . . . My grandparents, their oldest son who had a wife and two daughters, two of my uncles, two other uncles, two aunts, my parents, myself, and my baby brothers [who] were born in 1983."

Just as local households changed with the arrival of Central American immigrants in the 1980s, so too did neighborhood demographics shift significantly. In fact, one of the clearest ways that migrants produced, as well as responded to, context was through the changes that their presence wrought in Koreatown, Pico Union, East Hollywood, and other Los Angeles neighborhoods. Ruben Torres, whose family had emigrated in the 1970s, prior to the war, told me that El Salvador came to him in the 1980s:

> I saw that because, I mean, now as I grew up in like some of those — at the apartment complex I lived [at] in Hollywood — because we kept a lot of those contacts. They were also Central Americans, some were Guatemalans; there was a Nicaraguan family; there was also Salvadoran; there was like a Mexican family; of course an Armenian family there. So, you know, not just in Salvador, but all of sudden I was — like I — I'm aware that Central America was like — was there.

Some families moved to areas where there was only a small Central American presence, but many lived in communities where they met other Salvadorans,

Guatemalans, Hondurans, and Nicaraguans. For example, echoing the Tobar passage with which this chapter begins, Jessica Morales recalled, "Most of the kids that I played with were also either from El Salvador or Guatemala. I think I only had like two Mexican friends. . . . We used to play in the hallways of that big building." Rodolfo Martinez recalled that the Koreatown neighborhood where he grew up was "like a Salvadorian town. . . . You would only have to go to MacArthur Park and most likely you would meet somebody from back home, you know?" These children lived through the historic events that played out in Los Angeles, including celebrations when the Salvadoran peace accords were announced, the 1992 Los Angeles uprisings following the Rodney King verdicts (Gooding-Williams 1993), the 1994 passage of California Proposition 187 (which—though eventually ruled unconstitutional—was deeply stigmatizing because it would have required service providers to report undocumented immigrants), and the 1994 Northridge earthquake. Those histories are also their histories.

As children lived through and contributed to demographic shifts, they developed an intimate knowledge of *place* (Zilberg 2004). For example, Bayardo Morazan compared the communities where his family had lived:

> We actually moved to the Pico—Pico/Crenshaw area, you know, Pico Union. And I went to . . . junior high in Mt. Vernon, which was in the border of Koreatown, and the area, at that point, was more African American and a bit more Mexican as well. But there was [sic] already a few Central Americans who had moved into the area. I remember the building that we moved in was mostly Mexican, but there was another family that was from El Salvador, and another family that was from Honduras. . . .
>
> Silver Lake was completely different. There was more diversity in Silver Lake. And, you know, people from all kinds of walks of life. And in the Pico/Crenshaw area it was definitely more—definitely African American, I think that was the majority, and then next to that were Mexicans and Koreans. So it was a little difficult, you know, kind of trying to fit into that. But, you know, eventually I got used to it and it was like—it was home, you know, so. It became home.

Bayardo's concluding comment highlights the process that child migrants went through: they had to find a way to fit into existing neighborhood dynamics, but as they did so, they made these neighborhoods home, not only for themselves as individuals, but also for Central Americans more generally, thus changing neighborhoods in the process. Children's intimate knowledge of the neighborhoods and families they encountered is as much a part of their incorporation as the danger and violence that they experienced. Rafael Espinoza's account of how he met some of his first playmates illustrates the intimate distance of living in this gap between being a newcomer and becoming a member:

> Another one of my memories is that when we first got here, I was standing out in front of the apartment complex, and I saw some Black kids playing. And I had never seen Black kids before, so that was something new to me. It was really different. And I saw that they were playing tag. And I don't know how, because we couldn't communicate, but I approached them, and somehow we started playing together. I don't know how that was, because I couldn't talk to them.

As they created spaces for themselves within U.S. neighborhoods, many Salvadoran child migrants also found that their families were reconfigured through the migration process. In a sense, migrant children moved between and into families, even as they left other relatives behind. While it is certainly not the case that all enjoyed family stability prior to migration—for instance, in El Salvador, it is not uncommon for children to be sent to live with other relatives for periods of time, or for parents to start new relationships or have additional children—migration, for many, imposed periods of forced absence that disrupted familial ties. Children's narratives therefore remarked on the ways that their own family experiences deviated from an idealized norm of intact nuclear families surrounded by closely related kin such as grandparents, aunts, uncles, cousins. And, of course, some children moved with their families or at least with key family members. Nonetheless, changes in their family configuration struck many interviewees as significant aspects of their experiences as immigrants.

As discussed in chapter 1, separation from family members was part of the violence associated with immigrating without authorization (Abrego 2014b). David Zavala experienced such separation first at the age of five, when his mother left to work in the United States, and then again at the age of seven, when she sent for him and he left his father in El Salvador. David had been told that his father would follow as well, but "the day for him to be brought to the U.S. him [he] never came." For David, emigrating meant losing close contact with his father, though he did marvel at what it was like to rejoin his mother: "Waking up to 'I'm in a new house, a new place.' And just like waking up and seeing my mom, you know. Seeing my mom." As noted in chapter 1, though, some interviewees learned that the parents with whom they had long anticipated reuniting were often like strangers (see also Smith, Lalonde, and Johnson 2004), and some found it alienating to discover new stepparents or younger siblings who had been born in their absence.

In addition to experiencing such changes, many interviewees reported that their families regularly hosted new arrivals from El Salvador. Juan José Olvera Saldivar recalled with admiration the "help" that his father offered to others: "My dad used to help a lot of my cousins, so we never lived alone until we moved. There was always somebody in the house. Like he helped somebody come from El Salvador, so they were living with us for a month or two months until they got their work, and they could go off somewhere else. There was somebody always." For Juan José's friend, Mauricio Nuñez Arellano, such help extended to participating in the illicit migrant-smuggling economy, albeit on the receiving end: "Yeah, I remember also my cousins coming and my aunt coming and like picking them up from like where they were going to deliver them, where they were going to bring them, and just taking them home, and then them being there for a while." It is striking that for these interviewees, such ongoing arrivals of undocumented relatives were a normal part of childhood, as, gradually, more of their family members moved to the United States. Interviewees, who, as children, seemingly were not always informed of what was about to happen, often described the appearance of new relatives as something of a surprise. As Ruben Torres put it, "All of a sudden you have cousins that I didn't know also were like coming here." Ruben recalled the "sad and telling" comment that one of his newly arrived cousins made on such an occasion:

> At Christmas Eve when my family showed up. I remember it was a knock on the door. . . . And like, "Well, here's your cousin; here's your cousin; here's your uncle who's only seven years older than you." . . . There's a comment that my cousin made, she was eight at the time when she—and my uncle was twelve. . . . They always recount it because it was kind of cute, but sad and very telling. There's like, "What time are you guys—?" It's Christmas, right? It's like, "What time are you guys—are the fireworks going off?" I was like, "There's no fireworks here." They're like, "But it's Christmas." And that's something that's done over there [in El Salvador], you know? And over here it's like, "No, there's no fireworks." And they were very sad about that. You know, they were just—it was very weird to see that. There's pictures of us from that, I think, from that Christmas.

This story highlights the complexities that immigration introduced into family relationships. These relatives were close enough to be taken in on Christmas

Eve, but at the same time, Ruben had to be introduced to them. His little cousin's question about fireworks highlighted both the gulf between them—they now celebrated Christmas differently—and the loss that the newly arrived relatives experienced: in the United States there would no longer be Christmas fireworks; thus for them, Christmas, and presumably many other occasions, had changed dramatically. This poignant moment was captured in the retelling of the anecdote, which had become a family story, and in the photographs of "us," this newly reconstructed family, which had been preserved.

Some interviewees resented their relatives in El Salvador, who gained their parents' attention and sometimes also material goods. Moises Quintero told me a story that he characterized as "irrelevant":

> I remember that one year my mom had sent him [his cousin in El Salvador] a little Snoopy soap dish, an Avon Snoopy soap dish, and I wanted it. And my mom kept saying, "No, it's for your cousin Marc." And so when he came [to the United States], I was saying, "Oh," I go, "Did you get the soap dish?" And he was saying, "Yeah." And I go, "Oh, cool, can we play with it?" And he was saying—he was looking at me—he was older than I was, you know, I was a little kid. And I just remember looking at me—him looking at me like, "Wow, this is the retard in the family" sort of thing, you know, "He wants to play with a soap dish."

Like Ruben's story of his cousin's sad comment, Moises's account highlights both connection and distance. Moises and his cousin were connected through the Snoopy soap dish, a product that presumably was acquired through personal connections with an Avon salesperson and therefore might have been difficult to replicate, which traveled first to El Salvador and then, at least in Moises's mind, back to the United States with his cousin. At the same time, Moises's child-self placed more importance on this item than his cousin did, particularly given the context, as, when moving to the United States, his cousin may have been focusing on many other things besides this gift. Moises's comment that the story was "irrelevant" may echo his perception of his cousin's thinking about the irrelevance of a soap dish at such a moment. But, clearly, to Moises, the story was far from irrelevant. Perhaps to him, this movement (and nonmovement) of the soap dish and his cousin, as well as the difference in perspective that he had had as a child, captured something important about his relationship to such relatives.

Additions—whether through birth, marriage, or the continued immigration of relatives—gave rise to mixed-status families in which some were citizens, others were undocumented, and still others had temporary status (see also Dreby 2015; Fix and Zimmerman 2001). Such differences meant that opportunities and disadvantages were distributed differently within the same family. For example, Mauricio Nuñez Arellano, who has since naturalized, explained that his mother became a lawful permanent resident, and his younger brother, who was born in the United States, was a citizen, while for some time he and his father only had Temporary Protected Status (TPS). Mauricio recalled that his mother and brother "would go to visit El Salvador. They would go and come back, and I would be like, 'I want to go! I want to go visit my family!' Which was kind of hard not being able to go with them. But they would leave, and we'd just have to stay behind" (see also Abrego 2009; Menjívar 2002). Recall as well that interviewees who were part of mixed-status families worried about their relatives and therefore remained vulnerable to the effects of immigration law enforcement practices even after they became U.S. citizens. For instance, Veronica Reina was born in the United States and so had never experienced illegality herself. However, her aunt and uncle were still undocumented at the time of our interview:

> I know my mom's older brother, he came like five years before her like in the, yeah, early '80s, and he's still undocumented. He was actually arrested early January. The Immigration came to his house early in the morning and they arrested him. And, um, he was in jail for like a couple months until like late February. . . . [And] like my mom's sister, I know she's a single mother, and she's like—she's scared. She's undocumented. And she's scared that they're going to come for her. And she has a ten-year-old son. And she's just scared, you know, what's going to happen to him? They're separating her from him.

Differences in legal status, social experience, language skill, and cultural knowledge made relationships between child migrants and their parents complex. It was common for children, who quickly acquired English, to translate for parents, even about highly adult matters (see also Kim et al. 2003; Menjívar 2002). Recall that in the account that opened chapter 1, Milda Escobar, at the age of eight, had to translate for the police after her cousin was shot and killed at her home in Los Angeles. Similarly—though less traumatically—Juan José Olvera Saldivar had to translate legal documents for his parents: "I was like, 'Hey, you know, I understand how to read, but I don't understand this legal documentation.' It's like when they bought their first house, they made me read the mortgage, and I said, 'I can't understand any of this stuff.'" Other interviewees accompanied relatives to serve as translators at school conferences, doctor appointments, welfare offices, and other important meetings. As children gained new knowledge, they sometimes found that their parents couldn't provide support that they needed. Cesar Quintanilla, for example, reported that he tried to protect his mother from the realization that, with her fifth-grade education, she could not help him with homework:

> It was really hard for me. She wanted to help me; I know she wanted to really help me. She always wanted to be, my mom's been the best mother in the world. She would always try to do everything she could to help me, but I kind of stopped telling her to help me, because I could see it in her, that she wanted to help me, but she didn't know. So it was hard for her, you know? I tended to see that, and I was like I'd rather not ask her. I'll just wait tomorrow until I go to school.

Even as young people acquired knowledge that parents lacked, some parents also tried to exert control over their children. Fearful that children would join gangs, or, in the case of girls, become pregnant, some parents threatened or actually did send children back to El Salvador, where, they hoped, children would be removed from bad influences and exposed to more traditional values (see Haller and Landolt 2005; Orellana, Thorne, Chee, and Lam 2001). Some parents punished their children physically, either hitting them or making them kneel on grains of rice, a painful experience. Some interviewees observed that their parents, as Latinos, seemed to be stricter than "American" parents. Veronica Reina commented on this:

> I've noticed they're [my parents are] more strict and conservative compared to a lot of the parents, you know, American parents. You know, when I was invited to a sleepover, you know, they were like, "No, we don't know their parents." You know, they're more conservative and strict about what I'm doing. You know, like I noticed most girls like they don't have a curfew to them. And I had a curfew. I had to be home at eight and that was it, you know. I couldn't go out [by] myself. One of my parents had to be always with me. So I feel like, you know, Latino parents in general are more uptight with their kids, and who they're with, or what time do they get home, and what are they doing, and all that stuff.

Parental efforts to control children could give rise to conflicts, especially if children resented parents for "abandoning them," as one interviewee put it, and if, during earlier long periods of family separation, children had not needed parents' approval for their actions (Orellana et al. 2001).

At the same time, many interviewees reported having close relationships with parents, whom they considered inspiring. Eduardo Sanchez, for example, admired his father for gaining expertise as an auto technician who could then work on computerized vehicles. Eduardo also commented that, due to a paper he had had to write on feminist theory, he had questioned his mother about her relationship with his father and had gained new insight into his parents' interdependency: "They needed each other because they had no support." Cesar Quintanilla was impressed by what his mother, who had become a single parent when he was a baby, had been able to accomplish. Cesar, who had heard Eduardo's comment about his parents' interdependency, remarked, "And contrary to what he [Eduardo] was saying, my mom, after that, she's like, 'I don't need no man, I'm a strong woman and I don't need no man to help me out. I'm going to do it on my own.'" Cecilia admired her parents' educational achievements:

> My dad came here to wash dishes and then became an electrician. Now he's back in school because he wants to teach again. He wants to teach ESL [English as a second language]. My mom did the bakery thing, and she went to school, and she did real estate for a long time. Now she's been working with immigrant youth in the . . . school district, so like as a TA. And she's going to [Cal State] Northridge and getting her Spanish degree. So I mean I'm really inspired by my parents, just really humbled by what they've gone through.

The family relationships that young people forged and the ways that their presence reshaped neighborhoods helped to produce the social spaces of their childhoods. Context was not just inert, waiting to receive them; rather, child migrants themselves helped to create the social worlds where not only they but also U.S.-born children grew up. These were social worlds where Central American kids played in hallways, ran into peers from their home communities in public parks, joined in games of tag, received new arrivals who often entered the country without authorization, recalled Christmas being celebrated with fireworks, were capable of translating between English and Spanish, and in some cases—as we shall see in later chapters—joined or became affiliated with gangs. These new arrivals thus reshaped the very contexts where they were received.

Critiquing the notion that children are caught between "the 'worlds' or 'cultures' of their parents and the host society," Karakayali (2005:326) suggests both that there are more than two worlds (in that both parental and host societies are diverse) and that "the 'problem of the second generation' should be defined as how to realize the potentials engendered by a heterogeneous life, despite the obstacle of a social environment where the existence of such potentials goes unnoticed" (340). As they created spaces for themselves in neighborhoods where "Salvadoran" was not, initially at least, a known category, and as they joined—literally, brought together—families that had been transformed by the violence of immigration, child migrants realized such potentials. Their experiences, such as living in one-bedroom apartments with fifteen other people or driving to pick up undocumented relatives who were being delivered by a migrant smuggler, likely differed significantly from those of their middle-class white counterparts. At the same time, these children developed unique understandings of place, movement, family, marginalization, and possibility. These understandings also shaped and were forged by their experiences in schools and with peers, where they continually had to negotiate what it meant to be from El Salvador.

Identification and Misrecognition: Schools and Peers

As they encountered peers and entered U.S. educational institutions, interviewees discovered that race and ethnicity served as organizing (and sometimes exclusionary) principles in multiple situations. As Telles and Ortiz observe regarding the children of Mexican immigrants, "their acculturation is not only one of losing ethnic cultural traits but probably also of acquiring a strong sense of the American racial hierarchy" (2008:269–270). According to interviewees, race and ethnicity shaped friendship groupings, influenced where children sat during lunch at school, impacted teachers' interpretations of children's abilities, and defined gang affiliations and animosities. As they navigated these processes, Salvadoran youths also learned that, as a relatively new group, they fit existing categories only imperfectly (see also Brettell 2007). The categories "Latino" or "Hispanic," in which they were often placed, were, given the ethnic makeup of Los Angeles, often presumed to be equated with "Mexican," "Mexican American," or "Chicano." At the same time, many of their Mexican or Mexican American peers disparaged them for being different, mocking the way that they spoke Spanish or treating Salvadoranness as something negative or inferior. Youths responded to what they experienced as misrecognitions in multiple ways. Some sought to hide or downplay Salvadoran origins, adopting Mexican forms of Spanish and trying, generally, to blend in (see also A. García 2014). Others found a key individual, such as a teacher, who recognized their scholarly potential and supported their academic and other interests. And still others advocated for themselves by correcting others' misconceptions about Salvadoranness and refusing to let others' perceptions define their own senses of self. Like the ways that Salvadoran immigrants' presence reshaped neighborhoods, these diverse responses gave new meaning to racial and ethnic categories.

The continued pervasiveness of racial and ethnic divisions and hierarchies in the current so-called color-blind moment is well established (Bonilla-Silva 2014; Gómez 2012; Obasogie 2014). From jury deliberations to college admission procedures to funding awards to hiring practices, race, ethnicity, and gender have been found to shape evaluators' perceptions of merit in ways that produce disparate outcomes (Flores and Rodriguez 2006; Ginther et al 2011; Lynch and Haney 2011; Moss-Racusin et al. 2012). In fact, Sora Han (2012:84; 2015) has argued that race is foundational to the United States as a nation and also is an "absent presence" in the U.S. Constitution. She notes that, without the Constitution's fugitive slave clause, the states may not have come together to form a union but, at the same time, slavery is never actually mentioned. Though, historically, race in the United States often took the form of a black/white binary (Haney-López 1996), more recently, racial designations have become more fluid, with the U.S. Census now permitting individuals to indicate multiple racial and ethnic affiliations and even to write in their own categories (Lee and Bean 2010). Some have argued that this very fluidity, rather than simply opening up racial categories, is actually linked to neoliberalism, which treats individuals as consumers who are responsible for self-governance and who can choose among the array of commodities, values, and identities available in the marketplace (Urciuoli 1999, 2008). Race and ethnicity have thus become marketable—they are bases on which corporations appeal to consumers (Comaroff and Comaroff 2009) and individuals with "multicultural skills" are valued in the workplace (Urciuoli 1999). Yet such developments, which seem to suggest that the United States has overcome its racist past and that diversity is now something to celebrate, have occurred alongside the mass incarceration of people of color, seemingly ever more entrenched racial segregation in urban communities, and ramped-up immigration enforcement practices that particularly target Latinos (Chavez 2008; Inda 2006; Peterson and Krivo 2010; Simon 2007). This strange coupling of free choice and inequality is the essence of color-blind racism.

Salvadoran child migrants were caught in the interstices of these processes of racialization and color-blindness, of subjugation and the celebration of difference. Furthermore, anti-immigrant sentiment was particularly virulent in the 1980s and 1990s, as evidenced by the sanctions that the 1986 Immigration Reform and Control Act imposed on employers who hired undocumented workers; the passage in 1994 of California Proposition 187 (ultimately ruled unconstitutional), which required various service providers to screen individuals for their immigration status; and the restrictive immigration measures approved in 1996 with the passage of the Illegal Immigration Reform and Immigrant Responsibility Act (Martin 1995; Perea 1997). These public debates over immigration policies made race—and especially Mexicanness—more salient during the very period when interviewees were moving into U.S. communities and schools. Interviewees' experiences of recognition and misrecognition, interracial and interethnic animosities, and relationships with peers and teachers reveal the structures within which they were situated—structures that, contradictorily, treated race and ethnicity as biological essences, as a matter of self-definition, and as linked to merit. Because Salvadoran youths were seen as not fitting existing categories, they had the opportunity to forge their own forms of subjectivity and racial and ethnic identifications. In so doing, they drew on the legacy of earlier civil rights and social justice movements, notions of multiculturalism and respect for difference, and their own senses of their familial and national histories. Their accounts of school and peer relationships thus demonstrate the continued salience of race and ethnicity as well as the ways that their own alterity led them to question existing categories with an eye toward social justice rather than color-blindness. By seeking recognition on their own terms, youths simultaneously sought to re/member, to overcome silence about their own histories, and to create a world in which they belonged and had worth.

One of the first U.S. institutions where 1.5-generation and second-generation Salvadoran children experienced misrecognition were public schools, "strategic sites where youths struggle to make sense of the worlds they create and re-create with peers and adults" (Morrill et al. 2000:528; see also Suárez-Orozco and Suárez-Orozco 1995). Schools, seemingly, did not know quite what to do with them. Multiple interviewees reported that school officials in the Los Angeles area seemingly mistook their difficulties with English as an indication that they were "behind" academically and then placed them one to two years behind the grade level that they had already completed in El Salvador. Marta Dominguez recalled, "Math, that's all they gave me. No other thing because, I guess, because I couldn't speak the language. And then ... they put me back in third grade when I came. So it was kind of upsetting because I wanted to go to fourth grade." Likewise, Rafael Espinoza was kept in ESL classes even though he had mastered English. He told me, "By high school, I was fluent in English. . . . But I was still in ESL . . . so I told my teachers that I didn't belong there. They still insisted that I stay in the program, though, and they told me that I should take a test to see where I was. I took the test, and I passed all of them." Bayardo Morazan was placed in remedial classes due to speaking English with an accent. He recalled, "The counselor had put me in remedial courses. And so when I went and asked how come I was not in the regular courses? They said, 'Oh, your English—you don't speak English well.' And I did, you know, I have an accent and I had a thicker accent even back then." According to Marcelo Suárez-Orozco (1987), an educational anthropologist who did fieldwork in public schools during the 1980s, such practices were common. Teachers and counselors often made Central American students repeat courses they had completed and kept them in ESL classes longer than was necessary.

Such treatment made some interviewees feel that they were stupid. Cesar Quintanilla was placed in honors classes, over the opposition of at least some of his teachers, but nonetheless "felt like I was straight dumb. I didn't feel like I was prepared. Like the other students." Some interviewees linked such feelings of inadequacy explicitly to their race, ethnicity, and language abilities. Araceli Muñoz felt that her teachers generally expected minority students to do poorly: "And I guess that's the thing about, you know, education, they don't expect minorities to be, I guess, or don't expect them to be, I guess, in honors classes, and we were." William Campos recalled that, even when he was in college, he was publicly humiliated by a teacher, because he spoke English with an accent:

> It was an English teacher. She made ugly comments on my papers, and she told me that I didn't know enough, that I shouldn't be making those mistakes still, and that I needed to go back and retake the lower classes. And then in class she would embarrass me. I would say something, and she would just say, "What???? I can't understand you! What are you trying to say?" In front of the whole class. . . . And she made me feel like I couldn't do it, like I couldn't write, I couldn't speak. I became scared to write, scared to speak. It affected me for a number of semesters.

One lesson that interviewees learned in school was that race (and language, which is often a code for race) was inextricably linked to school officials' understandings of Central American students' aptitudes and abilities. Students were repeatedly misrecognized—as uneducated, inarticulate, and unintelligent. Some reported that teachers viewed them with mistrust. Cesar Quintanilla related that once, when he had a bloody nose at school, his teacher accused him of lying and would not allow him to go to the restroom, even though he was clearly bleeding. Frustrated, he left the classroom anyway and was subsequently punished. As new arrivals, interviewees experienced humiliating moments, such as a fellow student directing a male student to the girls' bathroom as a prank, or being unable to understand a teacher who repeatedly stated—in English—that a new student was in the wrong room, to the amusement of the rest of the class. Some female students reported that teachers sometimes expressed the stereotype that Latina women were more likely to have children at young ages. Veronica Reina, a student at a California State University campus in Southern California, said that one of her instructors had suggested that only half of the Latina freshmen would still be around as seniors, because the rest would become pregnant and drop out. Race and gender thus intersected in key ways—leading Salvadoran boys to be suspected of criminality and girls of promiscuity.

Despite these troubling raced- and gendered misrecognitions, interviewees in many cases found school fulfilling, and some considered their schools and programs to be of particularly high quality.[4] Marta Dominguez spoke glowingly of her experience: "I loved the school because it had like all these wonderful things. And toys and letters like, really cute decorated. I was like, I was amazed with the school. And then the fact that they fed us. That was just like new to me." One interviewee, who eventually earned a PhD, was placed in a gifted program in the third grade that she described as an "excellent program, with just diverse, fun activities, having scientists come and present, having actors come in and perform a play, and having a zookeeper come in with animals." Unfortunately, her family moved and her new school had no such program. Araceli Muñoz found kindergarten frustrating, due to the language barrier, but, by first grade, she had mastered both English and reading to such a degree that she was placed in an accelerated class.

As well—and in contrast to the misrecognitions described above—numerous interviewees described having their own potential recognized by particular teachers who served as advocates and mentors and who enabled them to succeed. Monica Ramirez reported having a quasi-familial relationship with a teacher: "I remember this teacher . . . I really grew to like, I don't know, it was just more than that, more than a teacher level, like she told me once she saw me like a daughter and I still remember her. . . . And she always tried to help me and just always [was] giving me individual attention, if I needed it." For Adelmo Ariel Umanzor, it was important that teachers recognized that, as a Salvadoran student fleeing a civil war, he had unique needs. He stated, "I started getting teachers that influenced me a lot too. They saw that I was from El Salvador and I came from the civil war. You know and they started giving me books about El Salvador. And then I was very interested in Che Guevara.[5] They would give me books about Che and [I] started reading about Roque Dalton."[6] Teachers who believed in students advocated for them with other school officials, told students that they had the potential to attend college, and countered perceptions that students were not intelligent. Graciela Nuñez had originally been placed in sheltered (ESL) classes in middle school, but her math teacher persuaded the school staff to allow her to transition to the regular English classes, a move that, she says, enabled her to enter the honors program in high school. Both Saul Henríquez and Nelson Almendrez told me about counselors and teachers who convinced them that they could attend a University of California campus. And Walter Olivar attributed his own college success to counselors and teachers who demystified the college application process.

At times, though, even such assistance encountered racial barriers. In eighth grade, Cesar Quintanilla was invited to participate in the Fulfillment Fund mentoring program (see www.fulfillment.org/mentoring) and was assigned a mentor. Cesar recalled:

> It was just, at the time, I met him when I was fourteen, fifteen years old. And you know, in our neighborhood, it was just *raza*, you know?[7] So, and this white man comes in, and he's my mentor, and it was funny, at the beginning, because I feel awkward. This guy was cool, as far as I know. It was embarrassing for me at the beginning when I met him. His job was to take me to places, to events, to college trips. He would just take me anywhere, anywhere he would take me, I used to love it, because it was a place that I wouldn't go if I would not have met him. So to the museum, to the opera, to the orchestra, because he used to play the violin. So we used to go see the L.A. Philharmonic or the L.A. chamber orchestra. So he would just take me different places. It was embarrassing at the beginning, because it's a weekend around here. You know, all of the kids on the weekend, everybody's playing around in the street, and here comes my mentor, [name deleted] like in a car, "Okay, Cesar, let's go!" And everybody's like, "Who is this fucking white guy? Where is he taking you? Is he your probation officer or something? Who is he?" It was funny!

It is striking that the level of racial segregation—some might say apartheid (Bourgois 2003)—and criminalization of Latinos was so high that in the late

1990s, Cesar's friends perceived his mentor, a white man, as Cesar's probation officer. It is also striking that, while Cesar says that he loved the cultural opportunities that this program provided, he was also embarrassed to participate, due to the ways that the program made him visible and set him apart. It felt strange to have a white mentor in a neighborhood where everyone was *raza* and to devote his weekend time to museum and orchestra trips while his friends played in the street.[8] These comments reveal the gulf that continues to separate low-income and minority children from their middle-class, white counterparts.

In addition to having their academic abilities misjudged, interviewees described repeated misunderstandings about their ethnicity and nationality on the part of both peers and teachers. As noted above (and see Dreby 2015), race and ethnicity were highly salient in public school settings. Jessica Morales described attending a San Fernando Valley high school at which seating during lunch was highly (though informally) segregated by race. She explained,

> All the white kids would hang out during lunch in an area that was known as Disneyland. Horrible. And then most of the Latino kids would hang out in another area that was known as little TJ [Tijuana]. And then there was the African American kids here, I don't think there was a name for where they used to hang out. And the Asian kids here. . . . I hated having to go where most of the Latinos were too because I felt like, "Well, why do I have to be here?" . . . So I just started going from group to group to group. . . . But even still like some people you could tell they didn't feel very comfortable or would make little comments, "Oh, what are you doing over here in Disneyland?"

Likewise, Manuel Cañas attended a middle school at which tensions between Latino and African American students were so high that violence sometimes resulted. Manuel himself had friends in multiple racial groupings and therefore felt somewhat protected.

Because Mexican Americans were the largest Latino group in Los Angeles, many interviewees reported that they were presumed to be Mexican, by both peers (including longtime friends) and teachers. Monica Ramirez said that when she told people that she was Salvadoran, they sometimes responded, "Oh, El Salvador, where's that?" or "What is that?" while Jessica Morales said that people sometimes asked her, "What part of Mexico is El Salvador?" Numerous interviewees described well-meaning schoolteachers who celebrated multiculturalism and honored Latinos only through a focus on Mexican traditions, foods, and history. Cesar Quintanilla described one such occasion:

"Alright," you know, you're at this school, you're supposed to trust this place. And then the teacher is telling you, "Alright." And the teacher most of the time being Anglo, at the time that we were growing up. . . . "Alright. You guys are Hispanic, and today we're having a celebration, Cinco de Mayo, and here is the flag that represents you guys," pretty much! And it's like, "Alright," we were little kids, coloring it, "Yeah, look! Our flag!" And we come home, "Mom, look!" You know? And it's like . . . , "What's wrong with you? You're not Mexican, you're Salvadoran!"

A few interviewees reported being taken for members of other ethnic groups, such as Filipinos or Indians. For Jessica Morales, ignorance about El Salvador was so widespread that it was noteworthy when a teacher discussed Salvadoran history. She recalled, "One time in, it was sociology class in high school actually, the teacher mentioned the civil war in El Salvador and I just felt like my heart racing because I felt like, 'Wow, somebody's actually acknowledging my country and what happened,' you know."

Even though they reported being taken for Mexicans or Mexican Americans, interviewees also stressed that Salvadorans and Mexicans were seen as distinct groups and that tensions between the two were high. In fact, interviewees talked much more about tensions between Salvadorans and Mexicans than they did about animosity between other national, ethnic, or racial groups. Such rivalry may, in part, be a continuation of animosities experienced in El Salvador, where there is some resentment of the ways that Central American migrants are treated in Mexico (Cruz Salazar 2011; Mendoza Aguilar 2013; Soto Espinosa 2014; Vogt 2013).[9] These tensions nonetheless seem to have taken some interviewees by surprise. For example, Monica Ramirez said that when she told friends that she was Salvadoran, they sometimes began to emphasize difference, referring to her and other Salvadorans as "you guys." She remarked, "Like, what do you mean, 'You guys?' 'Oh, she's Salvadorian, she doesn't know that.' But some people are like, 'Oh, she's from OVER THERE.'"[10] Many interviewees stressed that individuals who identified as Salvadorans were teased and looked down on by their Mexican American peers. Marta Dominguez recalled, "We were supposed to stay with our own [race], I guess, but within Latinos we are so diverse that Mexican kids were always being like, 'Oh you Salvi.'" Interviewees reported that they were called *cerotes* or *pupusas*, were looked on (to quote one interviewee) "as less Hispanics, or less Mexican, or less probably human," were accused of being loud, lewd, angry, violent, uneducated, and "Salvi-trash." Nelson Almendrez, who characterized himself as half-Salvadoran and half-Mexican, recalled that his friends seemed to expect him to simply accept such negative treatment: "I hanged with friends that were just Mexican and they were proud to be Mexican. And they'd always be saying a lot of negative things for Salvadorans. But they'd always throw out the 'Salvadorans—Salvadorans are so dirty, no offense.' That was always the punch line at the end, 'no offense.' And I was suppose[d] to be like, 'Oh, well, none taken,' or 'Yeah, it's okay you can talk all you want, it's okay.'"

Perhaps most virulent among these anti-Salvadoran attitudes was the stigmatization of young Salvadoran men as gang members (Zilberg 2011). Blaming media hype about gang violence, Eduardo Sanchez, Saul Henríquez, and Cesar Quintanilla complained that as soon as they identified themselves as Salvadoran, they were immediately assumed to be members of the Mara Salvatrucha or the 18th Street gangs. They explained:

> CESAR: It's like, for example, we're going to a party or something. This is an example. And there's a couple of friends that they had invited. "Oh, where're you guys from? Where are you born at?" "We're from El Salvador." "Oh, so you guys are *mareros* [gang members]."
>
> SUSAN: Okay. They'll just say that.
>
> CESAR: "Oh, you guys are like *mara*."
>
> EDUARDO: It comes up in conversation. You're meeting someone new, and you tell them that you're from El Salvador, and the first thing a lot of times they say, "Oh, are you from the *mara*?" It also has to do a little bit with the way we look. The profile of gang members. So the way we look and when we tell them we're from El Salvador, that's the first thing they think.

As college students who had grown up in neighborhoods where gangs were prevalent, Eduardo, Saul, and Cesar dedicated their time and energy to providing a positive role model to counter such stereotypes, as will be discussed further in the next chapter.

Ridicule of youths who identified as Salvadoran often focused on language, because their version of Spanish differed from the Mexicanized Spanish more prevalent in Los Angeles. Particular terms triggered jeers from other children. For Ruben Torres, the difference between *pajilla* ("straw" in El Salvador) and *popote* ("straw" in Mexico) stood out: "I never wanted to say *pajilla* around my friends. I never—it just sounded so, you know, funny amongst them. They'd laugh." Ruben reported that because he associated Salvadoran Spanish with family and home, he also lapsed into it when he was talking to particularly close friends. Even then, he recounted, Salvadoran Spanish was sometimes taken as a marker of difference rather than intimacy: "I can speak Spanish to certain people and they're like, 'Hey you're not, you know, you're Salvadoran.'" William Campos reported that even though he was a U.S. citizen, he was regarded as an immigrant due to his accent and appearance. Other children mocked him by saying "bad words, Salvadoran words. They didn't know what they meant, but I did." Araceli Muñoz, a college student who worked at a fast food restaurant, was annoyed that customers simply assumed that, because of where she worked, she was a monolingual Spanish-speaker. Often, she said, such people tried to talk to her in Spanish, even though her English was fluent and their Spanish was ungrammatical and heavily accented. Once, she was taking an order through a drive-through window and was having a hard time hearing a customer. She related, "I was like, 'I'm sorry. I'm sorry.' And I was trying to stick my head out the window and they kind of ended up saying, 'What? Don't you speak English?' Oh, my goodness. And I just kinda backed up and said, 'I'm sorry. Somebody else will have to come to the window because if he says something else I might explode.'" This racial insult was deeply offensive.

It is important to note that not all interviewees had tense relationships with non-Salvadoran peers. Some regarded teasing over identity or language issues as lighthearted, while others felt that their own friendship networks transcended differences between groups. One interviewee, who attended a predominantly white high school, formed close friendships with a small group of Spanish-speaking individuals from multiple countries of origin. He remarked, "We were a minority. And they [the white people] weren't bothered by us, or the other way around." Furthermore, even within the Salvadoran immigrant community there was differentiation. Ruben Torres related that after he was mocked for being Salvadoran, he sought out more recently arrived Salvadoran children: "I'd say, 'Hey, yeah, I'm Salvadoran too.' They're like, 'Oh, really, what part?' And this is in high school. I'm like, 'Well, I wasn't born there. I was born here.' And they're like, 'Ah, you're not Salvadoran,' you know. I'm like, 'Aw, man, what the hell happened?' They're like, 'Yeah, you're American,' and this is from other Salvadoran and Central American students who were immigrants in high school." Such misrecognition is a double displacement: Ruben (and presumably other youths) was ridiculed as "different" and "inferior" by non-Salvadorans, while, as someone who was born and/or raised in the United States, he was also excluded from the category of "real Salvadorans." Such double displacements—Latinos but not Mexicans, Salvadorans but not real—could potentially have left such youths nowhere.

Interviewees were not, however, left nowhere. Instead they developed multiple responses to the racialization and stigmatization that they experienced, and particularly to the presumption that they were Mexican, a presumption that was likely due, at least in part, to the ways that "immigrant" and "Mexican" were conflated in public debates over U.S. immigration policies. One such response was to adopt more Mexicanized forms of identity and ways of speaking, perhaps as a strategy for "passing" (see also A. García 2014). One interviewee reported that, due to the tensions between Mexicans and Salvadorans, he had, as a child, simply let others believe that he was from Mexico: "I got caught in that assimilation. . . . I was just, you know, another Mexican." For some, pretending to be Mexican was a defense mechanism, as Marta Dominguez commented: "Salvadorans, when I was growing up, because of that tension that there was in school, the majority were Mexican, they would deny who they were so they wouldn't get like beat up. Or picked on. . . . So we kind of like grew up as Mexicans, you know?" Others were less deliberate and simply absorbed the neighborhoods in which they grew up, as Marilyn Funes recalled: "I was fitting into the Mexican American bundle. And I grew up in South Central where there were more Blacks, so I—I kind of integrated with them. So I always looked like a mixed girl." Assimilating to Mexican American culture often meant losing distinctly Salvadoran Spanish. Bayardo Morazan was warned by Salvadoran friends and elders "'not to sound too Salvadorian,' because, um, well, one, because people make fun of your accent if it sounded different than Mexican; and, two, in case you were deported you can pass for Mexican."[11] Likewise, Moises Quintero recalled that because other children made fun of the way that they spoke Spanish, he and his brothers "just stopped speaking Spanish at school. . . . The word *vos* for some reason.[12] And it was just, 'Oh my gosh, that was wrong! You just didn't say that.'"

In contrast to those who tried, at least at one stage of their lives, to fit in by "passing" as Mexicans, other interviewees adopted a strategy of insisting on their Salvadoranness. William Martínez used a comparison to being adopted to emphasize the importance of recognizing one's origin—a theme to which I will return in chapter 5. Saying that the United States was like a "foster parent," he stressed, "I don't think I will ever kind of like deny being a Salvadorian because my skin is one of the proofs that won't make me deny it." William commented that his own curiosity about knowing his origins was similar to the pride that Chicanos felt in identifying with Mexico. Such comments treat origin as biological or innate. Marta Dominguez, in contrast, emphasized that her identity was real *because* it was socially constructed: "Society doesn't see me as just American. They see me as, first as a woman, and as a woman of color, and as a Salvadoran woman. So me saying I'm not Salvadoran is denying who I am or part of who I am."

And still other interviewees responded by seeking to create alternatives to existing identity categories.[13] Sandra Mejillas, for example, embraced the term "Chicana" as "a political identity. It's not so expansive that it takes up every aspect of one's identity. It's just an element." In creating such political alternatives, interviewees sought to be multicultural, in a way that did not reduce identities to equivalencies. One interviewee, for instance, raised the question, "The Chicanos invented the term 'Chicano' in the 60s, what are we going to call ourselves? My boyfriend is Mexican. And I want my kids to be Salvadoran. A lot of us may feel this way, we want our kids to be Salvadoran." Cesar Quintanilla insisted that, as a minority student who got good grades but who also failed to conform to behavioral expectations, he defied school officials' categories. "They didn't know what to do with me," he commented. Jessica Morales sought to turn double displacement into an advantage: "People that, you know, were Salvadoran always considered me American, and American culture would always say, 'No, you're Salvadoran.' So, I guess in some way it made me feel like, okay, I do belong here and I can be both." Multiple interviewees stressed that some form of in-betweenness—being both Mexican and Salvadoran, having a foot in El Salvador and in the United States, or being born in El Salvador but raised in the United States—was in and of itself a basis for identity. For Bayardo Morazan, it was important to emphasize that numerous identity categories have inflections, of being "able to say . . . 'although we share similar experiences and share some very similar cultural expressions, they're not exactly the same,' you know. . . . For example, the word *jota*, which is used for gay—derogatory term for gay, for Mexicans, but it doesn't mean anything to a Salvadoran. That word doesn't exist for us."

Thus, despite the educational disadvantage, stigmatization, and even violence associated with what they experienced as misrecognition, interviewees sought recognition not just of origin and history but of something that they were producing, a state of becoming. Origin could be innate, located in "skin," but also socially constructed. Schools staffed by teachers who erroneously imposed Cinco de Mayo festivals on Salvadoran students also sometimes recognized these students' academic abilities and encouraged them to pursue higher education. And Salvadoranness could be redefined, not as something in competition with other national and ethnic groups but also as enabling individuals to move between and to create new political categories in solidarity with previous struggles. These identifications—whether with Mexicanness, Salvadoranness, or alternative renderings—also are at least partially a strategic response to the racializing and anti-immigrant context in which they were situated. One interviewee commented that misrecognition on others' parts allowed her to play with identity. She remarked, "Somebody had come up to me and I guess they started speaking Spanish in that same way that they were assuming or something and because my friends have told me like if they don't—if they don't know your name you can actually claim that you're from somewhere else and I was like, 'Oh, I'm sorry. My family's from Hawai'i.' And they were just like, 'Oh, I'm so sorry. I'm so sorry.'" As someone who could fictitiously claim to be from Hawai'i—a state with a complex colonial past (Merry 2000)—this interviewee was able to turn a potentially stigmatizing moment into one in which the individual who immediately pegged her as Spanish-speaking turned out to be the fool. Identity, in such accounts, is far from fixed.

Transitioning to Adulthood: Movement and Stasis

As they transitioned to adulthood, interviewees whose presence had altered the neighborhoods in which they lived and who had struggled to create identities that were both recognizable and reflective of their own senses of self found that they had to assume adult responsibilities at early ages even as they faced uncertainty about their futures. Research on immigrant youths has found that, because public schools must admit all students, regardless of legal status (*Plyler v. Doe*), undocumented children are shielded from some of the effects of their immigration status (Abrego and Gonzales 2010; Gonzales 2011). When they reach young adulthood, however, they "awaken to a nightmare" (Gonzalez and Chavez 2012) in that they learn that, unlike their documented peers, they often cannot legally work, obtain driver's licenses, travel internationally, or qualify for the financial aid that would enable them to attend college. My interviews suggest that part of this "nightmare" is losing their childhood early, that is, fulfilling relatively adult roles, such as translating between their parents and officials, when they are still children and taking on work, childcare, and financial responsibilities at young ages (Jefferies 2014; Orellana 2001). Additionally, children are increasingly exposed to the secondary effects of intensified enforcement tactics, including fear that they or their relatives will be deported (Dreby 2012). In some cases, if their parents *are* deported, they accompany them, experiencing what Kanstroom (2012:141) has referred to as a "de facto deportation," akin to the "secondary prisonization" faced by relatives of the incarcerated (Comfort 2009; Dingeman-Cerda and Coutin 2012). Young people who are uncertain of their own futures, either because they are undocumented or hold temporary status or because they are "in between two worlds," as David Zavala put it, cannot go on to pursue their long-term objectives in education or work. So youths move quickly into adulthood but also experience stasis in that they cannot move toward long-term goals. And those with lawful permanent residency or even U.S. citizenship can experience this complex position, though to a lesser degree than do those who are undocumented or who have temporary authorization.

Youths' transitions to adulthood engage ideals about education and work forged in both the United States and El Salvador. In El Salvador, particularly among rural and low-income urban families, expectations about children's entry into the labor market differ from the U.S. middle-class ideal that childhood is a time for education and play, not for paid labor. A 2005 study found that, in El Salvador, 24 percent of individuals ages four to twenty-eight who reported not attending school cited their need to work as an explanation (Santacruz Giralt 2005). As well, in the United States, Orellana found that Central American immigrant families' understandings of childhood "contrast with bourgeois ideological notions of children as relatively helpless dependents in need of adult labor and care, living within protected spaces (families, schools), engaged in activities defined as play or learning (not work), and seen as individuals needing to be developed through adult intervention" (2001:377). At the same time, many Salvadoran parents hoped that, by emigrating, they could change this pattern of early work and thus give their children the childhoods that they felt they themselves had never had (Horton 2008). Early entry into the labor market was therefore simultaneously akin to experiences of many children in El Salvador but also a deviation from U.S. ideals and from at least some immigrant parents' aspirations for their own children.

As noted earlier, a key responsibility that Salvadoran child migrants assumed within families was that of translating for parents who were still learning English (Orellana 2001). Due to the greater ease of acquiring languages at a young age and to immersion in U.S. schools, most immigrant children learn English quickly (Rumbaut and Portes 2001). They are therefore able to serve as "brokers" between their parents and the new culture in which their parents are situated—a role that can potentially undermine the authority that parents hold over children (Kim et al. 2003; Menjívar 2002). Interviewees who translated for parents were exposed to adult situations (interacting with the police, reading legal documents) at young ages. Children as young as elementary school age translated for their parents when they met with immigration officials, at welfare offices, in schools, at medical appointments, and in many other settings. To again quote Juan José, "I used to translate, I still translate, everything for my parents, even when I was in elementary and middle school. As soon as I learned English, they would take me to the Immigration Office with them." Children had to describe family circumstances, such as why the recent death of a family member in El Salvador meant that their parents needed "advance parole"—permission to leave the country and reenter without jeopardizing their TPS. As a child, one interviewee translated as his mother tried to explain to welfare officials that his father had left them and would not be making the child support payments that a court had ordered his father to pay. Their roles as translators made interviewees intermediaries within legal matters even though they were legally underage.

By the time that they were teenagers, some interviewees took on significant family responsibilities, such as working and caring for other family members. Bayardo Morazan recalled that by the time that he was in high school, "I had become more of the person who took care of everything at home. You know, I took care of the bills; anything that had—any forms that they need to fill out I filled them out; you know, any letters they needed to write out or answer, so you know. And I was working by that time. I began working [at Burger King] from the ninth grade, so I was already helping the house, you know." Likewise, Rodolfo Martínez started to work when he was fifteen. "I was going to high school during the day and I would work at night. Loading and unloading trailers. From, as soon as I would get out from school I will, you know, grab the bus and, um, and I would go to work until maybe around twelve midnight." William Campos was born in the United States, returned to El Salvador with his family at the age of two, and then came back to the United States at the age of sixteen to complete his education. His parents remained in El Salvador, but his younger brother came with him. While struggling with depression and loneliness, William had to support himself and his brother even though he was still in high school. He recounted, "I came to live with my aunt and my uncle. I was only sixteen years old. And I had to work, which was something that I had never expected, not in a million years! . . . I had to work because my brother and I had to support ourselves. At first my aunt and uncle paid for everything, but then they couldn't keep it up. So they called my parents and asked them to send money, and they couldn't. That's when my mother called me and told me that I would have to get a job."

Such responsibilities—and it is important to note that not all interviewees took on such obligations—made it hard for young people to complete their educations. Some described almost Herculean efforts to finish high school or pursue college educations. Walter Olivar immigrated to the United States at the age of seventeen, somewhat older than most of the people I interviewed. He had not attended high school in El Salvador, but he still wanted to complete high school in the United States rather than enrolling in adult school. To do so, he had to complete four years of high school within two years, despite the fact that English was his second language. Walter described his schedule:

> I literally, literally had to be at school 7:30 in the morning to 9 PM. I was going to high school in the morning from 7:30 to 2:30, then to continuation school starting at 3:00 until 6:00. Then I had a break and then I had to go back to English classes to learn how to speak English from 6:30 to 9 o'clock. After that I had—I still had to walk back home . . . for twenty minutes; ate dinner because I hadn't eaten yet; take a shower; get ready; and then start doing my high school homework. I would go to sleep, literally, like at maybe like twelve midnight or 1 o'clock in the morning.

Walter not only graduated from high school but went on to finish a bachelor's degree and then, at the time of our interview, was working as an outreach counselor at a community college. Marisa Salgado described a similar schedule:

> I started working when I was—when I was sixteen. Like right when I turned sixteen. I don't even remember, but it was right after—like in the summer in my vacation, so I was working for two years. [She worked at a factory.] . . . I would have to come home around—right after school. Like I couldn't stay after school or talk to my friends. Eat. And, um, I usually get out at—I would get out at 2:30, I think, or 2:40, and I would have to be in—at work at 3:00, so no break at all. And like I kind of had to come home and eat fast, you know, and like try to be on time too. [Then she worked from 3:00 to 12:00.] . . . Sometimes I would like try to do my homework at lunch or during school, you know, like try to get it finished at—in class, or—and then I would try and do it before class like in some other period and to get to my other class and stuff. It was hard.

Despite this grueling schedule, Marisa was able to complete high school. She took Advanced Placement classes and qualified for admission to a private university, where she continued to finance her own education by taking out $25,000 in loans annually. A business major, she was confident that her degree would enable her to earn enough to pay back the loans. While pursuing her own educational goals, she also had adopted an almost parental attitude toward her younger siblings, advising them on such matters as what school program to enroll in.

Of course, not all who faced such responsibilities were able to complete their educations. Manuel Cañas told me that despite having a "good" year in the seventh grade and an "okay" year in the eighth grade, in the ninth grade he had a "bad" year. He explained why:

> The first semester, I did really good. And then the second semester I had to stay home to help babysit my cousin and my younger siblings. Because my mom was working nights, so she had to sleep during the morning, and she asked me, "Can you help me out?" So I did. And I went back to try to make it up. And the teachers set me up with extra work. And I tried it. But it was hard. I stopped going. . . . I only finished ninth grade. . . .
>
> I was in charge of everybody. I didn't have to cook dinner. But at the time I had to take care of my cousins and clean the house. And I would call my friends and tell them, "Come by and hang out." And they would be over. . . .
>
> Later on, I did try to go back to school at night to get my high school diploma. But I wasn't motivated. I really wanted a job. And they gave me a diploma for the ninth grade. So that's what I passed.

Manuel's first job after finishing the ninth grade was trimming sweaters at five cents apiece. He earned approximately $20 for eight hours of work a week. Next, he worked for $60 a week taking care of his relatives' children. Then he worked at a restaurant, where he was proud of his performance and was paid $7 an hour, and, at the time of our interview, he was earning $16 an hour working at the airport. While he experienced upward mobility in earnings, his early family responsibilities had prevented him from finishing high school or pursuing college, and his immigration status—he had TPS—prevented him from joining the U.S. Army, his long-term goal.

In addition to family responsibilities, lack of knowledge of the application process also hampered Salvadoran child migrants' abilities to pursue higher education. In some instances, as noted above, teachers or counselors assumed that interviewees were not college material. Moises Quintero related that high school counselors steered him toward the military rather than college, a path he took because "in my mind we just didn't have the money. And I wasn't going to get to go to any higher educational institution." He eventually left the military, went back to school, and, at the time of our interview, was completing a master's degree and contemplating PhD programs. Bayardo Morazan, who eventually graduated from UCLA, recalled, "I did not understand the whole college thing. I assumed that similarly to when I went from junior high to high school that, you know, I'd put in an app[lication]—I put in—I don't even remember—remember filling out some little form saying that I wanted to go to [my high school]. And I figured that I would do the same thing. If I were going to go to a public university." It was not until a friend on the bus mentioned that she had an interview with a counselor at UCLA and invited him to go that he became aware of what the college application process entailed.

> So I went with her. And then this guy started asking me questions like, "Have you started filling out the application? Have you taken the SATs?" And I was like, "What are the SATs?" Um, I mean, you know, even though I was in the honors and AP courses no one had ever like sat down with me to tell me, "This is what you do for college," you know. And it wasn't until I met this guy in the twelfth grade like sometime in September of the twelfth grade that he starts telling me, "You need to do this, you know."

Other interviewees had similar experiences. Jessica Morales, an AP student who was steered toward community college rather than a university by college counselors, commented, "Our teachers would sometimes say, 'Oh, when you guys go to college,' you know, but nobody ever said, 'Okay,' you know, 'Who's going to college? What are your plans? This is what you have to do?' Like it just never happened. And I had no idea how the system worked here. My parents don't know, they're not from here." Likewise, Juana Rocio described a gulf between her parents' knowledge and the knowledge that she had had to acquire:

> My dad he didn't finish his high school. He didn't even go to college. My mom didn't go—I think she did—the most she finished was the third grade. So I mean they don't really value that much, education. I mean for them I could have just gotten my high school diploma and started working, no college. So I mean with them they really didn't push me to go to college. It was more like my choice. And I mean applying to scholarships as well, I mean they didn't tell me to apply to scholarships. They didn't tell me, "Oh, go to this college."

Interviewees who overcame such obstacles to pursue higher education sometimes felt that they were the "chosen ones" who had to succeed for others' sake. As Cesar explained, he and his friends "came from gang-infested, drugs, violence, all that, you know, we seen that growing up. And all that has affected us for us to do something about it, you know? We're like how can I say it, the cream of the crop, I think. . . . But for us to come from [where we came from], have that street smart, and programs to give us a chance and for us to just be here, that's an accomplishment." Likewise, remarking that some of their childhood friends had now died, Eduardo Sanchez reflected, "And now some of those guys—like I see them around and some of them are in prison for life; some of them are like partly handicapped from being shot; some are 'rest in peace.' And those were all people I went to high school with, but I was already in Cal State and they were still right there trying to get through high school." Eduardo continued,

> Sometimes we think about that. . . . Sometimes I—just my mind just is crazy—sometimes I think we're like the chosen ones. Me, Cesar, all of us, I think we're like the chosen ones. We're like the first—the first to come over here really if you think about it in the early '80s. Well not the first, but the first mass—mass in the early '80s. We're like the first ones that came right here. And we're like, "Hey!" We're the ones that kind of like molded—started molding everything right here. Like we're the first ones to get exposed to the—to the whole U.S. and we still had a lot of that Salvi because they had just gotten here, you know. . . . I think we're like the chosen ones. We're like here for a reason. We got this education. Now we got to do something with it.

While such an attitude could inspire them to work hard and achieve, it was also a heavy burden to bear and one that is not uncommon among immigrant children, who are also well aware of the sacrifices that their parents made to provide them with better opportunities (Orellana et al. 2001). As chapter 3 will discuss, this sense of commitment inspired Eduardo, Cesar, and their peers to form new student organizations dedicated to helping underprivileged Central American youths pursue higher education.

Those who were undocumented or who had only temporary legal status faced added challenges trying to study and pursue professional careers. Students who were undocumented sometimes could not qualify for California in-state tuition (a situation that was changed with the passage of AB-540—see Abrego 2008; Gonzales 2008), state or federal financial aid, work permits, or even driver's licenses. Furthermore, if they successfully overcame these obstacles and obtained college degrees, then they would be unable to practice their professions without work permits. Those who had temporary legal status were disqualified from receiving some forms of financial aid, regularly had to renew work permits (a costly process), and did not know whether they would eventually be able to regularize their status or would instead be deported.

Marisol Sanabria's experiences illustrate the challenges faced by undocumented students attempting to transition to adulthood. When I first met Marisol in 2007, she was attending college at a local California State University campus, participating in the California Dream Network (a statewide coalition that sought financial aid eligibility and a path to citizenship for undocumented students), and she optimistically predicted that the DREAM Act would pass and that her goal of becoming a veterinarian and opening a shelter for animals would be achieved. When I interviewed her again in 2009, when immigration reform had stalled and the recession was at its peak, her fortunes had taken a turn for the worse. Her faith that the DREAM Act would pass had decreased, her employment opportunities had diminished, and her educational costs had risen. Without a driver's license, she had to travel to school by bus, which took two hours. She was saving everything she could to pay for her tuition but was still far short of the cost for fall. She was working five hours a week as a dog sitter, earning $100, but of that money, $20 was spent on bus fare. Her earlier goal of securing a PhD from UC Davis had been scaled back to completing her bachelor's degree and possibly pursuing a master's. She felt that her dependence on the bus had affected her academically, as she was unable to stay on campus late to participate in study groups with other students. Marisol also found the disparity between her circumstances and those of other students striking. She commented:

> I see my friends, you know, in school they have everything. Their parents gave them a credit card and they pay their ways, you know. The first year at a dorm . . . I remember my roommate she was from up north. And her dad was like a doctor. And she's like, "Oh, yeah, he gave me a credit card and I wasted $1,000 just the first week." You know, I'm like, "Wow!" Like if she knew how much I would have to work for $1,000, you know?

Marisol was very discouraged. She told me, "I used to have that mentality, saying, 'You know, I'm not even going to worry about it because I know I'm gonna get it [legal status].' But now, it's nothing. . . . I'm like, 'Oh, I'm going to start working,' but now I can't. [Inaudible] I don't know."

Other interviewees who were undocumented or temporarily authorized described similar challenges: fear of revealing their status to college counselors, worry about whether or not TPS was going to be extended, and the financial difficulty of attempting to pay for college while being unemployed, underemployed, or ineligible for financial aid. Under these circumstances, many had chosen to postpone college; attend a cheaper, local university rather than a higher-cost campus with a better reputation; or take a longer time to graduate.

As a result of these challenges, a number of interviewees faced uncertain futures, leading them to place key aspects of their lives on hold (Menjívar 2006; Mountz, Wright, Miyares, and Bailey 2002). Heightened immigration enforcement initiatives, such as SB 1070, the Arizona law that required law enforcement and other state officials to check individuals' immigration status (see Menjívar 2011b), led many to feel insecure. Numerous interviewees stated that they were "waiting for the DREAM Act to pass." Juana Rocio, a college student who was fighting an asylum case at the time of our interview, said that she was preparing for "two possible futures": one in the United States and one in El Salvador. Immigration challenges were exacerbated by the economic downturn. At our initial interview, Walter Olivar told me that he planned to naturalize, but when I met him two years later, in 2009, he had not yet done so. Walter explained that he let it go so long that he had to renew his green card to avoid falling out of status (in fact, those who do not renew green cards do not lose status; rather, they simply have no valid proof of status). Then he saved to pay the application fee for naturalization (in 2009, it cost $575 to file the application plus an $80 biometrics fee), only to instead loan the money to his sister-in-law. Tomás Marino-Vega, a student and TPS recipient, had to change jobs because, with the economic downturn, the company he worked for had failed. He quickly found a new job, but, unfortunately, his work permit was about to expire. He renewed his work permit as soon as possible, but his company still requested the new work permit three times before it arrived in the mail. Because of these difficulties, he had to withdraw from school and felt as though he was living in limbo. Tomás explained, "I've put my life like on hold, you know, to getting married and all that because I don't want to have that whole double issue of dealing with that until I get at least myself—my affairs straightened out."

Such uncertainty indicates that gaps—between El Salvador and the United States, law and illegality, violence and normalcy—did not disappear as interviewees acclimated to the United States but rather were transformed. As children became part of U.S. neighborhoods, schools, families, friendship groups, and, eventually, the workforce, they maintained linkages to El Salvador, to relatives who continued to migrate, and to pasts that could potentially become their futures. Such gaps are evident in the answer that Araceli Muñoz says that she gives when people ask where she is from: "I say, 'I'm from El Salvador' or

'I was born there, but I grew up here.' Like I always feel like I have to make that distinction for some reason. I always say, 'I was born there. I'm from there, technically, but I live here. I was raised here.'" The space created by this "distinction," by "technically" being born somewhere else, is filled by the lives that Salvadoran child migrants forge for themselves.

Conclusion: Making Something of the Gap

Interviewees' accounts of joining neighborhoods, reconfiguring their family relationships, entering U.S. schools, forming relationships with peers, and transitioning to adulthood demonstrate that the gaps that they have experienced between El Salvador and the United States, law and illegality, belonging and exclusion, and violence and safety are both sites of vulnerability and also opportunities for creativity. These gaps are not supposed to exist. In an ideal world, family members would remain together within their country of citizenship, or, if they immigrated, would do so with the full permission of the country that received them. As detailed in chapter 1, the violence of the Salvadoran civil war coupled with the restrictiveness of U.S. immigration policies created the gaps in which they were situated, positioning them in something of a nonspace, a place "offshore" or in the "shadows" (Chavez 1992; Coutin, Maurer, and Yngvesson 2002). Clearly, such a location marginalizes its residents, thus producing dis/memberment (a lack of membership and of recognition). Interviewees joined low-income neighborhoods, their families were disrupted, they were misrecognized by peers and school officials, their right to be present was challenged, and they had to take on adult tasks at young ages even as, in some cases, their abilities to transition to college or the workforce (especially as professionals) were curtailed. At the same time, by *living in* the gap, child migrants re/membered, that is, they stitched together that which had been broken apart. They transformed the neighborhoods that they joined: for example, making Los Angeles's MacArthur Park a place where people from the same village in El Salvador might run into each other. They and their families were part of migrant undergrounds, as new family members arrived, even as they also participated in U.S. civic rituals through the public school system. They navigated existing ethnic and racial categories while also striving to define—and redefine—what it meant to be Salvadoran in the United States. And they demonstrated a commitment to challenging structures that marginalize undocumented youths. As Karina Oliva Alvarado notes of second-generation Central American writers (see chapter 3), "being in the 'middle' allows them to envision identities that unbound the boundaries of nation, and tug at the restrictive ties of culture to nation" (2013:374).

Many interviewees clearly articulated the ways they had made something of the gaps in which they were situated. Their efforts demonstrate that, instead of merely being retrospective (recalling the past), re/membering is productive: it creatively recombines and redeploys persons and histories to create new often more meaningful versions. Thus despite having experienced trauma, children can be resilient and resourceful—a notion that Stuart Lustig and colleagues note runs counter to studies that rely on "Western, middle-class constructions of childhood" and that focus only on "loss and adversity" (2004:25). Milda Escobar said that, after returning to El Salvador as a teenager, she "reinvented" herself, developing a love of history and politics, fighting against Proposition 209, learning about the Movimiento Estudiantil Chican@ de Aztlán, and choosing to attend a four-year college where there was a Central American student association. In high school, Pedro Marroquín participated in an academic decathlon team on which half of the members were undocumented. Nelson Almendrez suggested that tensions between Mexicans and Salvadorans could be overcome by examining their common history. He commented, "The large indigenous population in . . . El Salvador, the Pipiles, were actually descendants of the Mixtecas, the Aztecs. So there's already a connection there showing that's how far back they go—that there's a connection." Cesar Quintanilla and other Cal State Los Angeles students felt compelled to work with students from the high school they had attended, encouraging these students to pursue higher education. As noted earlier, Jessica Morales developed a positive spin on being considered an outsider in multiple places, reflecting that she could be both Salvadoran *and* American. Cecilia Molina suggested that 1.5-generation and second-generation Salvadorans were "different, Salvadoran. We're different, different. . . . Our group that like grew—grew up here, studying." These and other comments indicate that many interviewees saw gaps as an opening, a place of connection, a chance to be creative.

Taking this creativity into account makes key contributions to existing literature on immigration, race, and childhood. First, it suggests that understandings of the "context of reception" that shapes immigrants' life opportunities might be made more dynamic by analyzing how newcomers' presence transforms and quickly becomes part of this context. While it is true that the context of reception has been understood as including "coethnics" who are already there, my point is that context is not inert in that new arrivals bring about their own transformations. Second, work on both racialization and on new forms of "color-blind racism" can be enriched by an examination of the ways that newly racialized groups, such as Salvadorans (see Baker-Cristales 2004b), assume the authority to add to, define, and redefine existing categories. Third, work on the ways in which immigrant children transition to adulthood might take into account both the ways that migrants are trapped—for example, denied work permits, granted only limited access to colleges and universities, consigned to uncertain futures—and the ways in which they are catapulted into adulthood early by, for instance, having to translate for parents and contribute to family finances. As one interviewee commented, "Maybe it will take one more generation" for students who were either undocumented or TPS recipients to achieve what peers who had already attained lawful permanent residency had been able to accomplish. Fourth, the experiences of 1.5-generation Salvadorans demonstrate the continued salience of race in producing belonging and exclusion, both among officials, such as teachers and school counselors, and, more informally, among children themselves.

Epilogue

JANUARY 18, 2008. I had arranged to meet with Julian, an eighteen-year-old TPS recipient, for an evening interview. We were originally going to meet at his apartment, but I wrote down the address incorrectly, so I had the right street but the wrong building number. When I called him to say that I couldn't find it, he was able to give me directions from where I was to a Denny's restaurant near Van Ness and Sunset. Then when I stopped at the wrong Denny's (who would've thought there would be that many Denny's restaurants so close to each other?), he drove over to meet me where I was. Although he was only eighteen, Julian seemed quite familiar with adult experiences like driving on freeways, commuting, and working.

When we met, Julian described, with pride, the challenges that he had had to overcome in order to graduate from high school:

> I used to go to school late. I was more into like—school started at 7:40, but I would be there at 8. I was like—when my teacher pressured me to be there early, but I told him, "Hey, man, I can just never wake up early." So I was like—so like he made a deal with me. He was like, "I'll let you come at 8, but you have to do all the work." And so—so I kind of made his deal. In the beginning of the course I was failing his class. But then I passed through it miraculously. I had to see my counselor every single day. My counselor

was always on top of me and like, "You got to do this. You got to do that." Yeah, "I applied for this and I applied for that." And then it's like, "You got to apply for college too." And I just never took the time to actually do it. Like I never took the time to actually apply to college and stuff, but I did meet all the requirements he told me because I wouldn't have graduated high school. The college thing, I really didn't do that. I didn't pay much attention, but right now, right now that I see—like I want to go to college, but for me it's kind of hard. It's kind of—it's not impossible, it's just too much money. . . . For me especially [be]cause I have no documents here, so it's like I don't even know if they'll take me, you know. . . .

Like ninth grade I really didn't put effort into it, until that second semester [be]cause like I had to play baseball and so . . . I was into sports. I played football my freshman year. . . . And then the tenth-grade year that's when I really messed up. Like I was far behind. And I had to go to school as like summer school, like in extended freshman and—which I never did. And then my senior year that's what I got—I had to make up all that—all that lost time I messed up on.

Oh, that was like to school, to the house, to like do what you got to do, go back to school. And so like I had to take like a—I had to take an extra class after school. So I could like get my credits. I had to get all my credits. So like I had to take a class from like 4 to like—from, yeah, from 4 to like 6. It was horrible. It was horrible. My teacher was great, but it was so long. It wasn't—it was like school was there. I really didn't like think about school. Like ninth grade—like I repeated all the grades—like when everybody would be [in] eleventh, I'd still be tenth. And so like I finally caught up on my senior year when I had all my credits. Just barely made it through.

Julian told me that he had not been back to El Salvador since he left at the age of three, and he had no memories of the country. Wondering aloud whether there was any record of him having been there, he commented, "I don't even know if I exist there." Like many other interviewees, he and his mother shared an apartment with another relative for part of his childhood, and he had grown up in a neighborhood where there was gang violence. When I asked him how he responded when people asked him where he was from, he immediately interpreted my question as being about gangs. He grew up in an environment that he described as mixed: "a lot of Mexicans, a lot of Salvadorians, um, Guatemalans, Nicaraguans, and all them." Though he was not an activist himself, Julian participated in the 2006 mass mobilization on behalf of immigrants' rights. He recalled, "And then just out of nowhere just like a big crowd of us was just pushing in front of us, so it was it like I guess we get—that just—it just happened. Like I guess—like we were concerned—like, you know, we were talking—we were talking about like—it affects—it has to do with us, you know. We were talking like, 'If people stand up first, then we will.'"

Julian told me that his long-term goals were to help his mother to get legal status, to make it possible for her to stop working, and to go to college where he hoped to study computer engineering or computer graphics. He also hoped to someday become a U.S. citizen. But, for the time being, he described himself as "stuck—I'm just stuck between two things, two countries, you know."

DECEMBER 20, 2007. After parking at a pay lot in downtown Los Angeles, I walked to City Hall, where a group of college students wearing caps and gowns were milling about on the steps below a huge Christmas tree. One student was dressed as Santa Claus, and other students placed brightly wrapped presents beneath the tree. Recognizing a couple of the organizers, I quickly greeted them and they thanked me for coming. I had learned about this event, the "Dreamer Holiday Celebration," via the list-serv of the California State University, Los Angeles, organization Students United to Reach Goals in Education (or SURGE, pronounced "soor-hey," which, in Spanish, means "rise" or "emerge"). According to an announcement circulated via the list-serv, this event was designed to

> keep the struggles of undocumented students alive and in the public eye . . . and just let the public know that those were our presents this year (raids, failure of Dream Act etc.). . . . Let the media know that those were our dreams. Hang up our dreams on the Christmas tree and let them fall as a symbol that forces beyond our control are preventing us from FULLY contributing to this society. While many people during the holidays will get what they want we are not asking for material things, but only for the OPPORTUNITY to CONTRIBUTE our talents, knowledge, and skills to America. . . . This event can also serve to celebrate our accomplishments as well. Despite all

the obstacles we encounter we still keep dreaming, fighting, and we will not give up until justice is serve [*sic*] to our communities.

I chatted with several students as organizers greeted the media—only the Spanish-language press came, not the English—and a few passersby stopped for a moment to look on curiously. It was a gray day, cold for Los Angeles, and I felt the chill through the wool jacket I had worn. Then the event began. Students took their places beneath the tree, Santa stood off to one side, and an organizer walked over to a podium to speak into a microphone:

> I'm the president of the student organization on campus called SURGE. . . . We advocate for higher education for students. So today we shall hear the voices of the present and future of America. Today young people in unison are here to tell this nation to live up to its creed that all men are created equal and that we are entitled to life, liberty, and the pursuit of happiness. This year many things happened to students all across the United States. We received many gifts from our government and from the American public who do not support immigration reform. Our gifts included the failure of the [federal] DREAM Act. The failure of the DREAM Act at the state level as well, that the governor vetoed. We have family separation that, you know, broke our families apart. And so today we just gathered here to tell Congress that next year we want something better. That next year we want immigration reform. We want the DREAM Act to pass because our dreams can't wait.

One by one, three students came forward to receive their gifts from Santa: Family separation. A 10 percent tuition increase. Failure of the federal DREAM Act. And each student gave his or her testimony. One talked about being determined to go to school even though she was undocumented and her mother suffered from cancer. Another discussed the ways that fee hikes disproportionately affected undocumented students. And a third described how his father had been deported to Peru after spending seventeen years in the United States. He said that while attending college he had to work at his father's gardening business on the weekends to support his family. As these students spoke, others stood silently, several holding signs that read "Deportation Order" and "Stop Police Brutality."

When the students' testimonies concluded, all gathered to give Santa a giant scroll containing their wish list for next year. I had seen the listserv exchanges, through which students had composed this list. As they unfurled the scroll down the steps of City Hall, the audience—me, several organizers and jour-

FIGURE 3.1 Student speaker presents a personal story at the Dreamer Holiday Celebration. Photo by author.

nalists, and a few passersby—was able to read the words that had been cut and pasted onto a large swath of butcher paper:

> Dear Santa: For Christmas, I DREAM for . . .
> - to have an equal opportunity to exercise my college degree
> - to start my own business
> - to go to college
> - to obtain a California drivers license and ID card
> - to be acknowledged as part of the American Dream
> - equal education for all
> - immigration reform
> - family reunification
> - to be the first in my family to graduate from college
> - to see more Latino youth pursue higher education
> - for my parents to stop slaving themselves in an underpaid physically demanding job

And more. As the event concluded, students chanted, "Education now, politics later. ¡Educación ahora! ¡Política después!" Then, after the media left,

FIGURE 3.2 The wish list that students presented to Santa at the Dreamer Holiday Celebration. Photo by author.

organizers and students gathered on the steps one more time, for a photograph. The resulting photo looks more like a class outing than a political protest.

One way in which some immigrant youths sought to challenge the dismemberment described in chapter 1 and to validate the social geographies described in chapter 2 was through activism. Although not all participated in activism, those interviewees who did were involved in three forms of student activism that I analyze here. First, as exemplified through the Holiday Dreamer Celebration described above, undocumented students and their allies sought passage of both the federal DREAM Act, which would create a path to legalization for students, and the California Dream Act, which would make undocumented youths who had graduated from California high schools eligible for financial aid for college. These efforts led to three successes: in 2011, the California Dream Act was approved; in 2012, President Barack Obama announced the Deferred Action for Childhood Arrivals (DACA) program, an administrative alternative to the DREAM Act (Zatz and Rodriguez 2015); and in 2014, the president announced that the group eligible for DACA would be expanded—

though, as of this writing, the expanded version of DACA is currently under injunction. Second, in addition to supporting the DREAM Act, which would benefit undocumented students, Salvadoran and Central American college students who felt that their own histories and communities were not adequately represented in existing ethnicity-based student organizations founded new student groups. Prominent among these was USEU (the Unión Salvadoreña de Estudiantes Universitarios, or Salvadoran University Student Union), an association that spanned campuses and, indeed, nations. Third, in addition to advocating for undocumented students and creating new student associations, student artists, writers, and entrepreneurs also began to found businesses, establish presses, form poetry collectives, and produce new literature. Through this array of activities, youths re/membered, that is, they sought to create a present that was both accountable for past inequities and in line with their visions for a more just future.

These three forms of activism are part of a broader new immigrant rights movement that captured national attention when, in 2006, unprecedented numbers of immigrants and their allies took to the streets opposing the Sensenbrenner bill, which would have made it a felony to be undocumented (Loyd and Burridge 2007). Scholars have attributed the new immigrant rights movement to a set of historical and social conditions that have given citizenship renewed significance. Benita Heiskanen (2009; see also Johnson and Hing 2007) sees the 2006 U.S. immigrant rights activism in racial terms, as an attempt to challenge black/white binaries by emphasizing the presence of Latinos. She further stresses the importance of viewing both immigration policies and immigrant rights activism in light of hemispheric power relations (see also Hayduk 2009; Robinson 2006). Susanne Jonas and Catherine Tactaquin (2004) suggest that, even before the 2006 upsurge, national security measures that targeted immigrants focused the public spotlight on immigration and thus, counterintuitively, created the opportunity for a conversation about immigration reform. In holding this conversation, immigrant rights activists created new practices and identities. Relatedly, John J. Betancur and Maricela Garcia (2011) suggest that the characteristics that enable a community to mobilize around a social problem can grow out of as well as precede protest.[1] Likewise, Irene Bloemraad, Kim Voss, and Taeku Lee (2011) argue that identities not only are a basis for mobilization but also can be recrafted during protest, while Alfonso Gonzalez (2009) characterizes the 2006 marches as a "counterhegemonic moment," deeply radical even if limited in its capacity to bring about real change.[2] Numerous scholars thus stress the breadth of the concerns that motivated activists, noting that instead of narrowly focusing on pending legislation, protestors sought justice for immigrants, and did so by employing creative tactics that went beyond traditional forms of political involvement (A. Gonzales 2009; Johnson and Hing 2007; Pantoja, Menjívar, and Magaña 2008; Walters 2006).

This chapter builds on this work by examining Salvadoran youth activism as a form of *generation* (see also Getrich 2008), that is, as a creative process that reconfigures the social and political landscape in ways that mark time and create new spaces for activism. As Karl Mannheim (1959) famously noted, generations emerge out of people's experiences of a common historical problem. For the youth activism analyzed here, this historical problem includes racialization, transnational connections, and the intensified enforcement tactics that led activists to emphasize immigrants' belonging even as some members of this generation were targeted for deportation. While there is, of course, variation within generations (Kansteiner 2012), such social and historical conditions can be key to establishing collective memory and identity (Eyerman and Turner 1998). At the same time, creating such memory and identity is particularly challenging for immigrants whose right to be present is suspect. Such activists are in what Michel de Certeau (de Certeau, Jameson, and Lovitt 1980:6) refers to as a nonspace, which "doubtless permits mobility, but requires amenability to the hazards of time, in order to seize the possibilities that a moment offers. It must vigilantly utilize the gaps which the particular combination of circumstances open in the control of the proprietary power. It poaches there. It creates surprises. It is possible for it to be where no one expects it. It is wile."

Youth activists have exhibited this "wiliness" as they have generated relationships, analyses, testimonies, organizations, literature, art, political thought, commodities, and political theater. In so doing, Salvadoran and Central American students, artists, and activists entered a field that was already defined by the generation before them, a generation that, with links to popular movements in Central America, was dedicated to challenging U.S. intervention, securing the rights of Central American immigrants and refugees, opposing deportations, and acquiring a political voice in the United States (Coutin 2005b).[3] They also entered a field defined by existing Latino student groups, particularly the Movimiento Estudiantil Chican@ de Aztlán (MEChA), which grew out of the Chicano movement of the 1970s (Oliva Alvarado 2013). While forming alliances with their predecessors and their contemporaries, Central American immigrant youths also sought to mark their own presence and establish their own agendas. Their work therefore not only targeted specific policy changes but also acted on their own understandings of their personal trajectories, their family and community histories, and their places in the United States and in their countries of origin. Immigration rights were only one component of their struggle, which sought not only legal rights but also full inclusion and acknowledgment from both authorities and their peers. The notion of *generation* captures both the innovative nature of youth activism and its linkages to earlier movements.

Though they sought to enact new social realities, student activists also found their practices shaped by the political circumstances that they encountered. Thus, students who were part of the Dreamer movement were potentially excluded from the United States due to their immigration status. These students therefore emphasized their "Americanness" and their ties to the United States, even as they were troubled by depicting themselves as stereotypical "achievers." In contrast to this focus on Americanness, the students who organized USEU pushed back against negative depictions of Salvadoranness (as prone to gang involvement, or as unsuccessful) as well as against what they perceived as a poor fit with college-based ethnic student clubs such as MEChA. They therefore emphasized and revalorized their nationality as Salvadorans. And Central American writers and artists pushed against received (especially nation-based) definitions of identity, instead emphasizing multiplicity, complexity, and hybridities. The identifications that were promoted in different forms of activism therefore had strategic dimensions. Analyzing youth activism thus reveals both the aspirations of its protagonists and the power relations within which it is enmeshed.

Dreamers

Activism on behalf of undocumented college students countered a key form of dismemberment, namely, the schism between students' histories growing up in the United States and a legal system that defined them as foreigners, nonresidents for purposes of college education, unauthorized to work in the United States even if they graduated with college degrees, and potentially subject to deportation (Corrunker 2012; Seif 2011). The challenges experienced by undocumented college students sharpened in the late 1990s and early 2000s as state legislatures distinguished more clearly between lawful residents and undocumented students, federal and state action made it more difficult for youths to obtain identity documents (such as driver's licenses or ID cards), and paths to legalization were closed by the immigration reforms of the 1990s (Gonzales 2008; Gonzales and Chavez 2012; Stevenson 2004). In the early 2000s, when calls for a new legalization program grew, students were one of the most sympathetic groups on whose behalf immigrant rights groups could advocate (Nicholls 2013). Students who immigrated to the United States as young children could be depicted as blameless in that their parents were the ones who had made immigration decisions. They could be depicted as familiar, in that most spoke fluent English, dressed like other students, and had graduated from U.S. high schools. They also could be depicted as deserving, because they had qualified to attend colleges or universities and their goals were to obtain an education and launch their careers—the epitome of the American Dream. The first version of the federal DREAM Act, which would have enabled undocumented college students who graduated from U.S. high schools to become legal permanent residents, was introduced in the U.S. Congress in 2001. Yet, in the wake of the anti-immigrant sentiment that followed the 9/11 attacks in 2001 and amid restrictionists' argument that the undocumented should be sent back to their countries of origin, regardless of age, students, like other immigrant groups, were unable to win passage. Activism by and on behalf of undocumented college students nonetheless persisted, as Dreamers—as these students came to be called—sought to make their legal status align with their senses of their own histories and futures (Milkman 2011; Nicholls 2013).

As discussed in chapter 2, interviewees who were unauthorized or who had Temporary Protected Status (TPS) were trapped in the temporal, legal, and geographic disjunctures that the DREAM Act was designed to bridge (Menjívar 2006; Mountz, Wright, Miyares, and Bailey 2002). Raised in the United States, but with neither lawful permanent residency nor citizenship, undocumented college students potentially experienced a deep disconnect between their pasts in the United States and their uncertain futures. For example, I interviewed Marisol Sanabria in 2007, when she was nineteen and attending a local California State University (CSU) campus. Marisol's mother immigrated to the United States shortly after Marisol was born, leaving her and her brother in El Salvador. When Marisol was six, her mother brought her to the United States with the assistance of a migrant smuggler. Raised in the Boyle Heights neighborhood of Los Angeles, Marisol did not realize that she was undocumented until she asked her mother if she could go on a school trip that would take her out of the state of California: "And I was asking my mom, 'I really want to go, I really want to go.' But I never knew that, to be honest, I never knew what was the difference to have papers and not have papers. Until that moment that she told me, 'Well, you can't get out of the country, you know, can't go out of the state.'.... And I'm like, I'll use my school ID, I'd do anything. I'm a student, you know." The contradiction between Marisol's sense that her school ID and status as a student *ought* to signify membership and the legal reality of her status as an unauthorized immigrant placed Marisol in an impossible position. When people asked her where she was from, she answered, "I grew up here," and hid her undocumented status: "I was so embarrassed. . . . How would they think about me?" Although Marisol was pursuing her college degree and hoped eventually to become a veterinarian, she did not know where her future would be. She had to act *despite* an uncertainty that only deepened over time (see also Morales, Herrera, and Murry 2011).

Undocumented college students' educational strategies reveal the complexity of their legal situation: these students were simultaneously *invisible*, in that they did not appear to be different from other college students (Stevenson 2004), and *extricated*, that is, sharply differentiated from others by the legal prohibitions that they experienced. Though California law permits undocumented college students who graduate from U.S. high schools to pay in-state tuition, these students were ineligible for federal and state financial aid and therefore struggled to afford their educations. Marisol, a stellar high school student, had been accepted into her "dream" school: the University of California, Davis, but she could afford neither the tuition nor living away from home. Students had to get to class without driving, because they were not eligible to obtain driver's licenses. They had to work under the table, as they lacked work authorization. And they had to study without knowing whether they would be able to practice their professions. They were of, but not in, society and were potentially removable. Beatriz Gonzalez, an organizer who had been an undocumented college student at UCLA, described how this felt:

> There is a constant reminder that you're different. As much as you feel normal, as much as you're with your backpack, chillin' at the quad and studying, you're different, it's different, because you probably can't even get a job on campus. . . . I remember I had to travel, like two hours, I had to get on the bus, and that took thirty minutes, and then I had to walk to the house [where she worked as a caregiver], so then I had to spend, even though I was only doing three hours, right, three and a half hours, then I'd have to do that, and it was already nighttime, and then I had to travel back. So, yeah, I

don't think you ever forget. Like, you *don't* forget. It is, it's a constant thing that's behind you in the back of your mind.

In short, undocumented college students had to pursue their educations without access to the jobs, financial assistance, and transportation systems that make studying possible and without the security of knowing that they would be able to remain in the country. They truly were "impossible subjects" (Ngai 2004).

DREAM Act activism was designed to transform impossibility into opportunity by placing youths in society and making their histories visible. My analysis here draws on my interviews with student organizers, immigrant rights workers who advised these groups, students who attended rallies and walkouts (A. Gonzalez 2009), and youths who supported this work but who did not participate actively.

According to these interviewees, a central strategy through which youths countered the deep stigmatization, isolation, and extrication associated with being undocumented was by founding undocumented student organizations, both in high schools and at the college level (Milkman 2011; Seif 2011). As the sociologist Leisy Abrego (2008:727) found, California Assembly Bill 540, which gave undocumented college students who had graduated from U.S. high schools the right to pay in-state tuition at public universities, "also granted undocumented students a new sense of legitimacy. As students, they can 'legally' and, therefore, legitimately request rights formally granted by the law." Marisol Sanabria experienced this sense of legitimacy. When she was in high school, she was afraid to reveal her legal status to others (see also Contreras 2009); however, when one of her teachers encouraged her to travel to Washington, D.C., for a school event, she told him that she was undocumented:

> He told me, "Why have you never told me this, you know?" He's just, "You're not the only one alone. You know there's more students. But they're afraid as you are because they don't want to come open about this. . . ." And then like, "Tomorrow we're going to have a meeting and you're going to start a club, you know. Not only for immigrants, but for everybody. And you're going to fundraise to have scholarship for you—for you guys, you know." And that's how I became open. And I started going to places, talking to people. And now I have gone to like—and now in college we have come to my high school from [her college campus] trying to make people apply to our school. . . . I was like if people are afraid maybe once we become open about more stuff, more people are going to be able to be more open. And

they were! I was surprised so many people . . . that I thought . . . had papers and like you know they have everything—and they were like, "We don't, we're like you."

After founding an AB-540 club at her high school, Marisol went on to found another club at her university. The AB-540 clubs were dedicated to educational outreach, "know your rights" campaigns, identifying scholarship opportunities that were open to undocumented students, raising funds for undocumented students, writing to politicians to urge them to pass the federal and California Dream acts, and carrying out public actions, such as rallies, in support of the federal DREAM Act. Together, the AB-540 clubs made up a coalition known as the California Dream Network, dedicated to sharing information and coordinating advocacy. The names of the participating organizations reflected the aspirations of student groups, as an organizer explained: "Some of these organizations are called like Rising Immigrant Scholars through Education—that's the organization at Berkeley. UCLA IDEAS, 'Improving Dreams, Equality, Access and Success.'"

Central to the work of AB-540 groups were public testimonies designed to identify commonalities among students, as Marisol described above, and to publicly counter negative depictions of undocumented immigrants (Corrunker 2012). Among student activists, giving public testimonies was risky, due to the possibility that such exposure would lead to deportation. Nonetheless, in social movements, including with Dreamer activism, oral testimonies can be a means of developing solidarity among movement participants and provoking emotional responses in listeners (Goodwin, Jasper, and Polletta 2000; Polletta and Jasper 2001; Polletta and Lee 2006). Beatriz Gonzalez described how she attended an AB-540 meeting organized by the Coalition for Humane Immigrant Rights of Los Angeles (CHIRLA) and then was recruited to speak at a press conference:

> And so I attended that meeting. And I think it was like twelve students, I don't remember. And they were talking about the next day, that they were going to have a press conference in support of AB-540. And they asked, "Who wants to speak?" So I think by this point in my life, I had already thought a little bit more about what it is to be undocumented. Because I had, you know, another younger sister who was going to go through the same thing. I had already thought a lot about it. And so it was very clear to me that this was very unjust. And that there was something like inherently

wrong with the fact that I couldn't go to college. So it was my first meeting, but I had already processed a lot of feelings, so I said, "I want to speak."

So the next day, I wrote my little speech. And I remember that when I wrote it—and I wished that I had kept it—but I remember ending it with like, "If you're depriving youth or students, you may be depriving the next Albert Einstein."

And so I say that because that's, it's interesting that at such a young age of seventeen, you do start thinking about these things, and it's because of the injustices that you're living. Whereas maybe another seventeen-year-old is not thinking about those things.

And so I spoke at the press conference, and it was good! Marco Fire-baugh was there, the author of AB-540. And so it was the last days of the campaign, the last months. And AB-540 became law in October 2001. And CHIRLA was the only organization that was able to bring students. And they brought two students. And I was one of those two students who was there when Governor Davis signed it into law.

Like Beatriz, other student activists had faith that personal stories could change attitudes and lives. During a 2010 interview, Pedro Marroquín, a student activist who had been president of his college's AB-540 club, articulated the philosophy that "sharing our stories," as he put it, was a way to overcome the divisiveness of immigration debates and the limitations of categories such as "illegal alien." He explained:

> The component I worked with is . . . realizing the power of personal nar-rative. . . . And using stories, I guess, as a tool to bring about change, you know? And get away from the political rhetoric of the debate around im-migration. Get away from talking about statistics and politics because that turns people off. And so I mean that's our assumption. And so we think that a better dialogue would be centered around our values that we share, our dreams, and aspirations. . . . I think people can realize that we share a lot. . . . We give this training on how we can speak from the heart, you know? As opposed to just speaking from the mind, I guess, or just talking about rational arguments, or things we hear in the media or on TV. But just how we focus our stories around the values of hard work, sacrifice, courage, faith, community, working together.

Pedro's approach to narrative was inspired by the sociologist Stephen Dun-combe's 2007 book, *Dream: Re-imagining Progressive Politics in an Age of Fan-*

tasy, a text that stresses the centrality of imaginative storytelling to developing new political thought. When I asked Pedro for an example of such a narrative, he gave me the following account:

> I would say something like, "My name is Pedro. My family came here in search of a better life because we had a dream and our dream was for . . . me to have a better education. And right now I'm going to college, and I work hard, and my family has sacrificed so much, and we're just as American as anybody else. And so we want an opportunity to be successful so that—I want an opportunity to be successful so I can give back.[4] And maybe I didn't come here with the right documents, but I have the right values. Ah, my mom has taught me the value of hard work. She works at a hotel, um, every day. And so she's given back to this country. She's paying taxes. And so I think you ought [to] just—I just want an opportunity to succeed and also give back to my community that I love, and give back to this country that I love and that has given me so much."

Pedro's narrative defines belonging as a matter of exhibiting "American values"—which he defined as sacrifice, love of country, contributing to the common good, hard work, and seeking opportunity—rather than having the right papers. Importantly, as noted above, the context in which Pedro and other Dreamers were located led them to emphasize Americanness and their ties to the United States. Accused of being "foreign" and "illegal," these students responded by insisting that they not only belonged but in fact were exemplary. The complexity of the identifications articulated at other moments—for example, the notion of being "half here and half there," encountered in chapter 2—drops out in this narrative. Note as well that Pedro's sentence "I think you ought [to] just—" remains unfinished, a false start that he cuts off before articulating. Pedro told me that he deliberately avoided demanding a particular action from his listener. In his view, stories were a means of building a moral justification for a desired outcome and were therefore more persuasive than simply making demands.

The sense of experimentation, of doing politics differently, also characterized other Dreamer actions (Seif 2011), such as mock graduation ceremonies or the Dreamer Holiday Celebration, described at the beginning of this chapter. To engage in these actions, Dreamers had to overcome their fear that public actions would expose them to deportation. Elena Aparicio, an organizer with the Orange County Dream Team, made up of AB-540 students from several

Orange County campuses, described an action that was carried out on the trains that run throughout the county:

> We went to the Santa Ana station and we rode the train over to Anaheim, like on the subway, and back to Santa Ana; down to Irvine; and back up to Santa Ana. What we did was pretty much get on the trains, and it was called, they're like Freedom Rides, it's based, so pretty much the whole point was to get on the trains; let people know, just like, "Like hi, I'm undocumented. This is my story. And this is what I need you to do," which is pretty much "I need you to call this number, this 1-800 number, and I need you to call the governor. I need you to let him know that I'm in this situation and I need you to call the Senate and let them know that I'm in this situation and that you care." And it was—it was definitely—that was definitely an experience for a lot of the people that participated in it because—well, see like before—like this—it was kind of a last-minute thing where we just saw the need and the hurry to do something to just express what we were going through. And a lot of people, especially from Los Angeles and the rest of the network, were very skeptical about participating with anything like that because they . . . see Orange County as extremely conservative, or even L.A., and they're like very afraid of just exposing themselves. They're like, "No, it's too risky exposing yourself." But we actually didn't even think about that. To us, Orange County is like home.

The Freedom Rides made undocumented students visible to train riders, demonstrating to them that the passengers' home—Orange County—was also home to undocumented students (see also Corrunker 2012). By demonstrating to riders that students who were otherwise indistinguishable from other passengers in fact held quite different legal statuses, students hoped both to raise riders' consciousnesses and to spur their fellow Orange County residents to take action.

The forms of activism developed by AB-540 students are revealing. Students were subject to a sharp and seemingly arbitrary differentiation from peers, a differentiation that was largely invisible but that denied them access to the basic opportunities—jobs, transportation, financial aid—that make education possible. This differentiation was deeply stigmatizing. Elena Aparicio compared discovering one's undocumented status to learning that one has a deadly disease, saying that it is only when they meet others who are in the situation that they realize, "Hey, maybe there is life out there. I can live." Beatriz Gonzalez described her own organizing work as part of "a healing process to being undocumented. Because you're undocumented, the law says that you can be mistreated, by allowing them to come into your house and pull your family apart. The law says that although you may have great talent, or have a great idea, still, 'I will not invest in you.' So, since you're at an early age, you're already hearing all these messages that you're a lawbreaker, you're a burden to the economy." In their own counternarratives, in contrast, youths describe themselves as assets rather than as burdens, as "American" rather than foreign, and as exhibiting "American values" rather than illegality. Youths' narratives were urgent, as speakers felt that there was a limited window of time in which to pursue degrees and launch careers. Youths' actions—forming AB-540 clubs, speaking out, political theater—enact the futures to which they aspire, futures in which they might achieve education, justice, political enfranchisement, citizenship, in short, normalcy. By acting as students, a status that both locates them in particular U.S. institutions and on an upward trajectory, youths sought recognition of their membership, recognition that sometimes comes in the form of being treated as constituents by the politicians whose support they seek to enlist.

Though it powerfully countered stigmatization, DREAM Act advocacy had several limitations. One is that narratives of student success can also draw an implied contrast with youths who drop out of high school, join gangs, or acquire criminal records, suggesting that the latter are undeserving. As a gang violence prevention worker complained to me during a 2007 interview, "Like in these recent marches, the immigrant campaign for legalization was divided. 'Do we stand up for the clean-cut immigrant? Or also for the criminal who is part of our community?' And they largely decided to stand up for the clean-cut immigrant." A second limitation, as noted above, is that students are caught in something of a double bind in that challenging the argument that they are "illegal aliens" leads to emphasizing "Americanness" over hybrid, local, or transnational identifications. And a third limitation is that arguing that child migrants are "blameless" can imply that their parents are culpable. To counter this limitation, undocumented students have more recently argued that they are "unapologetic and unafraid" (Seif 2011).

The fates of both the DREAM Act and of undocumented students have waxed and waned from 2006, when I began this study, to 2015, when I finalized this manuscript. The years 2006–2008 were a period of optimism. The 2006 marches led many interviewees to believe that passage of the federal and California Dream acts was around the corner and that their own futures were bright. By 2009–2010, when I conducted follow-up interviews, recession and prolonged immigration debates had taken a toll. Interviewees had lost jobs and were struggling to pay higher tuition costs even as the courses that they needed for completing their degrees were overenrolled. In 2009, one undocumented student interviewee was still in college but was discouraged: "I'm just tired of living like this. I have learned not to get my hopes too high, you know? Sometimes it doesn't happen and you learn how to deal with that. . . . There's no easy way out. They all want . . . the DREAM Act or something, but honestly it's not going to happen." Some had given up on finishing degrees, going to graduate school, and pursuing professions. Then, in 2011, under a Democratic governor, the California Dream Act became law, enabling undocumented college students who had graduated from California high schools to qualify for state financial aid. And on June 15, 2012, Obama declared that DACA would be available to individuals who had entered the United States prior to their sixteenth birthday; were under thirty-one as of June 15, 2012; had been in the United States continuously for the previous five years; and were either in school at the time of application, had completed a high school education or GED, or had been honorably discharged from the military. On August 15, 2012, when the DACA application period opened, legal offices were flooded with applicants. Unlike the federal DREAM Act, however, DACA only provides a work permit and defers deportation for two years. It does not confer legal permanent residency or the ability to travel internationally. Finally, in November 2014, Obama announced that DACA eligibility would be expanded to include individuals who had lived in the United States continuously since January 1, 2010, and that applicants no longer had to have been under the age of thirty-one on June 15, 2012. Yet on February 17, 2015, the very day before expanded DACA was to go into effect, a federal district court in Texas issued an injunction on the ground that the president had not followed proper procedure in announcing this expansion. As of September 2015, this injunction was still in place. Clearly, the status of undocumented and temporarily authorized students continues to be precarious.

Estudio y Lucha (Study and Struggle)

Unlike DREAM Act activism, which focused particularly on the needs of undocumented students, efforts to forge new Central American student associations targeted a range of political and social issues, such as homophobia, environmental justice, voting rights for Salvadorans living in the United States, and the rights of indigenous Central Americans. Centrally, such organizing work sought to combine "estudio y lucha" (study and struggle), to quote USEU, an association that was initiated in San Salvador in the early 2000s and then spread to the CSU and UC campuses. Through educational, artistic, social justice, and coalition-building activities, students asserted that Central American youths had unique needs and histories and that these could not be addressed adequately within existing student groups. In their focus on nationality rather than on pan-ethnic associations, these students were like other recent immigrant groups (Portes and Rumbaut 2001; Rosenblum, Zhou, and Gentemann 2009), but instead of emphasizing their Americanness, as did Dreamers, Central American student leaders stressed their origins in and connections to El Salvador and other Central American nations. More a movement than a set of clubs, new Central American student organizations pushed against the notion of the "ethnic club" associated with colleges' "strategic deployment of diversity" (Urciuoli 1999:289), even as this designation also led them to emphasize nationalistic definitions of identity.

My analysis of Central American student organizing draws on interviews that I conducted with students at California State University, Northridge (CSUN), which offers a major in Central American studies, and at California State University, Los Angeles (CSULA), which offers a Central American studies minor, as well as at other campuses and by attending several conferences that students organized. While this material is not necessarily illustrative of the dynamics on other campuses and cannot encompass the day-to-day organizing that takes place in planning meetings and regular club activities, it does shed light on the claim staked by the formation of these new groups, namely, that Central American students were becoming a significant presence on college campuses, in their communities, and to their nations.

The imaginative space that students sought to occupy is conveyed by one interviewee's account of her first encounter with CAUSA, the Central American United Student Association at CSUN. She recalled:

And [CSU-]Northridge was my first choice [for college], mainly because I learned about CAUSA. . . . And I imagined it as a huge association, because I was familiar with MEChA. I was so eager to go there, and to meet people, and to say, "Tell me! Tell me about the war! Tell me about El Salvador!" . . . And I remember, there was a summer bridge program for new students, and it was sort of an outreach activity. And I went there, and there were signs for the clubs, and I was looking around and I didn't see CAUSA. So I met a guy from MEChA. I asked him, "Where is CAUSA?" He said that he would take down my information and give it to them. . . . And I was telling other Central American students about CAUSA, and I was looking for them and couldn't even find the office.

Based on her prior experience with MEChA, a Chicano student association with chapters on many college campuses, this interviewee expected CAUSA, a relatively new Central American association, to be large, visible, and active. Her assumption that CAUSA would resemble MEChA is revealing. As Central American students developed a consciousness about their own national histories and came to perceive "Salvadoran" and "Central American" as nationalities or ethnicities (Baker-Cristales 2004b), they *expected* institutional recognition in the form of student groups that reflected their experiences. Such expectations do not arise automatically, but rather are products of identity politics in the United States,[5] where racialized immigration policies lead immigrant youths to experience nationality as an ethnicity more than as a legal status (King and Punti 2012),[6] and where underrepresented groups have critiqued the curriculum for omitting or distorting minority groups' experiences and have sought inclusiveness. The ethnic studies and Chicano movements of the 1960s and 1970s struggled successfully for alternative curricula, degree programs, and student associations (Rosales 1997). A legacy of this struggle is the fact that, in the 2000s, Salvadoran students who enrolled in ethnic studies courses or who participated in MEChA shared their predecessors' critique of mainstream accounts, even as these students also felt that they themselves were insufficiently represented in Chicano studies and ethnic studies curricula.[7]

As a result, some Salvadoran student organizers had an ambivalent relationship with Chicano and Latino groups (see Baker-Cristales 2004b).[8] Adelmo Ariel Umanzor, a student organizer active in the Juventud Farabundo Martí, an FMLN (Frente Farabundo Martí para la Liberación Nacional; Farabundo Martí National Liberation Front) youth group, recalled, "I was always organized in the, you know, Latino Awareness, student council, all of that, right? And we never had any spaces for Salvadorians or for culture. You know we were always imposed Cinco de Mayo, Mexican Independence [Day]." Likewise, Cesar Quintanilla, a CSULA student organizer, commented, "I'm not saying we're totally against that [MEChA], because we're not. We're cool with what they're doing. But all the Salvadorans, you know, we don't have anything. Also, we're trying to start something that hopefully evolves and Salvadorans when it comes to higher education, they're able to feel like there is something for them out there." Cesar felt that the increased presence of Salvadorans in the university ought to be reflected institutionally. William Campos of California State University, Long Beach, echoed Cesar's perspective: "We felt that the existing organizations didn't address our identity, and so we felt that we needed our own space. We were tired of groups that tried to instill other types of culture, like Chicano culture, or the Mexican culture that has developed in the United States. We felt that we didn't belong." Adrian Arroyo, a graduate of UCLA, was even more critical: "Salvadoreans being in MEChA, planning things for MEChA, thinking of themselves as Chicanos? I mean, come on! . . . While doing that, we deny our history."

Student organizers were also dissatisfied with established Central American community groups, many of which were founded during the 1980s as part of the Central American solidarity movement by the generation before them (Perla and Coutin 2010; C. Smith 1996). Students criticized these groups for a factionalism, linked to organizers' affiliations with the Salvadoran left, that prevented groups from coming together; for focusing too heavily on issues (such as immigration rights) that primarily affected first-generation immigrants; for having established structures that have "just become another job"; and, most important, for failing to prioritize issues of concern to students themselves. One activist summarized this critique:

> El Salvador is no longer under a civil war. Organizations need to restructure and should not focus only on immigration issues, but look at it more as a— look at the overall picture. . . . And I know that people don't want to bother with simple questions like, you know, when you go into a classroom, you don't start the class by asking, "What is history?" or "What is chemistry?" or "What is—?" Right? But you know what? Sometimes we need to ask the simplest questions. Why is it that people continue to migrate to the U.S.? . . . What is El Salvador doing in Iraq, anyway? What does it mean for El Salvador to emulate the societal [and] political paradigms of the U.S.?

The set of questions that motivated the student organizers whom I interviewed focused on identity, gangs, media stereotypes of youths, the impacts of the Salvadoran civil war, and community injustice—in sum, their own histories as distinct both from those of other Latinos and from the generation of Salvadorans before them. Note that in tackling these issues, student organizers addressed some of the very same structures and processes—criminalization, racialization, marginalization—that were described in chapter 2 and that made the deportees that I will turn to in chapter 4 vulnerable to removal. Student organizers argued that, as the first generation of Salvadoran youths raised in the

United States during the postwar period, it was important for them to define their own identities. As Milda Escobar queried, "The Chicanos invented the term 'Chicano' in the '60s; what are we going to call ourselves?" Youth organizers also sought to counter negative media that stereotyped them as gang members, as described in chapter 2. Likewise, a female student organizer challenged negative media depictions of women: "We are afraid of the media, because the media depicts us as maids, or as sexualized, or as gang members." Just as Dreamers found their student status to be a basis for organizing, so too did Central American student leaders hope that by forming *student* associations, they could counter negative media stereotypes of Salvadoran youths. At the same time, some of these student leaders felt that they themselves had narrowly missed the future that would have been predicted by these stereotypes. As one student organizer told me: "You use all that street knowledge, . . . just having that sense of what to do, when not to do, where to go, where not to go, what time, where to walk. . . . And for us, as students, not just students, but as kids, and living the lifestyle, and going along, partying, doing what we were doing, we gotta know where to go, how to like, pretty much like, you always gotta have an eye behind your head." Organizers also felt that they had to counter the impact of the Salvadoran civil war, which, one noted, had been "a very scarring experience" for their parents. Thinking aloud, another organizer summarized the challenges that she was attempting to address: "Now, the challenge is, how to bring young people to learn about their culture and history, and not just to learn but to analyze, and to be critical? How are we going to communicate to the older generation? . . . How do we build spaces? How do we create a movement?"

Although immigrant youths have not generally been found to replicate the transnationalism that characterizes first-generation immigrants (Menjívar 2002; Rumbaut 2002), the movement that Salvadoran student organizers sought to launch was transnational in nature. A case in point is the founding of USEU at CSULA. Several CSULA students who had gone to high school together had met Juventud Farabundo Martí organizers at the Salvador del Mundo celebration in Los Angeles and, after becoming active in that organization, were invited to the 2007 meeting of the Foro de São Paulo, an international conference of leftist organizations, in San Salvador. There, they met student activists from the Universidad Nacional de El Salvador. A CSULA student organizer recalled learning that students in El Salvador "face some of the same issues that we face. I mean lack of access to higher education, . . . how prices keep increasing and . . . promotion of higher education for younger people too . . . Salvadorian young people." Inspired by their San Salvador counterparts, who had formed a student association to address these issues, CSULA students decided to do the same. They drafted by-laws, secured faculty advisors, and formally launched USEU.[9] In the words of one organizer, USEU "grew out of not having an identity, of not knowing, us Salvadorans like, you know, like what's out there for us once you get to higher education."

Once founded at CSULA, USEU quickly grew, expanding to multiple university and community college campuses in California. This growth can be attributed to multiple factors. Students publicized USEU through their own networks, as an organizer explained: "We went to the MEChA conference, the Latino Youth Conference at UCLA, and—and we were able to expose USEU, like kinda tell about it. Like, yeah, we're here, we just need a new organization. And people from that started, like, 'Who are you guys? You know, could you give me your info? Could you email us,' you know? So people started becoming aware and they wanted to be part of it." Media-savvy students quickly created a webpage featuring information, photographs, and videos about USEU activities. Additionally, undergraduate students who were active in USEU graduated and went to other campuses to pursue master's or doctoral degrees. At their new institutions, some organized new USEU chapters. One organizer told me that he and his colleagues were even hoping to expand to the East Coast where there are large Salvadoran populations.

Some scholars have suggested that the politics of ethnic student clubs can be muted by the ways that universities celebrate diversity. Tara Yasso and colleagues (2009: 664–665) write:

> Universities celebrate diversity with ethnic food and fiestas while failing to provide equal access and opportunity to Students of Color. If, as research suggests, enrolling Students of Color helps White students become more racially tolerant, livens up class dialogue through more diverse points of view, and prepares White students to gain employment in a multicultural, global economy, then what is the role of Students of Color? Seemingly, in return for admission, universities expect Students of Color to enrich the experiences and outcomes for Whites.

Yet Central American student organizers exceeded the conceptualization of clubs as co-curricular offerings, securing recognition from political leaders both locally and in Central America. For example, USEU delegates were invited to attend the inauguration of Mauricio Funes, the first FMLN president of El Salvador. Delegations to Central America were also part of a political project that involved challenging existing U.S. and El Salvador relations. As an organizer explained, "We did want to think about how you export something good, not just the exportation of gangs from the United States, but how do you export consciousness?" USEU members also acted locally, conducting research regarding educational disparities at a Los Angeles high school, organizing an annual conference, and promoting higher education for younger Salvadorans. Organizers, who, as noted above, had confronted myriad educational obstacles, felt a tremendous responsibility to give back to their own communities, as Eduardo Sanchez explained:

> What I ended up creating in my mind was that I was the chosen one, that my parents immigrated to the United States, and I was born here for a reason, and that reason was to get the benefits, what little benefits I got, because the school I went to wasn't that good, but obviously, I had some educational benefits, compared to [those in] El Salvador. So I got more education than them, and I'm like the chosen one to go back and put it to use.

Salvadoran student leaders saw student associations as part of broader justice struggles and, perhaps naively, argued that their generation could solve entrenched social problems. As one student commented, "We're very talented and we can do a lot of things. We could—we could do anything basically." To realize change, students questioned the status quo. As Eduardo commented, "Things don't just happen, you know. Who's the one making this happen? Why is this normal? Why is it normal for us to get married, you know? It didn't just happen. Who created that? Why is the nuclear family normal? It has to do a lot with American government, and World War II, and the fifties, you know. There's a reason for all of this and we've got to question everything." Products of the digital age, students recorded their activities and also posted videos and photographs. The political moment, which was characterized by the 2006 immigrant rights marches and the elections of the first FMLN president in El Salvador and the first African American president in the United States, fueled student optimism. One organizer commented that he and his colleagues felt empowered: "There are a lot of things that are hurting us that we could do something about. So us being privileged to be in this position that we're at right now, we're students, so that gives us an advantage to get information, so that is a service we could provide to the community." Another agreed, saying, "We are going to use the power that we have been given."

Students' work was not without challenges. While being students gave them access to university resources, a valued social status, and an organizing platform, student organizations are potentially fragile, given that their membership is only on campus temporarily. One USEU organizer talked to me about the difficulty of recruiting new leadership on his campus when a cohort graduates, a perennial problem within student groups. Indeed, at some of the campuses where student groups were originally most active, participation has dwindled and the optimism that empowers students sometimes gives way to disappointment when goals are not achieved. One organizer, who had graduated and entered the workforce, told me of her realization that change comes slowly:

> I think that for a really long time especially after being involved in Central American studies, I think a lot of us, well, I don't want to speak for everyone, but I know I put a lot of pressure on myself for like you know, "We need to fix things," and "We have to make things happen," and just being very like young and idealistic about stuff. And then you start reading about all of these different communities that need to heal from war, and that takes a couple of generations. That's not just something that happens.

The broad range of activities pursued both by DREAM Act activism and by Central American student associations nonetheless is evidence of students' efforts to move beyond traditional organizational forms in order to "author who they are becoming" (Brettell and Nibbs 2009).

Literary Voices

Poetry without action is not poetry.
—QUOTE FROM A SALVADORAN WRITER
INTERVIEWED BY THE AUTHOR

For some interviewees, writing, performing, and other forms of scholarly, artistic, and cultural production were integral components of activism and political engagement (see also DeShazer 1994).[10] Inspired by work that they had read in Chicano and Central American studies courses, by *testimonio*, by U.S.–Central American literature (A. Rodríguez 2009), by Latin American writers and political thinkers, and by their own professors and mentors, new Salvadoran and Central American writers, artists, and scholars produced their own work, thus adding to the Central American literature and scholarship created by their predecessors (Chinchilla 2014; Escobar 2012; Oliva Alvarado

2009; Padilla 2012; A. Rodríguez 2009). These young writers and artists pursued or completed advanced degrees; founded publication outlets; and produced poetry, literature, and scholarly work. They did so collectively, as part of writing groups, artistic associations, and friendship networks. Their writing crosses boundaries between scholarship and art, documentation and fiction, the personal and the political, immigrant and Chicano movements, and the United States and Central America. Young Salvadoran and Central American writers and artists sought to transform literary landscapes and fields of study by documenting their own histories of repression, the injustices perpetrated within and against their communities, and legal challenges experienced by immigrants. Transnational, bilingual, Central American, multiethnic, heterosexual, and queer, these writers played with language, identity, and form as they sought to "create a space for our own U.S. Central American voices" (Chinchilla 2007). To explore the link between literary production and social activism, I draw on interviews with the Central American scholars whom I encountered through writing collectives, nonprofit organizations, social organizing, student groups, and friendship networks in Los Angeles between 2006 and 2010.[11] Their experiences reveal something of the currents that circulated around and intersected with DREAM Act activism, student organizing, and immigrant rights movements more generally.

Interviewees who formed writing collectives had multiple motivations. One was to produce scholarship about their own community rather than letting their community be defined by others. Interviewees recognized that literature by Central Americans was already being produced, both in the United States and Central America (see A. Rodríguez 2009), but they still felt that external forces—media depictions, political representations by U.S. and Central American officials, and social science scholarship—dwarfed the accounts produced by their own communities. One writer, who founded his own publishing company, explained that his goal was to enable "Central Americans here in the U.S. to control our ideas, information, education, in order to advance our culture." In producing their own work, writers sought to document their lives, articulating what was unique about their generation, while also connecting their experiences with those of generations that had come before them. One interviewee argued that it was only in the early 2000s that Salvadoran scholars and writers became visible. Another interviewee said simply, "We're coming of age, you know, in the Salvadorian community here in the U.S." Some interviewees were motivated to talk to me precisely out of a desire to document their communities' histories.

For many of the writers whom I interviewed, writing was a way to explore their own history and politics. One writer told me how, as a community college student, he first realized the connections between the Salvadoran civil war and the looting that had occurred in his own neighborhoods during the 1992 Los Angeles riots that followed the Rodney King verdict:

> At the library at PCC [Pasadena Community College], this was about '95, they had a photography book on El Salvador and it was about the war. And that was the first time I think I saw images. It was black and white photography—the corpses and—and, ah, it was very—I remember that—I'll never forget it. It was just an unassuming book. It didn't have the book jacket on it—a very thin book. And seeing the black and white pictures of corpses and—it really—it made me sick. That's the feeling I got—sick. And I became, so this was after the [peace] accords, and just, you know, looking back at the period, late '80s, and I'm like, "Wow!' This is what a lot of these people who are looting, or a lot of people that are in those neighborhoods where I grew up—these people must have—this was them too. You know, they came from this."

This realization along with his own experiences in grass-roots community activism made him want to travel to El Salvador to learn more about such "hidden histories." Several interviewees cited the critical educator Paulo Freire in explaining the importance of knowing and writing their own histories. One told me, "Doctora, I'll give you the—el hueso duro de mi filosofía, de donde sale. De Paulo Friere, *Pedagogy of the Oppressed*. Very simple. In order for someone to advance in society, in *any* society, they need to know where they come from. Where they're at. Politically, economically, and culturally." For some, writing was not a choice but a necessity, "animado por el dolor y el recuerdo" (motivated by pain and memory).

By producing their own work, writers sought to create a literary space that was uniquely Central American and in dialogue with other movements. Like interviewees who had founded Central American student groups, these writers described being inspired by but having a complex relationship with Chicano literature (see Oliva-Alvarado 2013). One scholar and poet recalled the excitement of her first encounter with this literature: "I went to East Los Angeles Community College. And that's where I took my first . . . Chicano classes and sociology, and a lot of literature courses, and encountered feminist theory. I was like, 'What??' So it was just really transformative." Now a published author herself, this interviewee related that her studies led her to pose the question

"Where *is* U.S. Central American literature?" Other writers stressed that even as they sought to create Central American literature, they also wanted to highlight diversity among Central Americans. One writer recounted his frustration, as a gay Central American man, with trying to fit in to existing groups. He felt that, as a child, he was shunned by Mexican Americans due to speaking Salvadoran Spanish, then by Salvadorans for being queer, and then by the gay crowd in West Hollywood for not being white (see also Roque Ramirez 2003). Another interviewee had participated in a Central American queer writing group "to kind of create a space where we could talk about . . . being a minority within a minority within a minority."

To create the space where they could both explore common histories and acknowledge differences, writers formed collectives where they shared their work and organized public readings. Several described the anthology *izote vos*, published in 2000 by Pacific News Service, as an inspiration (Kim, Serrano, and Ramos 2000; Oliva Alvarado 2013). Dedicated to dispelling stereotypes about Central Americans in the United States and to promoting artistic work by Salvadoran youths themselves, this "book/art/documentation project," to quote the editors (Kim, Serrano, and Ramos 2000, 3), features poetry, personal narratives, photographs, and artwork produced by Salvadoran youths in Los Angeles and San Francisco. The anthology's title was selected collectively by the writers and emphasizes transcending borders: "The *izote* is El Salvador's national flower, its fruit found in many native dishes. But the flower also flourishes in parts of California. *Vos* in Salvadoran Spanish means 'you,' but also conjures images of '*voz* . . . voice'" (2). Significantly, Salvadoran students' use of *vos* rather than the more common (in Mexican American Spanish) *tu* was one of the language differences for which they were stigmatized (see chapter 2), so incorporating this term in the anthology's title may have been a way to reclaim this term. This moving work pursues a variety of themes, including war, immigration, gangs, family, identity, gender, and sexuality. As Leticia Hernández-Linares writes sadly in the poem "Izote: A Flower for My Fathers," "Nothing in this realism is magical" (43). Deeply personal, it is simultaneously *testimonio*.

The *izote vos* project gave rise to new groups, as an interviewee who had participated in the literary collective Epicentro, made up of Central Americans with multiple national origins, explained:

> It [Epicentro] came out of a—out of a project that CARECEN [the Central American Resource Center] up in San Francisco was involved with in getting youth voices from L.A. and San Francisco. . . . And a few of the writers

featured in there from L.A. wanted to start something here with like Central American voices here—not just Salvadoran, but Central American. So there was a little circle—of those writers were students, graduate students. And it just started, you know, as I met them I was working at a coffee shop in Hollywood and I knew about the book. And I saw it and I was like, "Hey how come I'm not in this book, I write poetry?" I didn't even know it was something like this. It's just weird. And they're just like, not just 1.5, but there are second-generation people. . . . In this writers' group, they wanted to feature different voices. Because there was queer voices; there was transgender voices; there's Salvadoran; Guatemalan.

Likewise, another participant explained: "I was going to this coffee shop called Expresso Mi Cultura on Hollywood and Gramercy. And it was there I saw people reciting poetry. I got up and recited a poem. In front of a room. It was quiet. And a lot of the audience was people from Epicentro. That's how I got involved in Epicentro."[12]

Such writing collectives provided participants with performance venues, social support, mentorship, and the opportunity to explore the boundaries of their art form. They thus created what Yasso and colleagues (2009:660) refer to as a *counterspace*, that is, a culturally supportive environment in which students and scholars navigate between the worlds of home and the university. The participants in these groups included not only those who sought to become professional artists but also those in social sciences, medicine, and other fields, for whom artistic endeavors were linked to other forms of documentation and scholarship. Their poetry was explicitly political, as they sought to challenge hegemonic structures responsible for violence and injustice. For example, during an interview, one Epicentro participant argued that it was important "to develop a new school of thought. How can we gain independence? And I don't mean geographical independence, I don't mean economic independence. [I mean] mental independence. How can *we* grow out of the Western thought? Can we develop a Latin American philosophy that is, that breaks away from Western thought? And that is not all indigenous?"

This desire for alternatives is reflected in the poetry published by these writers (Arias 2012). For example, the poem "Central American American?" by the poet Maya Chinchilla explores identity, history, and language, asking "Centralamerican American/does that come with a hyphen?/a space?" (Chinchilla 2014; Chinchilla and Oliva Alvarado 2007; see appendix). The poem references her own history as a Central American who eats "black beans and white rice" in thick tortillas, feels bombs and gunfire in her heart, suffers through "backlists and secrets," and had "mysterious people/passing through my home." Her poem denounces those who reject Central American immigrants, who "tell us the American dream is the truth/but that our stories of escape from horror are not." Where, she asks, is her home? The poem concludes with questions: "Are there flowers on a volcano?/am I a CENTRAL/ American?/Where is the center of America?" These questions destabilize terms in which identity, geography, and history are construed. Perhaps being a Central American means being at the center of America, an unknown and, the poem suggests, shifting location that might encompass the multiple homes through which Central Americans have passed. And perhaps, if they are central, immigrants will be able to live, instead of having to make further sacrifices.

The bilingual poem "hybrideities/hibrideidades" by the Guatemalan poet GusTavo Guerra Vásquez also plays with language to explore identities (see appendix). This poem, written in both English and Spanish, lists "hybrid names," drawing on slang terms for people from El Salvador, Guatemala, Mexico, Central America, Los Angeles, and elsewhere: "GuateMayAngelino/GuanaMex/ Guanachapín/GuanaChapílena." As the hybridities are listed, the gender of the identity referenced shifts from a masculine "o" ending to feminine "a," and in some cases it is gender neutral. The list of shifting hybrid names implies movement, recombination, and change as location redefines identity, producing new names, even as the elements of these names reference past histories and are only understandable if one is an insider who can decode the terms. Though a finite number of hybrid names appear in the poem's list—there are nine altogether, culminating in "TicoGuanaCatraChapicanAngelina"—the poet gestures toward the future: "and the list continues . . . ," suggesting a perhaps infinite and at this moment unknowable number. In these namings, the poet locates both "struggle" and "hope"—the hope that comes from movement, from continuity, and from invention.

Like DREAM Act activism and the founding of new Central American student organizations, the work of these new writers seeks to know the past in order to imagine more just futures. Arturo Arias (2012:301–302) observes of groups like Epicentro, "Their Central American–American identity challenges both our traditional understanding of Latino communities and our comprehension of nationalistic diasporas." Though their goals and practices differ, these three forms of activism—which have overlapping protagonists— reshape the terrain on which belonging is determined.

Conclusion

The activism practiced by young Salvadoran and Central American students, organizers, and writers demonstrates the breadth of the immigrant rights movement in content and scope. Though youths certainly engaged in traditional political activism, such as holding rallies and protests, and many participated in the 2006 marches, interviewees also developed a host of other political practices, including political theater, conferences, and poetry readings. Although they sought particular policy changes, such as passage of the federal and California Dream acts, youths also pursued broader justice claims, denouncing violence against women, seeking inclusive curricula, and supporting political struggles within Central America. Though clearly inspired by previous movements, particularly the Chicano movement and the Central American solidarity movement of the 1980s, youths' political practices were also situated in relation to the university context, their ties to Central America, and the political and legal structures that define U.S. citizenship. In creating a new Central American student movement, youths responded to the particular injustices that they had experienced and also sought to generate more just alternatives.

Commonalities in the form that their activities assumed thus reveal the power relations within which students are embedded. First, the forms of activism discussed in this chapter seek to counter the historical erasures that make re/membering necessary. Dreamers recounted personal histories both to demonstrate the deservingness of undocumented students and to explain how and why these students and their families came to be in the United States in the first place. As Pedro Marroquín stated in his example of a personal story, "My family came here in search of a better life because we had a dream and our dream was for us to—for me to have a better education." Founders and participants in Central American student associations also sought a deeper knowledge of history by sending delegations to Central American countries (which represented youths' pasts), interviewing parents about family history, or doing research. Likewise Central American writers produced historical accounts, among others, whether these assumed a documentary form, as in the family photos in the *izote vos* collection, or a literary one, as in Maya Chinchilla's poetic account of her history as a CENTRAL American. Knowing one's history simultaneously produces resemblance (to other groups that also have histories) and differentiation (in that one's history is unique) (Greenhouse 1996). Though it in some ways resembles nostalgia, which can idealize the past, this quest for historical memory highlights injustices and serves as a form of social critique. Publicly articulating histories that highlight injustice (the war, "black lists and secrets") and aspirations (the dream to have a better life) substitutes for the *absence* of history that leads some Central American kids to be taught that Cinco de Mayo is their holiday or that immigrants entered the United States for selfish reasons. For these youths, re/membering is key to creating alternative futures in which undocumented youths are granted lawful permanent residency, Central American youths from low-income families go to college, and college graduates pursue social justice campaigns. Memory practices therefore can have a "presentist" focus in that they deploy the past in order to make arguments about present and future conditions (Berdahl 1999; Bissell 2005).

Second, these forms of activism also incorporate performances that make youths' social geographies visible, thus enabling youths to *generate* rather than merely consume media images. When Dreamers stand up on a train to announce that they are undocumented, when student groups post videos about Central American student delegations on a campus website, and when Central American writers publish their work, youths both assert presence and also reconfigure spaces within which presence can be performed (Arias 2012). A train becomes a site where the arbitrary nature of distinctions between documented and the undocumented is revealed, a campus news report records images of Salvadoran youths encountering political leaders in El Salvador (www.youtube .com/watch?v=vM6iucztUNY&feature=related), and a coffee shop becomes a place where the experiences of queer and transgendered Salvadorans can be explored. Such performances interrogate the legal categories, national boundaries, and hegemonic understandings that delimit presence even as they, at times, reproduce hegemonic understandings of "deservingness" as linked to demonstrating values (e.g., hard work, sacrifice) presumed to be "American." Strategically, activists may highlight particular dimensions of identity and belonging. For instance, Dreamers emphasized the "Americanization" of high-achieving college students, while organizers who founded student associations on their campuses emphasized national identities as Central Americans. Collectively, however, student activism also points to other possibilities, in which national categories are deemphasized, citizenship can be practiced transnationally, and identities can be multifaceted. These complex relationships are explored further in chapter 5.

Third, for these students and scholars, articulating history and performing presence are political acts. These actions give students a public voice, enabling them to *act as citizens* who are entitled to have a voice in influencing policy, shaping curricula, governing universities, or producing both literature and fields of study. They thus challenge both the marginalization to which Central Americans have historically been subjected in the United States, as well as the political and economic structures that, in Central American countries, have fueled emigration. In so doing, they seek to bring social and legal membership into alignment and to make citizenship full, thus countering racial, class, and gendered disparities that make some individuals' citizenship "second class," even within activist circles. Furthermore, these youths do so transnationally, as even Dreamers, who are not able to travel internationally due to their immigration status, recount personal stories that begin with their entry to the United States from elsewhere. In this work, notions of "origin" are complicated. On the one hand, "origin" can be depicted as "natural" just as "the figure of the homeland" comes to be associated with particular language groups, racial or national designations, or time periods (the time "before") (Axel 2004:43). On the other hand, by unfixing origin, which, activists suggest, can take place in Central America, the United States, Los Angeles, a particular school, or all of the above, "origin" becomes a destination, something that can perhaps be deferred to the future, a process of becoming that is not pinned to a single place or point (Axel 2002). This work thus acknowledges the "bi and multiple rooting that occurs for immigrants with numerous 'homes' in the United States and Central America" (Oliva Alvarado 2013:371).

Finally, by dreaming, Central American youth activism establishes new organizations and practices alongside those created by the generation of Central Americans who immigrated as adults during the 1980s. With support from their predecessors and allies, youths focus their activism on the issues that concern them, such as media representations of youths. They thus re/member both the United States and Central America. As one writer told me, "I like to say I'm Salvadoran from L.A. . . . I claim my space here in L.A. . . . You know, L.A.'s got that distinction of being the fifteenth department [of El Salvador, a country divided into fourteen departments]. . . . I could say that playfully too like in Spanish to some people." As the "fifteenth department" of El Salvador (Rivas 2014; A. Rodríguez 2005), Los Angeles becomes a transnational space. By revisiting their own histories and enacting alternative futures, these youths seek to occupy this space, making it visible. The organizational forms through which students create spaces (and counterspaces), though, are sometimes transitory, in that student organizations must contend with changes in leadership and membership as students graduate and in that collectives and friendship networks can coalesce and/or disperse over time. These forms nonetheless lay the groundwork for future intellectual and professional endeavors.

One other difference, though, between these youths and their parents' generation is the intensity of the immigration and criminal justice enforcement tactics to which they have been subjected. The forms of activism discussed in this chapter were carried out, to some degree, in the shadow of these tactics. Dreamers struggled against the prospect of being deported, USEU members challenged stereotypes that Salvadorans were gang members and sought to increase educational opportunities among high school students who were at risk of joining gangs, and Central American writers and scholars denounced social injustices, including incarceration, police brutality, Immigration and Customs Enforcement raids, and deportation. The next chapter turns to the experiences of 1.5-generation Salvadorans who were subjected to the experiences that these activists struggled against, namely, criminalization and removal to El Salvador.

Boundaries

AUGUST 17, 2012. I sat in the offices of a Central American community organization in Los Angeles on the third day after the DACA program began. Since 2011, I had been doing fieldwork and volunteer work in the legal services department of this nonprofit organization; I shadowed legal service providers, translated documents, and provided support to the legal staff.

As hundreds of would-be DACA applicants and their parents arrived at the nonprofit in search of advice and legal services, I was asked to help the organization screen potential applicants to ensure that they met the eligibility requirements for DACA.[13] Picking up a completed intake form, I called out a name, and a young man from Ecuador approached. We sat at a desk in a crowded room, and I began to review the materials that he brought with him. Handing me his passport, where his entry date was clearly stamped, he explained that he first came to the United States when he was fifteen and a half. One of the requirements for DACA was to be a "child arrival," namely, to have entered the country when one was under the age of sixteen. Looking at his birth date, which was also visible on the passport, and the entry date, I quickly did the math in my head. He had been sixteen, not fifteen. I asked, "Are you sure that you were fifteen when you came to the U.S.?" He said that he was, and he called to his mother, who was sitting in a nearby waiting area. "Wasn't I fifteen when I came to the U.S.?" he asked her. "Yes," she said. Not trusting my math, I pulled out a piece of paper and calculated again. "If this entry date is correct, then you were sixteen," I told him. Disbelievingly, he pulled a calculator from his pocket, entered some numbers, and saw the answer: 16. "Surely there is some flexibility," his mother insisted. I explained that to my knowledge there was not, and I apologized, pointing out that I was not the one who made up these rules. "You mean that if I had entered the United States three months earlier, I would qualify?" the young man asked me. I said that, unfortunately, that was the case. As he and his mother got up to talk to someone else, in case there was still some way for the young man to qualify, I reached for the next intake form. Recalling the compelling stories that I heard from the student activists who had sought DACA, I reflected on the arbitrariness of the lines that the law draws around the deserving.

JULY 2008. I met Pablo, Francisco, and Jorge Ramirez in San Salvador in the office of Central American Resource Center (CARECEN) Internacional, an immigrant rights nongovernmental organization (NGO) that was helping me to set up focus-group interviews with 1.5-generation Salvadorans who had been deported. These three brothers had been removed from the United States in 2006, along with 11,050 other Salvadorans who were deported that year (U.S. Department of Homeland Security 2007). They would have fit in quite well in the United States, but in El Salvador, as they related, they stood out. All three were dressed in what struck me as stylish attire: polo shirts, jeans, and tennis shoes. Francisco had longish curly hair, pulled back by a black sports band, as well as piercings in his cheeks. They each wore single-studded diamonds in their ears, and Pablo had on a puka shell necklace. The three were despondent about their circumstances. When I asked how he was doing, Francisco responded, "It's a Tuesday, just like any other Tuesday. One more day to get through, that we have to be here."

Over the course of two interviews on different days, I learned how, after having gained lawful permanent residency in 2001, Jorge, Pablo, and Francisco came to be deported only five years later. The three brothers' parents had immigrated to the United States without authorization in the late 1980s, when El Salvador was at war. Jorge recalled, "I used to go outside in the morning and see the helicopters. I remember that it used to stay still, and then start the bombs. Bomb! Bomb! [sound of bombs falling] And then just like shootouts, everywhere! It was crazy!" After arriving in the United States their parents worked for a year or two and then, in 1990, fearing that their children would be forcibly recruited by combatants, they hired a migrant smuggler to bring their seven children to the United States.

Once the children arrived, the family applied for political asylum and obtained work permits while their applications were pending. The children grew up in New York where their father worked as a landscaper and where they encountered forms of misrecognition much like those described in chapter 2. Francisco related that, in the eighth grade, "there was [sic] more Hispanics. So it was difficult because I was not Dominican or I was not Colombian or I was not Puerto Rican. I was Salvadoran. There was always a barrier there. I don't know why."

In 1998, the family moved to Georgia, to remove the children from pressures to join gangs, and in 2001, Pablo, Francisco, Jorge, and their siblings were awarded legal permanent residency through the Nicaraguan Adjustment and Central American Relief Act (NACARA). The brothers did not seem to fully understand the legal process that they had gone through, as Jorge explained: "My parents first, they applied for asylum. Then they didn't go for asylum because it was over. Then they went and my pops, since he was over here for a long time, he went and applied for some program that they had. I forgot the name of it."

Although moving to Georgia enabled them to avoid gangs, the children still encountered difficulties. Francisco's girlfriend became pregnant and he had to drop out of high school to support his daughter. By the eleventh grade, Pablo got married and had a daughter, and he too dedicated himself to work. Then the three brothers were (separately) convicted of minor crimes, including driving under the influence of alcohol, carrying a gun without a permit, and drug possession. After short periods of probation or jail time (the same penalties that a citizen would have faced), all three were placed in removal proceedings. Terrified of being deported to El Salvador, which by the mid-2000s was wracked by gang violence, they applied for political asylum, but, after being detained for a year, they agreed to sign deportation papers, believing that by doing so they would earn the right to return to the United States more quickly. (In fact, it is very difficult to secure waivers to reenter the United States following deportation or removal.)[1]

In 2008, at the time of our interview, the three brothers were still hoping that eventually, through U.S.-citizen relatives, they would be able to return to the country legally. In the meantime, Francisco told me, "I'm already here. I'm going to have to deal with it now. I've gotta suffer through it. And there's nothing I can do now but suffer through it."

As the Ramirez brothers' experiences illustrate, some 1.5-generation youths who were raised in the United States were eventually deported to El Salvador where, rather than being able to practice the sorts of activism described in the last chapter, many had to renegotiate their pasts and futures. *Deporting long-term residents is, like emigration, a form of violent dismemberment.* Deportation breaks apart families, strips individuals of any legal status that they have acquired, and essentially exiles them from the country that they may have come to call home. In the process, many deportees lose possessions, suffer psychologically, and experience physical deprivation and even danger. No one is intrinsically deportable; rather, individuals are *made* deportable through policies that criminalize youth culture (resulting in criminal convictions), prevent unauthorized migrants from regularizing their status (resulting in illegality), and treat immigration as a matter of security rather than humanitarianism or labor (Dauvergne 2008; de Genova 2004). Despite the current effort to focus deportation policies on serious criminals, a wide net is being cast: in 2012, 12 percent of deportees were serious offenders, 21.4 percent were convicted of drug-related offenses, 40.4 percent were convicted of other crimes (more than half of which were traffic offenses), and 23.8 percent had immigration offenses (Treyger, Chalfin, and Loeffler 2014; see also Kubrin 2014). Scholars have attributed the policies that result in deportation to structural determinants, such as capitalist needs for an expendable yet compliant workforce (de Genova 2002) or neoliberal efforts to shape behavior by reinforcing normative (and racialized) understandings of citizenship (Dowling and Inda 2013; Inda 2006). Yet the disproportionality between deportation's effects on the lives of deportees and the circumstances that most commonly give rise to deportation suggests that these explanations tell only part of the story. In addition, deportation appears to be an irrational excess of security policies, one that, much like going to war in the name of peace, leaves a trail of insecurity and uncertainty in its wake (Kanstroom 2007, 2012).

Given that I interviewed both 1.5-generation Salvadorans who were highly successful (e.g., they secured legal status, obtained jobs, and/or went to college) and those who were less so (e.g., they may have developed a criminal record and/or been deported), it is tempting to compare the narratives of each group in order to identify the factors that led to these very different life outcomes. Such a comparison might reveal what predicts deportation. In this chapter, I deliberately resist this temptation, primarily because while individuals' life outcomes (at least at the time of their interviews with me) may have been strikingly different, the deportees whom I interviewed stressed the *normalcy* of the lives that they lived *prior* to being deported. Like the individuals described in chapter 2, most deportees grew up in U.S. neighborhoods, went to U.S. schools, learned English, joined and formed families, struggled to understand their place in their new communities, encountered challenges (including family tensions, impoverished schools, and gang pressures), formed friendships, and entered the labor market, often at young ages. Many also encountered legal difficulties associated either with their immigration status or with criminal offenses ranging from petty infractions to more serious crimes. Some interviewees ascribed these difficulties to their own wrongdoing. For example, Francisco Ramirez, who had been convicted of selling and possessing drugs, told me regretfully, "When you're young, you *do* make bad decisions. But in the end, it always hunts you down, especially if you're not from there [the United States]." Yet focusing on such "bad decisions" would direct attention away from the institutional structures that resulted in deportation. These institutional structures include immigration policies that denied asylum to Salvadorans, socioeconomic segregation that forced new arrivals into crime-ridden neighborhoods, intensified policing in those neighborhoods, the criminalization of aspects of minority youth culture (including drug use), the 1996 reforms that prioritized the deportation of noncitizens with criminal convictions, and the unavailability of state-appointed legal counsel in removal proceedings.

Thus, while it might be interesting and instructive to identify what enabled some youths to overcome these challenges while others did not, my point here is that (1) focusing on differences that led to eventual deportation would overlook the commonalities, at earlier life stages, as described in chapter 2, between interviewees who had been deported and those who had not; and (2) emphasizing differences would reinforce the popular rhetoric distinguishing the "criminal aliens" targeted for deportation from other noncitizens, when in fact the policies directed at "criminal aliens" have by and large "removed the pettiest of violators" (Kubrin 2014:329). At the same time, it is important to recognize that deportees and nondeportees who were interviewed had quite different attitudes toward and relationships with El Salvador and the United States. As we saw in chapters 2 and 3, growing up in the United States led to complex identifications, in which interviewees who were living in the United

States often stressed both their "roots" in El Salvador and sense of identity as "Salvadoran," even as they also insisted that they belonged in the United States. In contrast, deportees generally stressed their alienation from El Salvador and their identification with the United States. This contrast, which was shaped by individuals' legal experiences and life circumstances, is consistent with the notion that identity is at least in part situational (Okamura 1981). So, while emphasizing commonalities, I do not mean to imply that there are no differences between these groups.

I therefore focus on the ways that, despite encountering institutional challenges, youths who were eventually deported sought to re/member, that is, to make lives for themselves, both before and after being removed. Like other 1.5-generation children, these deportees became part of U.S. neighborhoods, and in fact the crimes of which some of them were convicted are evidence of the degree to which they joined in local youth culture. According to Alejandro Portes and Min Zhou's theory of segmented assimilation (1993; see also Portes and Rumbaut 2001), immigrants who have experienced negative contexts of reception assimilate, but to marginalized sectors of U.S. society, including those subject to increased policing—though in fact (and contrary to popular perception) neighborhoods where there are significant foreign-born populations have lower crime rates than do neighborhoods populated by those born in the United States (Ousey and Kubrin 2009; Sampson, Raudenbush, and Earls 2007). Youths who experienced such negative assimilation and who were placed in removal proceedings often fought their cases, remaining detained while they either exhausted the legal process or became exhausted by being repeatedly told by both guards and other detainees that their legal efforts were futile. And, after being deported, interviewees struggled to re/member, returning to the United States with or without authorization, seeking jobs, and sometimes re-creating aspects of their U.S. lives within El Salvador.

The security policies that resulted in the Ramirez brothers' deportation have entailed a broad escalation in the size, scope, and technological sophistication of removal. By the early 1990s, immigrant-receiving countries in various parts of the world ratcheted up their enforcement tactics (Cornelius, Martin, and Hollifield 1994; Walters 2002), restricting irregular migrants' access to employment and services (Perea 1997), militarizing border crossings (Nevins 2002; Rosas 2006), imposing harsher sanctions on those who defied restrictions (Welch 2002), and expanding surveillance (Fassin 2011). In the United States, police have increasingly joined federal agents in detecting unauthorized migrants (Decker, Lewis, Provine, and Varsanyi 2009; Varsanyi 2010). Also new detention center complexes have been constructed to hold those apprehended (Welch 2002), massive numbers of individuals have been displaced through deportation, and the law has changed in ways that both propel and accommodate these practices (de Genova 2004; Hing 2006; Kanstroom 2007; Menjívar and Kanstroom 2013). A case in point is the Illegal Immigration Reform and Immigrant Responsibility Act (IIRIRA) and the Anti-Terrorism and Effective Death Penalty Act (AEDPA), which, in 1996, expanded the range of crimes that could result in immigration consequences and eliminated waivers through which "criminal aliens" could fight against deportation (Kanstroom 2000, 2007; Morawetz 2000; Nevins 2002). The impact of these legal changes was swift. In 1995, the year before these reforms, 50,924 individuals were removed; in 1996, the year of the reforms, this number grew to 69,680, and in 1997, one year later, it escalated further to 114,432.[2] By 2013, 368,644 individuals were removed from the United States.[3] For a country like El Salvador, whose economy has come to depend on migrant remittances, the impact of escalated removals has been severe. In 2013, El Salvador was the fourth most common destination of deportees from the United States, with 21,602 individuals removed.[4] These arrivals exacerbate already high unemployment rates and have fueled public panic over crime (McGuire 2011; Moodie 2011; Zilberg 2011).

By placing deportation within its institutional context while also attending to experiences of individual deportees, I make several contributions to deportation studies. First, by attending to law's *archaeology*, I seek to advance understandings of the legal technicalities involved in the "illegalization" of migrants (Peutz and de Genova 2010). Scholars who have analyzed illegalization have tended to focus on its structural determinants (i.e., capitalism's need for a cheap and expendable labor force). These structural determinants, however, play out through laws whose content may vary historically. To excavate such legal histories, I examine how the categories and distinctions used to deny status at one moment in time become part of legal history such that when new policies are developed, these earlier meanings are also reproduced. As refugees fleeing an oppressive government supported by the United States, Salvadorans were largely denied asylum during the 1980s (Silk 1986). This denial was reproduced in subsequent policies such that 1.5-generation youths who could otherwise have naturalized were still noncitizens and therefore vulnerable to deportation at the time that the 1996 immigration reforms were implemented. Second, focusing on the *geography* of deportation reveals how the spatialized tactics involved in removal transform both deportees and the nations where they reside (Mountz 2010). Removal has been thought of as a process that removes someone who is already "illegal" from one clearly demarcated nation to another. Yet deportees' accounts of apprehension, detention, and deportation suggest that this process *makes them illegal*. Experientially, deportation strips away their earlier identities while also redefining the territories that they occupy, making the country to which they are removed an extension of the detention they experienced. Third, examining the ways in which deportees have responded to their own removals suggests that "wiliness," exhibited by 1.5-generation youths who have to navigate something of a gap or nonspace (de Certeau, Jameson, and Lovitt 1980), is not extinguished through removal. Rather, from a place of extreme marginalization, deportees nonetheless claim membership in ways that challenge both removal and social exclusion.

My analysis in this chapter derives from interviews that I conducted in 2008 with forty-one 1.5-generation migrants who had been deported from the United States to El Salvador. Two Salvadoran NGOs helped me to recruit interviewees. These were the San Salvador offices of CARECEN Internacional and Homies Unidos, a gang violence prevention organization. Interviews, which each lasted approximately two hours, were conducted at these organizations' offices and also at a hotel in Usulutan, in order to draw on more rural populations. The majority of individuals interviewed originally left El Salvador during the 1980–1992 Salvadoran civil war. On average, interviewees were 10.6 years old at the time that they left El Salvador, and they had lived an average of 16.2 years outside of El Salvador before being deported. Approximately half of the interview sample had become legal permanent residents (LPRs), while the other half was undocumented, temporarily authorized, or of unknown legal status. Most had been convicted of a crime prior to being deported. In some cases, the crime was quite serious, such as homicide, but most often convictions were for fighting, drug possession, joy-riding, petty theft, gun possession, or driving while intoxicated (offenses that are generally punished through only fines, probation, or short jail or prison terms). While they were in criminal justice proceedings, interviewees (many of whom had been LPRs) shared the same due process rights as did U.S citizens, but after they completed sentences and were placed in removal proceedings, their lack of U.S. citizenship suddenly became a defining factor in their legal futures. The majority of interviewees were deported between 1996 and 2008, precisely when immigration reforms in the United States were being implemented. Thus, they were caught up in the intensification of immigration enforcement that occurred following the 1996 reforms (Kanstroom 2007; Morawetz 2000).

The first section of this chapter analyzes the legal history through which some 1.5-generation Salvadorans were rendered deportable. This history echoes and elaborates on the legal violence and dismemberment described in chapter 1. The second section draws on interviews with deportees to recount the ways in which, as children, they felt undifferentiated from other U.S. youths even as, through criminalization and illegalization, they were eventually extricated and excluded. The third section examines the ways that detention and deportation stripped individuals of status, redefining their national identities and their legality. The fourth section examines deportees' experiences in El Salvador, where they had to forge new relationships and reconsider their own futures even as practices of spatial exclusion led them to perceive their time in El Salvador as an extension of their confinement in the United States. Their accounts of these experiences are themselves a form of re/membering as they shed light on the ways that, even in the midst of extreme deprivation, 1.5-generation youths attempted to shape their own and others' futures.

Producing Deportability

Understanding how the Ramirez brothers and other Salvadoran youths were made deportable requires reexamining in greater detail the legal violence described in chapter 1. As readers will recall, during the 1980s, Salvadorans who entered the United States (the country supporting the Salvadoran government in its war against guerrilla forces) were generally denied asylum; in the 1990s, they were granted temporary remedies—Temporary Protected Status (TPS), Deferred Enforced Departure (DED), and status as *American Baptist Churches v. Thornburgh* (ABC) class members with pending asylum applications— and eventually were able to apply for lawful permanent residency through NACARA. As well, in 2001, immigrants who had arrived more recently or who had failed to apply through these earlier programs were granted TPS due to two major earthquakes that struck El Salvador. Although these remedies resulted in status and even citizenship for a number of immigrants, the slowness of this process and the limitations of temporary statuses meant that Salvadorans who could have naturalized if they had been granted asylum when they first arrived were instead still LPRs, temporary residents, or even undocumented when the 1996 immigration reforms were implemented. As noncitizens, these immigrants were vulnerable to deportation, especially if convicted of crimes. Deportability was produced through this institutional process.

To understand the legal technicalities through which Salvadoran youths were made deportable, I attend to law's archaeology, that is, to the layering of documents, statutes, court cases, notices, and records through which law is constructed (see also Merry 2004).[5] Examining this layering helps to overcome the ways that "wider historical contexts . . . over time are repeatedly silenced through the institutionalized legal processes of denial and forgetfulness" (Darian-Smith 2007:61). Crafting a statute, writing an opinion, creating a file, and issuing a document entail *entextualization*, that is, excerpting elements of other texts, documents, or records to be redeployed in a new case or context (Bauman and Briggs 1990; Richland 2008). Textual redeployments invoke texts that have already been deemed authoritative, make use of agreed-upon language, ensure that a new policy applies to a previously delineated population, and occur as part of corrective law-making cycles (Halliday and Carruthers 2007; Riles 1998). Each instantiation of law therefore builds on prior instantiations, even as redeployment in a new context alters existing law, making it part of a new legal conversation, and creates a new administrative moment (Urciuoli 2008). Entextualization thus enables law to *refer*, to look forward and backward in time, to "preserved possibilities . . . which act on the future out of the past" (Nelson 2009:312). Law therefore exhibits what Judith Butler describes as citationality, the "double-movement . . . where 'to be constituted' means 'to be compelled to cite or repeat or mime'" (1993:220) as well as what Bruno Latour (1999) calls "backward causation," the retroactive creation of something that was always already there. As "memory carries with it traces of past temporal and spatial relations . . . through such things as material artifacts" (Micieli-Voutsinas 2014:50), law can itself be understood as a materialization of memory. The reproduction of preexisting legal elements allows law to *return* to and reconstitute a prior moment, but such reproduction also brings prior legal moments forward through time. The redeployment of legal artifacts therefore creates potential reinterpretations but reproduces a historical trace or shadow that makes it difficult to leave prior moments entirely behind (see also Corsín Jiménez and Willerslev 2007). Such "histories that cannot rest" potentially disrupt the present (Coddington 2011:748).

A trace or shadow that has continued to haunt Salvadoran immigrants' subsequent legal experiences was the denial of asylum during the 1980s (M. García 2006). The rationale for such denials was stated at a 1984 U.S. congressional hearing on the status of Salvadorans and Guatemalans, when Assistant Secretary of State Elliott Abrams depicted these migrants as indistinguishable from other undocumented immigrants: "El Salvador . . . is a country with a history of large-scale illegal immigration to the United States" (U.S. House of Representatives 1984:67). Immigration and Naturalization Service (INS) executive associate commissioner Doris Meissner agreed, attributing immigration from El Salvador to "the poverty and lack of overall economic opportunity that people in that country face" (91). Indeed, at the same hearing, INS commissioner Alan Nelson raised the specter that granting Central Americans safe haven would open the floodgates to the world's poor, asserting, "Basically everybody in the world would be better off in the United States" (110). Consistent with these attitudes, the U.S. State Department, which was required to weigh in on asylum applications, routinely advised INS district directors to deny Salvadoran and Guatemalan asylum cases. These recommendations were generally followed (Silk 1986). As a result, during the early 1980s, asylum applications filed by Salvadorans and Guatemalans were denied at rates of 97 and 99 percent, respectively (Silk 1986).

Throughout the 1980s, this broader political context played out at the level of individual asylum hearings, where Central Americans' accounts of persecution were transformed into something other than violence, or into violence that could not be linked to race, religion, nationality, social-group membership, or political opinion. Transformations were accomplished through a number of devices, including challenging witnesses' credibility, requiring nonexistent documentation (such as copies of death threats) that would be dangerous for migrants to possess, delinking the decision to emigrate from the experience of violence, treating individual experiences as instances of generalized suffering, defining violence as criminal rather than political in nature, and defining "indirect" threats, such as the assassination of neighbors or family members, as not rising to the level of persecution (Anker 1992).[6] For instance, at an asylum hearing that I attended in Tucson, Arizona, in the mid-1980s, a Salvadoran applicant testified that, as a soldier in El Salvador, his life had been threatened by a sergeant who had been involved in a relative's assassination and who accused him of being a guerrilla sympathizer. The applicant had deserted and attempted to hide but, upon being recognized, had fled to the United States. During the hearing, the attorney for the INS countered that Salvadoran authorities had a legitimate interest in apprehending deserters, that the applicant was at no more risk than the general population, and that the government had had the opportunity to persecute the applicant when he was in the armed forces, if it had desired to do so. This latter argument is something of a catch-22 for asylum seekers: if they escape, then it is difficult to prove that their lives were in danger, but if they are killed, danger is proven but then they are not in the United States applying for political asylum. At one hearing that I attended, an INS attorney asked an applicant who had been threatened by the guerrilla forces, "But they in fact didn't kill you?" as though merely being alive undermined her claim (see also Coutin 1993:99–102; 2001). In contrast to the treatment received by Salvadorans (who were fleeing a country governed by authorities whom the United States supported), a special program was created to enable Nicaraguans (who were fleeing the leftist Sandinista government, to which the United States was opposed) to remain in the country (M. García 2006).[7]

By the end of the 1980s, circumstances changed in ways that made it possible for Central Americans to remain in the United States, but the view of Salvadorans and Guatemalans as "economic immigrants" made the statuses that they were granted tenuous. The INS was under pressure to reform its asylum procedures; the infamous assassination of six Jesuit priests in El Salvador had drawn international attention to human rights abuses and made it more difficult for the United States to continue to provide military aid to the Salvadoran government, the war in El Salvador was at a stalemate, migrant remittances had become key to the Salvadoran economy, the Salvadoran government advocated allowing Salvadorans to remain in the United States, and the *American Baptist Churches v. Thornburgh* case, which charged that the United States was administering asylum law in a discriminatory fashion, was entering the discovery phase, which was likely to prove embarrassing to the U.S. government (Blum 1991). In this context, the ABC case was settled out of court and the U.S. Congress passed the Immigration Act of 1990, which created TPS and awarded Salvadorans eighteen months of this new status. TPS and ABC were linked in that applying for TPS defined an individual as an ABC class member (Guatemalans, who were not eligible for TPS, had to register as class members). Together, ABC and TPS created a potential remedy and applied this remedy on a mass scale, but this remedy was limited by the temporary nature of TPS and by the need for individual asylum adjudications. Moreover, although the 1991 ABC settlement was written in anticipation that adjudications would begin shortly after the agreement was reached, in fact, hearings on Central Americans' asylum claims did not begin until 1997.[8]

The 1996 immigration reforms threatened these tenuous statuses, but Salvadorans were able to obtain relief, though not without once again reproducing the disparities that had led them to be denied asylum in the 1980s. An unlikely alliance of immigrant rights advocates, U.S. and Central American officials, and Nicaraguans, Guatemalans, Salvadorans, and their supporters were able to secure passage of the NACARA.[9] This legislation incorporated earlier eligibility dates and thus allowed the population that had been carved out through ABC and TPS to remain in the country. Passing this legislation was an extraordinary accomplishment, coming only one year after the adoption of highly restrictive immigration measures. Yet, for advocates, this accomplishment was marred by the fact that the cold war ideology that seemingly had influenced asylum approval rates during the 1980s produced a disparity within the legislation. ABC class members, TPS recipients, and certain other Salvadorans and Guatemalans with pending asylum applications were to apply for a "special rule cancellation of removal"—basically a suspension of deportation. In contrast, NACARA allowed Nicaraguan Review Program (NRP) participants to adjust their status to that of LPRs. The Nicaraguans, who had fled the leftist Sandinista government, fared much better, because the remedy created for Salvadorans and Guatemalans, who had fled right-wing governments, was lengthier, more expensive, more cumbersome, and less certain. National-level political considerations were influencing individual-level access to refuge and residency.

Salvadorans and Guatemalans who obtained LPR status through NACARA were also subject to the increased securitization of immigration law that began in the mid-1990s with the passage of IIRIRA and AEDPA and continued into the 2000s (Miller 2005). Although noncitizens who were convicted of crimes had faced deportation prior to the 2000s, IIRIRA and AEDPA created a new class of deportable migrants who, prior to 1996, either would not have been subjected to deportation or would have been eligible to apply for relief. A number of factors are responsible for this intensification of enforcement efforts. During the 1990s, U.S. public concern over unauthorized migration intersected with the war on drugs and other criminal justice policies that subjected youths of color and low-income neighborhoods to policing (Simon 2007). Targeting "criminal aliens" was an easy way to simultaneously increase removal statistics and "fight crime," and, as a government report noted, removing noncitizens immediately after completion of prison sentences was more efficient than releasing them into the interior, where they would then have to be apprehended (U.S. General Accounting Office 1999). Improved apprehension and record-keeping techniques also gave larger numbers of illicit border crossers criminal and immigration records (Heyman 1999). The 9/11 attacks increased security concerns and derailed advocates' efforts to create a new guest worker or legalization program for unauthorized migrants. Detention center populations grew, the numbers of individuals removed from the United States increased, and migrants were increasingly prosecuted and sentenced to prison time for immigration violations, such as entry without inspection and reentry following deportation. In fact, a Bureau of Justice Statistics report attributes 14 percent of the growth in the federal prison population between 1985 and 2000 to increases in the incarceration of immigration offenders (Scalia and Litras 2002), and, by 2005, immigration offenses made up 25 percent of the caseload of federal prosecutions (U.S. Department of Justice, Bureau of Justice Statistics 2005).

The deportees whom I interviewed in El Salvador in 2008 had lived through this transformation. Significantly, these deportees' experiences of the Salvadoran civil war were much like those of ABC class members and NACARA beneficiaries, suggesting that their need for refuge was similar to those who eventually were able to qualify for residency under NACARA. For instance, Enrique Lemus, whom I interviewed in El Salvador after he was deported, recounted that, as a child, he and his friends used to climb trees to pick mangos in an area that was near a guerrilla hideout.

> We used to see helicopters from the army actually go down. One time we saw an execution when we were on top of the tree. . . . They put four guys out onto their knees. They had a bag [over their heads]. And they just executed them there. And afterwards, they left on the helicopter, and we got off the tree. We actually went and played with the bodies. . . . I would look at the blood spilled, and sometimes we would see guts spilled out. Something that a normal seven-year-old kid shouldn't be watching. But the environment that I was in, it was kind of becoming normal for me to see that.

Likewise, Edgar Ramirez, a deportee who later became a gang member in Los Angeles, recounted that as a child he had seen "buses on fire. Shots everywhere. Headless bodies. . . . And on the way to school, I saw two or three dead bodies thrown there. . . . Psychologically, I was traumatized" (see also Hume 2008). Witnessing an extrajudicial execution might place an individual at risk of persecution and could constitute grounds for an asylum claim, and being in an area where there were shootings, beheadings, dead bodies, and buses on fire clearly indicates that an individual is at risk of falling victim to violence him- or herself, even if the individual was not directly targeted.

Interviewees also were caught off-guard by changes in immigration enforcement. Earlier, during the 1980s and early 1990s, when the securitization of U.S. immigration law was just beginning, a simple entry without inspection or reentry was unlikely to lead to prosecution, detention was not mandatory for those who were apprehended on immigration violations, waivers for convicts facing deportation existed, and border enforcement was not as stringent (Miller 2002–2003). Noncitizens who were used to these earlier practices found it difficult to believe that, after 1996, criminal convictions would basically result in irreversible exile from the United States. For example, Roberto Orellana had immigrated to the United States in 1989 legally, at the age of seven, when his father obtained a family-based visa through Roberto's grandfather. Roberto saw himself as like everyone else: "I was feeling free, I was confident. I feel like an American because I had the same rights. I had no issues going places, like to TJ [Tijuana, in Mexico] or to a bank." Roberto planned to become a U.S. citizen. He joined a gang, however, and, after getting into a fight, was charged with assault and battery. He pled guilty to the charges in exchange for a reduced prison sentence of one month. After being released, he was caught riding in a stolen car, and, under pressure from his public defender, again pled guilty. Believing that he had already automatically become a citizen, because his father had naturalized when he was underage, Roberto did not anticipate that his conviction would affect his immigration status. Conversations with his fellow inmates convinced him otherwise. Roberto explained, "They told me that if I did more than a year, I qualified for deportation. I told them, 'No, man, I've got papers.' They said that it doesn't matter, that if you've got a criminal record, you've got felonies. . . . 'Okay, that's it . . . You're going back!' I couldn't believe I was going back."

This excavation of Central Americans' legal history has demonstrated that, rather than being intrinsically deportable, individuals are made removable by particular histories, policies, moments, and movements. In the case at hand, the illegality that tainted the status of Pablo, Francisco, and Jorge Ramirez and their families at earlier moments in their lives was reactivated at the moment of their deportation. Cold war definitions of "refugee" that rendered Salvadorans and Guatemalans "merely" economic immigrants resulted in liminal legal statuses such as TPS and DED and also influenced the disparity within NACARA, which in turn delayed adjudication of NACARA applications. The trace of the 1980s denial of asylum therefore remained, within liminal statuses and bureaucratic delays, to be reactivated by stripping away the LPR status of noncitizens convicted of crimes.

Integration and Extrication

The ambiguity of the liminal statuses afforded to Salvadorans meant that those who were still noncitizens in the 1990s and 2000s were integrated into U.S. communities but also always potentially removable. Like the interviewees described in chapter 2, deportees spent their childhoods in the United States in a gap between legality and illegality, but in their cases, this gap officially closed, leaving them formally "illegal," a status that they contested during interviews. Thus, the youth activists described in chapter 3 and the deportees who are the subjects of this chapter had similar childhood experiences of immigrating to the United States, growing up in marginalized neighborhoods, encountering recognition and misrecognition in school, and having to assume adult responsibilities at early ages. Indeed, my conversations with deported Salvadoran youths were replete with references to sites, knowledge, and experiences that placed them in the United States. As Herbert Osorio told me, "*I was there*. I could be American, I could be from North America" (emphasis added). By collectively citing markers of "having been there," youths who had formally been removed, who were forbidden to legally reenter the United States, and who were struggling to adapt to life in El Salvador articulated alternative measures of belonging. According to these alternative measures, belonging ought not to be invalidated by the unauthorized entry, undocumented status, or criminal convictions that had resulted in these individuals' deportation. The fact that, in their cases, belonging *had been* invalidated demonstrates that extrication is always a risk for noncitizens, one that, given the right (or wrong) set of circumstances, can become a reality.

When Herbert Osorio and other interviewees stressed that their years of presence in the United States ought to have conferred legal recognition, they were, perhaps unknowingly, invoking legal notions of territorial personhood. According to U.S. law, regardless of immigration status, territorially present persons gain limited legal rights (for example, to trial by jury if accused of a criminal offense, to due process in determining removability) not enjoyed by individuals who are outside of U.S. territory (Motomura 2006, 2014).[10] The relationship between territorial presence and legal recognition is also reinforced by the fact that particular immigration remedies or statuses require fulfilling specified periods of continuous presence or being physically present in the United States on or before specified dates. Examples of such remedies include cancellation of removal, the legalization program authorized by the 1986 Immigration Reform and Control Act, awards of TPS, Deferred Action for Childhood Arrivals (DACA), and naturalization. When interviewees who had been deported cited their prior lives in the United States as a basis for belonging there, they were making an argument that has some grounding in immigration law. Furthermore, 73 percent of the interviewees who had been deported actually had held some form of legal status in the United States prior to being deported (46 percent had been LPRs; 22 percent had work permits, which likely means that they had temporary authorization; and 5 percent said that they were asylees). So their invocations of territorial personhood also sought to reclaim these earlier statuses.

A key form of "evidence" of presence proffered during interviews was the naming of particular locations that were important in interviewees' childhoods and young adulthoods. For example, when Edgar Ramirez described his elementary school experience, he named each school that he had attended: "I was in fourth grade in elementary school. It was called Walgrove Elementary School. On Venice [Blvd.] . . . [Then] I went to Kittridge. Kittridge Elementary School. I started sixth grade. And then I finished that and went to junior high. Madison Jr. High." This recitation of schools, which evokes a résumé, locates Edgar's childhood not only in Southern California, but also in public institutions that teach children about the United States. Jorge and Pablo Ramirez, two of the three brothers I introduced earlier, had been carpenters before being deported for minor offenses. They stated proudly that they had performed custom finishing on a number of important buildings in Georgia, including the state capitol building, the Atlanta courthouse, an aquarium, and the Georgia Institute of Technology. These buildings presumably still bore the traces of their carpentry skill, even though Pablo and Jorge had been removed.[11]

In addition to citing places, interviewees also recalled their localized U.S. knowledge. Amilcar Mejía, Pablo Ramirez, and Jorge Ramirez laughed at their shared memory of the buses that they had ridden in kindergarten:

> AMILCAR: ESL [English as a second language] came in [to the schools] when I was in kindergarten. I used to go, like they said, I used to ride the bus for twenty minutes.
> JORGE: The little buses?
> AMILCAR: The little buses. [Pablo and Jorge laugh.] To go to ESL. The yellow ones with the tinted windows.

Likewise, David Mardoqueo, Enrique Lemos, and Carlos Alas shared memories of childhood games they had played in school, particularly those that involved teasing girls:

> DAVID: I liked messing around, especially with the girls. I remember we'd [he touches Enrique to demonstrate] "I got you!" And we'd run off! And play around. The girls used to get mad. But I enjoyed it.
> ENRIQUE: Do you remember "Bloody Mary in the Mirror"?
> [all laugh]

DAVID: "Bloody Mary in the Bathroom."
CARLOS: "Give me your lunch ticket." [They laugh.]

Interviewees also placed themselves in the United States by citing details of their arrivals there. Lorenzo Gómez recalled the date of his arrival: "So we finally got to the U.S. We were in San Diego. And in San Diego, a black Regal, a black car picked us up. And a lady drove us to Los Angeles. And that was on October 31, 1978. Halloween day." Victor Castillo actually brought his U.S. documents to the interview, to show me. Victor had been adopted by a U.S.-citizen father at the age of eight, an act that generated a new birth certificate but that did not prevent him from being deported almost forty years later: "I even have a birth certificate from California. This, look!" My notes from the interview read, "He handed it to me. Sure enough it was a birth certificate issued in California, with his adoptive father listed as the parent, and with El Salvador still listed as the birthplace." To Victor, this "rebirth," documented by the state of California, placed him legally in the United States. Likewise, Pablo Ramirez stressed to me, "We thought with the green card, we were citizens, basically."

The gap between "basically" being U.S. citizens, as Pablo put it, and being deportable baffled interviewees, who articulated deep connections to place. U.S. childhoods, cultural knowledge, memories, relatives, and language skills were all cited as indelible markers of belonging. Francisco Ramirez stated, "I actually grew up in New York. . . . I had grown up in the States, basically. I went through elementary school, high school, junior high, having my first daughter there, being married there. My entire life was basically there. . . . I had grown up there, my culture was there, I had adapted it to be my own, because I had grown up there," while Amilcar Mejía insisted, "We thought we were U.S. citizens. Our life is over there. Everything, our memories, our childhood is over there. We don't have no childhood over here. We don't know what it is to play with a top [as some children do in El Salvador]. With marbles. Why? In the States, we don't play with things like that. What memories do we have here?" Roberto Orellana explicitly rejected birth as a basis for nationality, stating, "I don't think being an American is where you were born. It's where you were raised and the memories you have and most of your life." Numerous deportees referred to the United States, rather than El Salvador, as "back home."

Deportees' descriptions of their childhoods in the United States stressed the normalcy of their daily lives. Interviewees characterized their U.S. school experiences, such as hanging out at the YMCA, playing basketball in the public parks, joining sports teams, earning trophies, being on the honor roll, dating, and making friends, as typical. Yet, even as they joined U.S. communities, interviewees were also set apart in key ways. Jorge and Pablo Ramirez marveled that their New York school, which, at the time of their arrival in the early 1990s, was predominantly African American, had created an ESL program for their benefit. Jorge recalled, "After a while the school put us in a program to teach us English. ESL. They didn't used to have ESL in that school; it was all Black people. They put us in ESL, and we were like, 'Dang!'" ESL classes treated Jorge, Pablo, and other youths as community members who deserved services, but also as "different," in that they could not speak English.

Like the interviewees described in chapter 2, deportees entered the workforce at early ages and even, in some cases, went to college. Their accounts of such experiences appear to claim a moral worth that, interviewees contended, had been inadequately recognized. Victor Castillo, for example, named the retail outlets where he worked, the crafts he mastered, and the county where he worked: "I've done everything. McDonalds, when I was sixteen. K-Mart, selling with a tie. Unloading trailers. Warehousing. Mechanic. Various things. But I went to a technical school for drafting. And carpentry. I liked it and was trained. When I worked in South Orange County." Likewise, Lorenzo Gómez reenacted his job as an AT&T operator for me during our interview: "One of the best jobs I had was an AT&T phone bilingual long-distance operator. . . . People would call the operator. I was an operator. 'Okay, where do you want to place your call?' 'The Florida Keys.' 'Okay ma'am, this is the area code, and who do you want to call?' Stuff like that. It was fun! I made friends. You talk to people." Citing jobs they had held at recognized U.S. businesses, the services they had provided to others, and the positive responses that they had received put forward indirect membership claims and challenged the rationale behind their deportation. Reynaldo Rivas, for instance, spoke of his educational achievements: "I'm a graduate. I went to junior college, DeVry. And then because of my intelligence and football experience, they sent me to Penn State." Language skills acquired at young ages were also a focus in some interviews. Lorenzo particularly stressed his English skills:

I have very good grammar, and I can speak English fluently. That helps me to get a better job here. Or work as an English teacher. Because I can write good too. I have very good spelling and grammar. And that is something that, as a child, when I was growing up in elementary, I started to notice . . . that I was in love with the English language at that point. You know? And I was so fascinated with it that I became a little bookworm. I would grab books, go through them, and read them. I was interested with the English language. . . . And then throughout junior high and high school, I couldn't live without the newspaper. I had to really learn words and how to spell them. My English class was my favorite class. I remember I had Mr. [name deleted], that was back in junior high. He was my English teacher. And I never missed that class. I'd miss math, homeroom, and a lot of other classes, but not that class.

Given the association between English skills and U.S. citizenship, Lorenzo's depiction of himself as a bookish child who was in love with English stakes a claim to belonging (Chavez 2003; Coutin 2003; Perea 1997; Sánchez 1997).

Unfortunately, other parts of the normalcy experienced by these migrant youths were crime, gang activity, racial tensions, and a police presence— something that the activists who were discussed in the last chapter also struggled against. As Alejandro Portes and Rubén G. Rumbaut (2006:255; see also Portes and Rumbaut 2001) note, "The central question is not whether the second generation will assimilate to American society, but to what segment of that society it will assimilate." Many interviewees described becoming part of schools and neighborhoods riven by ethnic rivalries, gang relationships, petty delinquency, and encounters with the police. Victor Castillo, for example, described how the lack of parks in his Southern California neighborhood forced youths to gather in other territories, creating hostility:

It was a barrio. . . . And you could only enter through Rose Hills. On the border of Whittier and Pico Rivera. . . . They jumped me in when I was thirteen, into the gang of that barrio. . . . And because the police, the Pico Rivera sheriffs, entered, and there were no parks. Our barrio was the only place that had no parks. So to go somewhere else to go to the park, we ran into problems [due to gang rivalries]. So we were concentrated there. And there were a lot of us. So that's where I lost myself, in drugs, the police bringing me to jail.

As they became inscribed in urban neighborhoods, and sometimes also in gangs, many youths who were eventually deported also acquired criminal records. Manuel Urquilla, for example, described his own petty offending as part of "hanging out" with friends and as "not uncommon":

I was getting involved in minor possession of alcohol, and driving without a license. I used to get caught doing a lot of stupid things, when I was sixteen, seventeen. It was the people I was hanging with. I got caught with a stolen car. Three times. But it was so funny because I was never the one who used to steal the car. I used to hang out with this Puerto Rican kid, and he would say, "Just watch! Just watch!" And he'd go take the car, and I would just stand on the corner. It was something to do, I guess. We didn't even sell the car. Just for rides.

Youths' localized knowledge of neighborhood dynamics included a familiarity with the youth authority, juvenile hall, and second-opportunity high schools: the result of limited opportunities in the inner city and of the criminalization of youths—particularly racialized minority and immigrant—cultures. Their inscription of particular schools, neighborhoods, and institutions therefore also became the basis for their eventual extrication through what Tanya Golash-Boza and Pierrette Hondagneu-Sotelo (2013:272) have referred to as "gendered racial removal," due to the assumption that immigrant men of color present criminal threats.

Thus, as they assumed adult responsibilities, youths found that the sense of relative normalcy they had enjoyed as children evaporated as the legal differences between themselves and their U.S.-citizen peers became only too clear (but see Dreby 2012 regarding the fear experienced by children who are undocumented or have undocumented relatives; see also Abrego 2011; R. Gonzalez 2011; Gonzales and Chavez 2012). Young people who had assumed that their futures were in the United States found that, as noncitizens, their abilities to forestall their removal to their countries of origin were limited. Instead of being "Americans in waiting" (Motomura 2006), they were redefined as aliens who lacked a legal basis for remaining in the United States.

Detention and Deportation

Detention and deportation have been conceptualized as practices that target noncitizens who are illegally present in the United States and who pose a public threat. For example, a March 2, 2011, memo in which U.S. Immigration and Customs Enforcement (ICE) director John Morton detailed ICE's enforcement priorities stated that enforcement targets are part of the "illegal alien population in the United States" (Morton 2011:1). Although this phrasing suggests that individuals are illegal *before* they are apprehended, interviewees described detention and deportation as a stripping away of the legal personhood that they acquired through living in the United States. This erasure left only the alienage created by their origins elsewhere, making them socially unreal, an "interminably spectral" presence in the communities in which they once lived (Butler 2003:22).[12] Detention and deportation can therefore be understood as something of a rite of passage that forcibly transforms the individuals who go through it. Spatial movement is key to this rite in that, just as deportees' legal personhood was acquired through territorial presence and civic participation, so too was their transformation into "illegal aliens" wrought spatially, through movement into the detention center, disruption of familial and community relationships, and, ultimately, removal to another national territory.

Immigration detention has become more prevalent due to intensified enforcement strategies. A rise in apprehension rates coupled with the elimination of bail for most detainees has meant that more noncitizens are spending more time in detention.[13] Detention is an administrative form of custody rather than a punishment, so while a U.S. citizen and an undocumented immigrant who are charged with crimes share the same due process rights throughout their involvement with the criminal justice system (M. Taylor 1994–1995), this formal equality appears to evaporate as soon as prisoners are transferred into immigration custody, where their lack of U.S. citizenship becomes particularly salient. This evaporation of formal equality is also a product of a shift between the mandate that states and local governments treat immigrants as "persons" under the U.S. Constitution and plenary power, which allows the federal government to treat migrants as "aliens" or "nonpersons" and therefore as subject to "rules that would be unacceptable if applied to citizens" (*Mathews v. Diaz* 1976:1891, quoted in Varsanyi 2008:879).[14] As "portals" where noncitizens are "removed" from the public at large and held before being transferred to other countries, detention centers are spatially ambiguous, located within and yet potentially leading outside of the nation at the same time.

As individuals enter this space, they are transformed from potential citizens into removable aliens. For example, Pablo Ramirez was at home, getting ready for work, when ICE agents arrived to detain him and his brother Jorge. Pablo recounted:

> We had papers. We had our green cards. And we thought with the green card, we were citizens, basically. I remember that when ICE came to pick us up at the house, they said, "Where's your green card?" And usually I used to carry it in my wallet. I took it out and said, "So what're you going to do now?" And he's like, "Well, you ain't an American citizen. So you're going back to your country no matter what." And right then and there, he just, boom! Flipped it over and broke it in half.

I heard similar stories from other interviewees: the destruction of a detainee's green card at the moment of apprehension appears to be something of a ritual. This act symbolically removes the legal protection that permitted migrants to remain in the country. Furthermore, once they are in immigration custody, migrants often discover that they can never again return to their homes and communities. One interviewee who had had this experience was Marcus Lopez, who was taken into immigration custody while on probation for statutory rape (having sex with an individual who is under the age of consent, a crime that, during our interview, he denied committing). One day, when he presented himself to his probation officer, "There were two guys sitting on the desk. They just told me, 'You got a warrant to get you deported. This is INS.' Locked me [up]. I lost everything. My car just got thrown in the streets. The house [was lost]." Although he had simply been performing a routine activity, Marcus found himself seemingly irrevocably pulled into another space, the detention center, where he was removed from the people, places, and relationships that made up his life, and where his only means of exit was deportation.

In detention, the territorial personhood that unauthorized immigrants had enjoyed previously is considerably eroded. Detainees are not charged with crimes, are not serving a specified sentence, have no predetermined release date, do not have public defenders, often lack the right to be released on bond, and frequently become convinced that it is useless to fight deportation because they cannot win. They are serving what one interviewee referred to as "dead time"—"time that you're not guilty of. You're just locked up." Their family, community, and employment relationships are disrupted, and they are subjected to frequent and unannounced transfers to other detention centers. Of course, detainees technically have not yet exited the United States. They may have a right to an immigration hearing, they can still receive visits from relatives, they have the privilege of hiring an attorney at their own expense, and there is always a chance that a few could prevail in court and win release. Detention center conditions nonetheless seem designed to convince migrants that they are on their way out.

Marcus Lopez described the many frustrations that he experienced after being detained during the visit to his probation officer. Marcus had immigrated to the United States at the age of twelve to live with his father. He completed high school and married his U.S.-citizen girlfriend, with whom he had a child, and he qualified for a work permit through a pending application for residency under the NACARA. Before he could become a resident, however, he was convicted of petty theft and for committing a sexual offense with a minor (a charge that he said was fabricated). He was attempting to turn his life around when he was taken into immigration custody.

> They wouldn't even let me see the judge. I requested it so many times. Even though when the detective, officer, from INS took me to the headquarters of INS in Baltimore, I told him, "I'm married to a U.S.-born citizen." He said, "We don't care. That's not the way we work." And we got there, finger-printed me. He said, "Would you like to see a judge?" I say, "Yes." He said, "If my supervisor approves it, you're able to see it." He did not. They denied it. I would send letters from the detention center requesting a judge or a trial or something to fight the case. They would never respond. They would just be a pain to us. . . . They would force you to sign your own deportation, saying that you are agreeing to get deported. . . . So that's what they'd say. "Okay, if you don't want to sign, just stay here. You're going to be here twelve years, if you want to. . . ." And the treatment when you get deported is like you're a dog. To them, it is like we are clowns. Almost like we are from another planet. That's how they treat you.

Practices such as frequent transfers, denying detainees a hearing before an immigration judge, lengthy procedural delays, and continual pressure to sign deportation papers appeared designed to convince detainees that it was hopeless to attempt to return to their previous lives. Like Marcus, many interviewees were told repeatedly by guards, immigration officials, and fellow detainees that fighting their cases would lead only to endless detention. Mandatory detention policies significantly undercut exercise of the appeal process. For example, Amilcar Mejía won his immigration case, only to have the judge's decision overturned on appeal. Because he did not want to remain in detention, Amilcar chose to sign deportation papers rather than continuing to appeal.

As their territorial personhood is eroded, detainees experience themselves as foreign (see also Yngvesson and Coutin 2006). Many interviewees were LPRs or at least work-permit holders prior to being detained. Their criminal convictions made them ineligible to retain their residency, thus stripping them of their U.S. legal personae and leaving only an alienage that was not even temporarily authorized. This stripping away was akin to banishment. According to Cesare Beccaria, banishment "nullifies all ties between society and the delinquent citizen. . . . The citizen dies and the man remains. With respect to the body politic, [civil death] should produce the same effect as natural death" (quoted in Walters 2002, 269). The "man" who remains after ties to society have been nullified is nothing but a body, an extralegal being, an alien, potentially subject "to the gaze of others, but also to touch, and to violence" (Butler 2003:15). Interviewees, who in many cases thought of themselves as quasi-citizens, discovered that, through detention, they became this alien. Francisco Ramirez, whose experiences were described above, used an analogy to explain how, through detention and deportation, a single facet of an individual's experience or being comes to dominate and thus erase all else. Picking up a mug that happened to be sitting on the table during our interview, Francisco commented, "See this cup? You don't see the white [background], but what stands out more is the black spot, that logo there. That's what they see. They don't see what's around it; they only see that one little dot, that one little stain."

The stripping away of a prior legal identity is a violent act, as demonstrated by Victor Castillo's experiences (see also Seattle School of Law 2008). Victor had entered the United States legally during the 1960s, at the age of four. Because he was adopted by a U.S. citizen when he was eight, he believed himself to be a U.S. citizen as well, so he never applied for naturalization. In his forties, after several drug-related convictions, he was placed in deportation proceedings, having lived for forty-one years in the United States. When immigration officials told him that they were going to take him to the Salvadoran consulate to verify his nationality (thus establishing his alienage), he refused to go. Victor described what happened next:

> They give you a little jumpsuit, elastic waistband, it fell to my ankles, I was shackled hands and feet, and they kept me in that condition, naked, for at least an hour. Then when a major finally came in, he didn't have no feelings for me: "You know what? You're gonna go or you're gonna go." And I'm like, "I promise you, I'm gonna go. But let me pull my pants up." "Okay." "Now, put your shoes on." "No, I'm not going." Boom! And they twisted me in a knot. It was an experience. Traumatizing. All I was trying to do was present my case.

Victor told me that he was beaten so badly that he had to be hospitalized with a broken back. But the beating worked. He no longer resisted deportation: "I wasn't about to refuse again and get my butt kicked again." As Victor's and other interviewees' experiences indicate, in the space of the detention center the part of them that was "normal" was ripped away such that the illegality—which in this case was also foreignness—was no longer confined to a segment of who they were but rather became the totality. As Victor explained, "I was American in my heart, my mind. And for them to just uproot me, and just throw me [away]. . . . I've been *banished* from my country . . . and they said forever!"

The securitization of immigration and the spatial implications of enforcement tactics contribute to the reformulation of citizenship and membership more broadly. There are clear connections between the territorial splintering that is entailed in confinement and what Mae Ngai (2004:5) refers to as the "impossibility" of the illegal alien as "a person who cannot be and a problem that cannot be solved" (see also Bosniak 2006). These migrants embody contradictory legal identities—unauthorized yet territorially present, prohibited yet retaining traces of a prior legal existence, foreign yet national. Deportation would seem to resolve ambiguity by sorting out the legally authorized and unauthorized. Nevertheless, within their countries of origin, deportees can once again experience themselves as foreign. This foreignness is not only a matter of acculturation to U.S. society but also of the imposition of a legal identity—"Salvadoranness"—defined in relation to what deportees are *not*—not U.S. citizens, not LPRs, not present within U.S. territory, not permitted to reenter the United States. This redefinition is made clear in the following exchange between two deportees who were interviewed in El Salvador:

> AMILCAR: Our mentality [living in the United States], our thought was, we thought, "Wait a minute, I'm a green card holder, that should automatically make me a citizen. My mom's a citizen, my dad's a citizen, my sister's a citizen. Everybody over there's a citizen!" So it's like why am I not a citizen?
>
> JORGE: Because you're Salvadorean, man.
>
> AMILCAR: Now, I'm Salvadorean.

In this excerpt, Amilcar says, "Now, I'm Salvadorean," suggesting that he *became* Salvadoran, in contrast to his earlier legal identity as a green card holder and quasi-U.S. citizen, *through* the process of detention and deportation. His Salvadoranness is not simply what is "left" when his U.S. legal identity (in his case, as an LPR) is removed; rather it is in some sense *newly reconstituted.* Even though Amilcar probably also considered himself Salvadoran at earlier points in his life, through deportation he became *legally* Salvadoran in a way that he had not been previously. Their legal identity as Salvadoran citizens resituates deportees within El Salvador even as the fact that this legal status, established definitively in the United States prior to their deportation, sets them apart. To deportees, such redefinitions define legal status as seemingly arbitrarily allocated, potentially alienable, and something that can be constituted or removed through security procedures. Such redefinitions are consolidated through removal even as some deportees attempt to challenge the conditions in which they are situated.

Exile

Interviewees who were forcibly returned to their country of origin through deportation experienced their new lives in El Salvador as akin to being exiled from the United States, the country where they were raised and where they had expected to continue living. For deportees who had spent a significant portion of their lives in the United States, therefore, *presence within* their country of origin was simultaneously *absence from* the United States. Furthermore, deportees' prior history—the normalcy that they established in the United States and that was erased through detention and deportation—continued to differentiate them from other Salvadorans, placing them apart and creating internal spatial boundaries. Such differentiation was potentially life-threatening, as interviewees were harassed by police, security guards, or gang members. The risk of harassment (or worse) hampered deportees' abilities to move within their own national territories and thus further extended the confinement that these migrants had already experienced in the United States. The deportees I interviewed nonetheless tried to remake their lives, whether through returning to the United States illicitly, assisting each other, attempting to adapt, or recreating something of their U.S. lives within Salvadoran territory. They thus continued to exhibit the wiliness that characterized the youth activists who were described in chapter 3, albeit in a very different context.

Deportees' sense of El Salvador as a place of exile or confinement was conveyed by their practice of describing their lives in El Salvador as a "sentence." For example, when asked to describe his future plans, Amilcar responded, "I guess I have no plans. . . . This [living in El Salvador] is just part of my sentence. I'm just going it day by day. Just a little bit more freedom. I guess I haven't settled in yet; it hasn't kicked in. That I'm destined to be here for the rest of my life. I guess it hasn't set in that this is a life sentence. I just don't want to accept it." The temporal suspension of the detention center—"dead" time, seemingly endless detention while fighting deportation—continued through such uncertainty, even as judges' specifications of the penalties that deportees would incur upon reentering without authorization appear to limit the time that deportees had to spend outside of the United States. For instance, Javier Ayala, who had lived in the United States from the ages of eight to twenty-five, commented, "I went before the judge, I signed the deportation, and the judge said, 'We're going to give you five years [during which time] you cannot enter the United States. If you do, we're going to give you up to twenty-five years, and a fine of $25,000.'" Interviewees were unclear what would occur at the end of the specified period—could they then reenter the United States legally, if they were eligible for a family visa petition? Or would the convictions that, in many cases, resulted in their deportations also make them ineligible for legal reentry? In essence, the exile that they were experiencing appeared to be indefinite, and, in fact, aggravated felons and those who reenter the country without authorization following deportation are subject to a permanent bar on lawful reentry (Chacón 2007).

Of course, deportees were not actually confined and therefore enjoyed much greater liberty than they had when they were in detention, a fact that many interviewees appreciated. Remarking on what appeared to him to be the greater permissiveness of Salvadoran law, Wilbur Quezada, a deportee who had been convicted on drug-related charges in the United States, commented, "Because one is in one's own country, one has more freedom to do what seems appropriate to one. . . . Here, one has more liberty." In El Salvador, deportees potentially could work, form families, and enjoy leisure activities.

Deportees nonetheless experienced severe restrictions on their movement and activities. Deportees complained of being discriminated against in public settings, and multiple interviewees told me of friends of theirs who had been murdered. Nicolás Serrano told me that he and other deportees were regarded as failures, that others thought, "You were deported because you were worthless in the United States. You are nothing here." The high degree of suspicion with which deportees were regarded was conveyed by a story that Manuel Urquilla told about being violently accosted by police when he was on his way home from work:

> One day I had some scissors in my back pocket, and I was coming from work, in Santa Ana, and they [the police] stopped me. "What do you want this for?" And they hit me with the rifles. "Stay like this! Stay still!" I was with my girl. "What's the matter? We're coming from work!" I was helping out at work. We were doing *sembrando la esperanza* [planting hope; presumably the name of a social program], we were giving some food for the poor, and I was helping them out, tying up the boxes, eggs, and all that. And I forgot the scissors and put them in my back pocket, and they wanted to take me for that. If my girl wasn't there . . . [his voice trailed off]

To cope with the risk of harassment by police, security guards, and gang members, those interviewees who had the economic means to do so avoided areas that were known to be gang territory, rented homes in middle-class (and therefore relatively secure) neighborhoods, and purchased cars so that they would not have to travel by bus. Some interviewees prominently displayed their work badges when they were out in public so that they would not be mistaken for gang members. Cesar Rojas, who had put his English skills to good use by getting a job at a call center, told me, "Every time I walk, I walk with my badge. 'I work, man!' I wear it on my days off." Francisco Ramirez and Marcus Lopez, neither of whom had ever belonged to gangs, described the continual harassment that they nonetheless encountered in El Salvador:

MARCUS: I just get pulled over. All the time. Just getting arrested. Because the way I look. The way I dressed. The way probably I talk. . . .

FRANCISCO: They call us gangbangers.

MARCUS: It's not usual to them here. . . . I used to get just disrespected from the police. Just pulled [over] from that. With not proper words. Just, "What the fuck are you doing here?"

FRANCISCO: We got beat up by the cops. Me and my two brothers [who were also deported]. They told us, "We don't want you deported guys here."

MARCUS: And even in the malls.

FRANCISCO: Harass you.

MARCUS: The [security] guards.

FRANCISCO: That's why I don't like going to the malls here. Because especially with my two other brothers, they think we're up to something. Even though we're just walking around being like a normal person. They just follow us and make us go through all this embarrassment, in front of everyone. "Pull up your shirt! Let me see if you have a gun!" Search us. And everyone starts looking at us like—

MARCUS: —like we're criminals.

Such differences constituted deportees as the inverse of what P. J. Spiro (2006:208) refers to as "external citizens," that is, "the growing populations of citizens who reside outside of their countries of citizenship." Instead, deportees are de facto aliens in their country of citizenship. Marcus explained, "You don't even have to say anything [for people to know you are from somewhere else]. The way you cut your hair, the way you walk, just anything, they will just *know* you're not from here." It is particularly striking that it is in a San Salvador mall, a space that Cecilia Rivas (2014:15) describes as one "where consumers can envision an escape from violent imaginaries," that Francisco and Marcus encounter violence and exclusion. Likewise, interviewees described boarding buses, only to have other passengers grab on to their purses and look away. Employers were reluctant to hire deportees, particularly those who had tattoos. Even friends and acquaintances seemed to regard interviewees as foreign. Victor recounted, "I'm like, 'These are my people! I was born here. But I'm a stranger here.' They don't—people don't look at me like I belong here. They look at me like I'm a stranger. 'This guy can't even speak Spanish. You know, he's saying he's Salvadoran. He ain't Salvadoran, he's gringo!' That's what they say, 'He's gringo.' 'He was born here but that don't mean he's *from* here.'"

Some deportees actually found themselves entirely without resources, living in the streets and hopeless regarding their future prospects. Victor, who, as noted above, had believed himself to be a U.S. citizen before being deported, was in this situation.

> And so I don't have a country over there, I come over here, I'm not even accepted, right? And it was like I was hating everything. I actually wanted to kill myself. I thought suicide. I was sharing that yesterday, my testimony at a bible study. It was to a point where I was in this apartment, fourth level, and I said, "I'm out of money. I just blew $350 in two days. I know my family ain't gonna send me more money. I'm going to sell my clothes, and as soon as my clothes is gone, I'm jumping!" . . . And I sold my clothes. And then I just felt the Lord talk to me and said, "Sit down. I'm going to get you out of here soon."

Victor's thoughts of suicide, though extreme, were not uncommon among interviewees. Deportees linked depression and thoughts of suicide to their sense of being trapped. This sense of being trapped is *anticipatory*, much as extraterritorial enforcement of U.S. immigration law is "*anticipatory in space;* . . . based on the future contravention or infringement of U.S. immigration law (i.e., undocumented entry), and . . . thus doubly *anticipatory in time*" (Coleman, 2007:620, emphasis in the original). Cesar Rojas, for example, described his fear of future confinement, saying, "If I go back [to the United States], I could have to do more time. But then again, do I want to go to prison in the United States? Or do I want to go to prison over here [in El Salvador]? Or do I want to get killed? At least in the United States, I'm not gonna get killed. I might go to jail, but over here, it's 50 percent that they're gonna shoot me." Faced with a choice between what one interviewee described as a "death sentence" in El Salvador and possible incarceration in the United States, some deportees despaired of improving their life circumstances.

In short, although interviewees were not formally confined, their lives in El Salvador were defined in relation to the (im)possibility of returning legally to the United States (see also Shachar 2007). Some interviewees had attempted to return, only to be deported again by Mexican or U.S. authorities. Interviewees found themselves weighing the possibility of being reunited with family members (including their U.S.-born children) and securing more lucrative jobs in the United States against the risks of traveling without authorization, the high fees charged by smugglers, the possibility of prison time for unlawful reentry, and, even if they successfully evaded detection, the pressure of having to live as a fugitive. Victor commented, "It's *feo* [ugly] to live under this fear. Trapped. You want to do what is right, but no, 'the things of the street,' 'hide yourself, they'll pick you up.' No, *hombre!*" Lorenzo, who had been an LPR before being deported due to drug convictions and who had already served a four-year prison sentence for unlawful reentry, explained his thinking about making another reentry attempt: "I'm scared. Because if I get busted crossing, I'm going back to the BOP [Federal Bureau of Prisons]. For reentry again. This time, I'm gonna get double time. Eight years. So I really don't know what to do. I'm so confused. I need time. I miss my family so much! I'm really hurt!!" One interviewee had seriously considered paying doctors to alter his fingerprints so that he could return to the United States with a new identity; however, he feared that his fingers would melt or that he would be left with no sensation. The severe deprivation that makes such extreme actions conceivable demonstrates the way in which deportation traps detainees.

Despite their dire circumstances, deportees, like the student activists described in chapter 3, found ways to resist deportation. In a sense, deportees' resistance is on a continuum with the forms of activism practiced by Dreamers, student organizers, and Central American scholars. Elana Zilberg (2011) has documented the sorts of "cultural production"—tattoo artistry, rap—in which some deportees have engaged. Among those I interviewed, resistance took more prosaic forms. Many deportees returned to the United States without authorization, despite increased border enforcement and federal prosecution of immigration violations, while others deliberately re-created aspects of their U.S. lives within El Salvador. While neither of these approaches changed the structural conditions or institutional processes responsible for deportation, each suggested that connections between personal histories and territorial belonging are powerful. Returning to the United States at great risk could potentially allow deportees to return to their former lives, albeit with the constant risk of being incarcerated or removed again. And, when deportees re-created aspects of their former lives while continuing to live in El Salvador, they suggested that deportation removes not only persons but also the landscapes to which they are attached.

An example of the ways in which some deportees tried to re-create their former lives following deportation is provided by Roberto Orellana:

> At the house, it's totally 100 percent English. My sister-in-law, she was raised in Kentucky too. Her husband, he was raised in L.A. So her family and me, when we get together, we speak nothing but English. The baby? We don't talk to him nothing but English. . . . And sometimes, I don't know if you remember, there's a lot of helicopters [in Los Angeles] at night. Tch-tch-tch-tch. [Roberto's imitation of the sound of helicopters.] So right here, sometimes when one passes by, I just close my eyes and I feel the breeze at night. I could picture I'm [there]. I miss the whole thing a lot.

Similarly, deportees who had secured jobs at call centers in El Salvador[15] proudly cited instances when their customers had recognized their Americanization, as in the following exchange:

> PABLO RAMIREZ: Sometimes people call me, and they say, "Thank God I'm speaking to someone in the States!" And, inside of me, I'm laughing out loud!
>
> AMILCAR MEJÍA: And I'm not in the States.
>
> JORGE RAMIREZ: They ask you, "Where're you located at?" And I say, "I'm in Central America. El Salvador." They're like, "What? I'm calling over there?"
>
> PABLO: They're like, "Am I being charged for calling over there?"

Likewise, Ed Casals and Frank Sandoval, who also worked for U.S. companies' call centers in El Salvador, recounted instances in which they surprised customers with their cultural knowledge:

> ED: The other day, this customer called me, right? I answered the phone. The dude was like, "Where are you located? Central America?" I'm like, "Naw, downtown San Salvador." "Where the F is that at?" I'm like, "Central America, El Salvador, sir." "Man, you guys don't know nothing about the States." I'm like, "Alright, let's hear it, right." I was like, "Do you know anything about my nation?" He goes, "No." I'm like, "I know pretty

much everything about your nation." He goes, like, "Tell me the Pledge of Allegiance." Boom! And it came right away, like, "Where the fuck have you been that you know it like that?" "It's where I've been all my life, in California, sir. I was there and now I'm in this different country. This is my nation and I'm proud to actually take your culture." You know and that's why he always asks for me.

SUSAN: So you really impressed him. Wow.

ED: You know, a lot of people actually call me and tell—and sometimes I tell them, "Where you located?" I never say, "Central America, El Salvador." I say "Downtown San Salvador." And they like, "What part of the States is that?" I'm like, "No, it's not in the States, dude. Central America, El Salvador, back into Guatemala and Honduras." And they go, "Man, your English is good!" And I'm like, "Thank you!" No, but sometimes it happens, and I told my wife that, sometimes. And they are like, "Dude, you sound like a gringo!" Damn! We actually, we still took our culture from the States.

By citing their cultural knowledge, their English-language skills, and others'—especially Americans'—recognition of their Americanization, these interviewees countered the rejection that they experienced through deportation. They also attested that rather than being aliens or foreigners, they *belonged* in the United States. By asserting such ties, speaking English, and "tak[ing] their culture from the States," these deportees defied removal, giving landscapes and territories a degree of portability and permeability that belied strategies of territorial confinement.

Conclusion

By conjoining "exile" and "home," two places that are normally considered antithetical, this chapter—and indeed, this book—has explored the complex realities that are created through U.S. immigration and deportation policies. In the case of 1.5-generation Salvadorans, deportation removes individuals who may have come to identify with the United States, forcing them to return to a country where, though technically they are citizens, they are treated by many as foreigners and even criminals. Much like Daniel Kanstroom's (2012) contention that deportation has produced an "American diaspora" by displacing what are essentially American noncitizens along with, in many cases, their U.S.-citizen spouses and children, the notion of being "exiled home" through deportation conveys the fundamental contradiction between the legal notion that deportees are being sent "home" and deportees' own experiences of deportation as exile from their U.S. homes. "Home" has been defined as entailing physical security, familiarity, community membership, and a social position that enables individuals to plan for the future (Löfving 2009:150), all of which, as we have seen, were denied to deportees. Deportation thus produces yet another dismemberment in that it breaks apart families and communities, while erasing the territorial and legal personhood deportees acquired in the United States and also ignoring the years that they lived there, the ties that they developed there, and the circumstances in which they originally immigrated. This dismemberment continues in El Salvador itself, where instead of being welcomed as members of Salvadoran society, interviewees all too often experienced social exclusion and repressive policing strategies. When they recounted their life histories; insisted that they "could be American"; returned to the United States; continued to walk, dress, speak, and act as they had before they were deported; and insisted on their social legitimacy in El Salvador, interviewees sought to counter dismemberment by re/membering, thus reconnecting their presents and pasts in ways that, they hoped, would allow them to envision a future. Some interviewees told me that, despite such efforts, they had no future plans, and this shows how difficult it is to overcome the trauma and social dislocation of being deported.

The deep ties to the United States that interviewees articulated suggest that, instead of being a rational approach to securing the country from unauthorized entrants, current high levels of deportation, which have set records under the Obama administration (Thompson and Cohen 2014), are an irrational excess of securitization. The war on terror, racial profiling, criminalization, and fiscal concerns about expenditures on social programs have led to immigration law enforcement practices that actually reduce immigrant integration, foster distrust, break apart families, and create an immigrant underclass that, due to having a record of prior deportation, can never legalize (Calavita 1996; Chavez 2008; Inda 2006; Hernández-López 2010; Peutz and de Genova 2010; Volpp 2013). Significantly, this excessive securitization is carried out through legal institutions. As we have seen, in the case of 1.5-generation Salvadorans, cold war fears of Communism led both to U.S. involvement in Central American wars and to the denial of asylum to Salvadoran and Guatemalan victims who sought safety in the United States. The trace of this denial continued to shape immigration law, such that the remedies created for Salvadoran and Guatemalan asylum seekers were temporary in nature, reproduced political disparities based on country of origin, and were implemented slowly. The deportability of the 1.5-generation Salvadorans whom I interviewed in 2008 was a product of this history in that, if they and their families had been granted asylum in the 1980s or early 1990s, they could have naturalized and thus secured their status in the United States.

Excessive enforcement, like other forms of legal violence that 1.5-generation Salvadorans have experienced, erases histories by treating individuals' criminal convictions and noncitizen statuses as the full definition of their personhood. Recall Francisco Ramirez's comment that U.S. immigration officials had seen only the "black spot" of his transgressions instead of the totality of his life. In contrast to political rhetoric implying that only certain people (the worst of the worst) are removed (Paige 2011), interviewees' accounts suggest that their childhoods in the United States were not that different from those of their counterparts who were not deported. While many of the deportees I interviewed had been convicted of crimes, they also shared numerous commonalities with interviewees who had not been deported. Members of both groups had grown up in U.S. neighborhoods, learned English, attended U.S. schools, adapted to local styles of dressing and comportment, held jobs, joined or started families, and, in some cases, started college. Yet, in the case of interviewees who were deported, securitization, criminalization, and detention transformed them into expendable foreigners whose unauthorized entry or subsequent transgressions had abrogated the right to remain in the country. The contention that deportation is not a form of punishment is hard to fathom when deportees' narratives of belonging are contemplated.

As it transforms persons, deportation simultaneously transforms territories, in this case, putting the United States and El Salvador into a relationship in which El Salvador is defined as "outside" the United States, even as both countries are also internally differentiated through the presence of socially excluded individuals. Deportation is thus an instance of what Kal Raustiala (2009:5) refers to as intraterritoriality, "when different areas within a sovereign state have distinct legal regimes," and extraterritoriality, which occurs "when domestic law extends beyond sovereign borders." This extension is accomplished by manipulating space—by relocating targeted noncitizens in the ambiguous space of the detention center and then by removing them "elsewhere." Deportees' perception that being in El Salvador is part of their sentence suggests that, for them, the confinement they experienced earlier continues still. There are therefore connections between the spatiality underlying deportation on the one hand and immigration enforcement practices more broadly on the other. Alison Mountz (2011) has documented how removal to remote islands, which are, for immigration purposes, treated as being outside of national territories, has become key to the international asylum regime. She writes that the "violent colonial histories" of islands have produced "residual material landscapes [or] sites where past usage haunts present occupants as they often serve as convenient built structures" (118). Such spatial and temporal distortions echo the ways that, far from efficiently sorting citizens from noncitizens, deportation leads to confusion, as individuals who thought that they were from the United States rediscover themselves as foreign.

This confusion raises questions about origins, temporality, and accountability. Can re/membering rather than ignoring originary violence lead to accountability and thus disrupt the cycle in which past violence continues to haunt future generations? If so, then how might membership itself be transformed, such that individuals could locate themselves within official histories, presence could confer status, and multiple affiliations might be acknowledged? By citing their prior histories in the United States and attempting to reconcile their present circumstances and past lives, the deportees interviewed for this book have gestured toward such a future.

More American?

JUNE 6, 2014. I arrived ten minutes before the second-grade musical at my son's elementary school began, and I successfully snagged one of the few remaining seats in the far back corner of the room. The auditorium was filled with parents, grandparents, and siblings, who strained to record the event on cellphones and iPads. Many had to stand in the back, given that the school now served a much larger population than it was originally designed to hold.

The curtain opened and something like two hundred second graders dressed in red and blue performed a patriotic tribute to America. The children sang "Yankee Doodle," "Erie Canal," "I've Been Working on the Railroad," and a few multicultural pieces such as "The Navaho Happy Song" and "La Raspa." Luckily my son was on one of the top rows of the risers onstage, so I was able to see him.

Listening, I was struck by one of the songs that the students sang with particular enthusiasm. "What's More American?" composed by Kadish Millet, repeatedly asks "What's more American than _____?," filling in the blank with iconic aspects of American culture, such as cornflakes and rock-n-roll, or with patriotic symbols, such as the fourth of July. Each time that the students sang this question, they then sang out the answer: "I am! I am! I am!"

As the song continued, I found myself thinking of Francisco, Pablo, Marcus, Victor, Lorenzo, and the many other deportees I met in El Salvador. Did they ever participate in these sorts of school musicals? What do "American" and "I am" mean when performed in schools in this fashion? And would any of the other children who sang so heartily onstage in front of me someday be removed?

OCTOBER 30, 2007. Sipping coffee, Sandra Mejillas and I sat at an outdoor table at a bookstore near a college campus where she was teaching. She had agreed to participate in an interview about her experiences immigrating to the United States. As our interview wound down, I asked her whether she had ever naturalized. She answered vehemently that she had never naturalized because of "a personal experience that . . . to me was just so traumatic at the time that I did *not* want to become a U.S. citizen" (her emphasis). She then told me the story of this experience:

> I was on a train from L.A. to San Diego, going to the zoo. Went there, you know, great visit. I was on my way back. With my husband, at the time. I was also pregnant. And I was feeling a little ill. So my husband went to try to find something for me to drink, and crackers or something. And I was sitting alone. You know. And I noticed a man walk by and stare at me. He did that a few times. And I was like, "Oh my gosh! What a pervert! I'm pregnant! What's he doing? Why is he staring at me that way?" So, and then he comes over, and he says, "I need for you—Do you have your documentation?" [Incredulously] "*Documentation?*" I respond to him in English. He asks in English and I respond in English. I'm like, "What are you talking about?" "You know what I'm talking about. I'm asking for your documentation." I'm like, "My documentation. You mean like my ID?" I'm like, "What type of ID

are you looking for?" I'm like, "Because I have many! I have different kinds! I have a school ID. Do you want to see my driver's license?" So we start going back and forth, arguing. And we're both, very, I don't know, there's just a lot of animosity between us. And I knew what he was asking for!

And so eventually I say, "Are you asking me to show you my green card? Is *that* what you want?" "Well, you know what I'm asking you for! Show it to me! If you don't show it to me, I could arrest you. Do you want me to arrest you?" I immediately replied, "Arrest me! Arrest me!" He ended up being an INS [Immigration and Naturalization Service] agent. . . . They were, I guess, scanning the aisles for potential, you know, illegal immigrants. And then he says that if I don't show him my green card, he could arrest me and deport me. And I start telling him, "Why are you harassing me? I was just sitting here. Why are you — ?" And I knew that he was, you know, *picking* on me. At the time, I didn't know to use the term *profiling* me or something. But, I just said, "Why are you picking on me? Why are you harassing me?" I'm like, "This train is *full* of immigrants." And it was! Because, I — that was something that I had already paid attention to, all the languages that were being spoken on the train, you know. German, Japanese, it was, obviously, everyone had gone on a weekend trip to San Diego. And he was picking on *me*. I was *very* mad!

And my husband shows up. And my husband's wearing a big USC sweat-shirt. And they both suddenly start talking to each other as if I'm not there. And, "Sorry officer," type of attitude. "She's pregnant," just. . . . So that pretty much took care of it. And the agent left.

But what happened was that I started crying. And I cried for *a while*. And not only that, I just felt like, oh my gosh! I went to school here, K through 12. I put my right hand over my heart! And there was no reason why this man would even pick on me! He was going by the color of my skin! By my big belly because he was afraid it was just another immigrant woman having a child in the U.S.! And wow. It was so hurtful to me that I thought to myself, "I will never belong to this country. Obviously, that man just showed me that. So why even try?"

In this narrative, Sandra describes how a routine train trip was transformed as she was pulled into someone else's narrative about her life. To the official who questioned her, she was seemingly a potential undocumented immigrant, perhaps Mexican or Central American, who, instead of simply returning home from an outing to the San Diego Zoo, might have been illicitly entering the

United States in order to give birth to a U.S.-citizen child. The official's alternative narrative, which was implied by his increasingly angry demand for Sandra's documentation, exemplifies a broader U.S. narrative about the "Latino threat" posed by (allegedly) illegal aliens who were encroaching on and even taking over the United States, including by coming to the United States to give birth (Chavez 2008). The racializing and sexualizing nature of this experience, which Sandra says she later recognized as profiling, was deeply humiliating,[1] one that she resisted by deliberately refusing to enter into his narrative, asking, "What are you talking about?" and insisting that she had many kinds of ID. Language, a marker of belonging and exclusion, and racialization were key to Sandra's experience. She notes that both she and the agent spoke English and that other passengers who spoke German and Japanese were also likely immigrants but were not targeted. The request for documentation singled Sandra out from the rest of the passengers, and she was further "removed" through the conversation in which her husband apologized to the officer for her behavior, as if she wasn't there. Like the individuals described in chapters 2 and 4, Sandra cites the civic rituals of attending school and saying the Pledge of Allegiance as evidence of who she was. For Sandra, the official request for documentation was a traumatic betrayal from a country to which she had sworn loyalty as a child. This betrayal demanded accountability, which came in the form of her decision (at the time of our interview) not to become a citizen of a country in which she was always already suspect.

Like Sandra, many other 1.5-generation and second-generation Salvadorans whom I interviewed had complex relationships with the nations they were part of, relations that defined them as incomplete or partial legal subjects. Although they had similar biographies—in most cases, birth in El Salvador, emigration during the civil war, and growing up in the United States—legally they had a variety of statuses, including U.S. citizen, lawful permanent resident (LPR), Temporary Protected Status (TPS), political asylee, and, in some cases, no status at all. Many argued that their biographies made them quasi-U.S. citizens even if they still had to contend with the legal realities of being noncitizens. To convey the limitations and ambivalence of their statuses, some compared their relationship to the United States to that between a child and a foster or adoptive parent—that is, an approximation of but something not equivalent to a "natural" relationship (see Yngvesson 2010). Those who were deported to El Salvador found that their relationships to El Salvador were also, in some sense, an approximation, as law enforcement officials there continually questioned their right to be present (Coutin 2013). And interviewees who were drawn to El Salvador by a desire to visit their relatives, reencounter their pasts, and learn about Salvadoran history discovered that they were sometimes treated as "gringos" by those around them.

In this chapter, I focus on the cluster of temporalities, geographies, and legal forms created through interviewees' claims for membership in, recognition by, and the right to return to both the United States and El Salvador. First, regarding temporality, when migrant youths seek to reconcile their own transnational biographies with national histories and legal forms, they re/member the past, that is, they revisit the past in light of the presents that they inhabit and the futures that they seek to realize. According to linear notions of time, in which the past has already happened (Greenhouse 1996), such reworkings could appear fraudulent. Yet, for interviewees, deepening and revising their understandings of the past can overcome silences, broaden the scope of relevance through which their biographies may previously have been interpreted, and counter other stories that, by either vilifying or glorifying immigrants, erase personhood (Garrod, Kilkenny, and Gómez 2007; Madera et al. 2008; see also Greenhouse 2008). Re/membering the past thus potentially connects individual biographies and national narratives in ways that challenge exclusionary policies.

Second, regarding geographies, just as spatial tactics of exclusion are key to the enforcement practices discussed in chapter 4, so too do the relationships that interviewees seek to forge with the United States and El Salvador take unique spatial forms. As discussed in earlier chapters, immigrant and deported youths experience disjunctures between their countries of origin and residence: as occupants of excluded spaces they are often misrecognized and they can be an absent presence in the territories they have left behind, even as they connect these territories through their relationships and their returns. By initiating claims from the "nonspaces" that they occupy, youths seek to re/member geographies, that is, they seek to be recognized as members within countries from which they have been excluded and to return to places where they used to live. Efforts to re/member stitch together spaces that have been forced apart, and, in that sense, resonate with notions of liminality, borderlands, and hyphenation that have been key to the literature on race and migration (Anzaldúa 1987; H. Bhabha 1994; Pérez Firmat 1994). As Behar (1996:82) writes, "Memory—which is a form of knowing—always takes place elsewhere, . . . it is always 'other.'" Liminal spaces (such as the space of the undocumented) are both beyond or outside of the law but also constituted by law (Motomura 2014) in that national territories are divided by borders but also linked through the enforcement practices and migrant movements that transcend these borders

(Zilberg 2011). Therefore, the "elsewhere" or "beyond" (beyond law, beyond borders) from which youths stake claims is a space that is already, in a sense, there. Attending to these spaces deepens understandings of transnationalism as a phenomenon that is both within and beyond the nation-state form.[2]

Third, regarding law, re/membering pasts and geographies forces encounters with the fraught nature of temporal and spatial origins (Benjamin 1978; Derrida 1992) and thus exposes both law's power and its pretensions. If origins can be resignified from the future, then they cannot fully originate; likewise, if locations that individuals occupy are simultaneously elsewhere, then legal efforts to demarcate boundaries appear unfounded. Therefore, when it references or ignores origins in an effort to place or exclude people, law is a powerful, even violent, force but also one that appears to abandon some of the principles that grant it legitimacy. For example, as we shall see, numerous deportees remarked on their shock at having been told by judges that they were being "sent back," regardless of their ties to the United States or the dangers that they might encounter in El Salvador. Decisions to send them "back" appear to ignore considerations of equity and proportionality that are central to law's legitimacy (Kanstroom 2012). Furthermore, many deportees contested the understandings of origin and membership implicit in the idea that deporting them to El Salvador was sending them "back." A law that re/members would take multiple equities and origins, including lives in the United States, into account (see Bosniak 2006; R. Smith 2014).

To further explicate the temporalities, geographies, and legal forms associated with re/membering, this chapter revisits three types of accounts in which interviewees' claims about their relationships to the United States and El Salvador were highlighted: first, U.S.-based interviewees' understandings of and encounters with U.S. immigration law; second, deportees' accounts of how state security concerns came to be superimposed on their own biographies; and third, U.S.-based interviewees' accounts of their return trips to El Salvador. Throughout, I attend to ways that, by seeking to re/member, interviewees simultaneously sought more inclusive relationships with the nations they had called home.

Unrecognized Child Subjects

U.S.-based interviewees' accounts of their relationships to the United States reveal what it is like to be an unrecognized child subject, in other words, a legal subject who claims a quasi-"natural" relationship to a state that does not recognize him or her. Unrecognized relationships are ambiguous: they do and do not exist. As a result, claims for recognition reference both an incomplete past and a future that is not (yet) realized. As Judith Butler (2003:31) notes, "To ask for recognition . . . is to solicit a becoming, to instigate a transformation, to petition the future." Interviewees' requests for recognition convey the ambiguity of their relationships to the United States: their legal relationships can only mimic "real" relationships established by birth (see Yngvesson 2010), and their "real" relationships are not always legally recognized. This distinction between "real" and "as if" relationships is also experienced by colonial subjects. For instance, Homi Bhabha writes that colonizers and their subjects were "almost the same, *but not quite* . . . [which] becomes transformed into an uncertainty which fixes the colonial subject as a 'partial' presence" (1994:86, emphasis in original). As "partially present" subjects, legally unrecognized migrant children experienced seemingly arbitrary outcomes and procedural irregularities. While many felt that their biographies placed them in the United States as quasi-, naturalized, or U.S.-born citizens, their families' origins elsewhere also rendered them suspect to others, regardless of their legal status.

To convey the sense of being treated as illegitimate offspring of the United States, some interviewees resorted to the analogy of being an illegitimate, foster, or adopted child who sought acknowledgment from its parent. For example, Beatriz Gonzalez, an activist who helped to organize the California Dream Network and who herself had been undocumented, characterized the United States as like "a mother who *raises* you, who nurses you, that to some extent chose to raise you." Undocumented youths, she said, are asking this mother, "Recognize me! How could you not recognize me as your own? If everything I did was *right*, the way that you said that I should do it?" Similarly, William Martínez, a TPS recipient, said that he was like a foster child of the United States; Deris Posada, who had been deported, told me that his dream had been "for the United States to adopt me as a son"; and Araceli Muñoz, also a TPS recipient, explained, "I feel like I have a country; it just feels like the country doesn't really acknowledge me." Juana Rocio, who was in removal proceedings fighting an asylum claim, pointed out to me that without any memory of El Salvador, "It's as if I was born here!"—a view echoed wistfully by Marisol Sanabria, who was undocumented and who commented, "I wish I was just born here."[3]

Strikingly, these interviewees' characterizations of their relationship to the United States invoke notions of *legitimation* that are key to the legality of a parent-child relationship.[4] Historically, in both the United States and many

Latin American countries, children could only inherit goods (including their surnames) from their fathers if their parents were legally married or if their fathers formally acknowledged them. Legitimation of children is still part of U.S. immigration law. To this day, children born out of wedlock outside the United States can only acquire U.S. citizenship through U.S.-citizen fathers if they are legitimated through law in their country of origin, acknowledged by their fathers in writing under oath, or have their paternity determined by a court. In contrast, children born out of wedlock to U.S.-citizen mothers need only be living in the United States in their mother's legal and physical custody to qualify.[5] As deployed by interviewees, however, calls for legitimation are a form of critique in that they fault the United States for failing to fulfill its "parental" obligations to its "children."

On what basis can interviewees depict themselves as "children" of the United States, legitimate or otherwise? The answers to this question are twofold. First, some interviews attribute their presence in the United States to unjust policies that the United States adopted toward El Salvador. Marta Dominguez, who at the time of our interview was a naturalized U.S. citizen, commented:

> If there had never been a war or if the U.S. would have never, like, penetrated, you know, El Salvador [and] created a war, many families would not have left and my mom and my dad would have been able to find a job there. I feel like . . . they robbed me of, of me being able to grow up with my parents. They forced me to this migration experience and all this discrimination that I have to face. . . . This is also the place that maybe robbed me of my other life.

Likewise, Adelmo Ariel Umanzor, a student activist, described coming to the United States as entering "the jaws of the beast. You know I was caught like not directly and so violently like in El Salvador, but I got caught in the system. I became part of the system, you know. My taxes are paying the wars that we're [the U.S. is] leading in El Salvador." Bayardo Morazan, who was in the process of naturalizing at the time of our interview, also explicitly attributed his presence to the United States: "I'm a result of those policies. The reason I'm here is a result of those policies, you know. The war was well funded." If the United States *produced* emigration by supporting the Salvadoran government and funding the war then, interviewees suggested, it needed to take responsibility for the immigrants it produced.

Second, the idea that the United States is like an adoptive or foster parent implies that migrant children's relationship to the country mimicked the country's relationship to its "natural" citizens. The notion that those who are "like" U.S.-born citizens have a claim to belonging relies on what some have called "social citizenship" (Bosniak 2006; Hammar 1990) or "contingent citizenship" (Boehm 2011, 2012), that is, de facto membership in the community, with the added element of having lived in the country at a formative age. Indeed, numerous interviewees said that they thought of themselves as U.S. citizens, even if they had not yet naturalized. Walter Olivar, who was an LPR, told me that when people asked him where he was from, he explained, "I'm a U.S. citizen from El Salvador," while Manuel Cañas, who held TPS, reflected slowly, "I think I'm more [pause] a U.S. citizen than a Salvadoran one."

Such comments, from noncitizens, suggest that Salvadoran child migrants came to see citizenship as more than a legal status, as encompassing affiliation, identity, connections, and memory. Indeed, it was interviewees whose legal status was the most tenuous who tended to emphasize their connections to the United States. Juana Rocio, for example, who had a pending asylum application, characterized legal status as something "plastic," "a card," that other people took for granted but that she, due to not being born in the United States, could not. Many resorted to biographical rather than categorical accounts of identity to convey who they were, through such phrases as "I was born in El Salvador, but I was raised here," to quote William Martinez. As we have seen, others used terms like "technically" and "basically" to convey the relative weight that should be given to law and biography in determining their nationality. Araceli Muñoz, for example, said that she tells people, "I was born there. I'm from there, technically, but I live here. I was raised here." Likewise, Tomás Marino-Vega told me, "I consider myself basically a U.S. citizen, though not legally, right?"

As chapter 4 demonstrated, however, being "basically, a U.S. citizen" has limitations in that noncitizens can be deported. David Zavala, a TPS holder, drew attention to these limitations, commenting that he could not yet see himself as a U.S. citizen: "It's like I'm not fully here. It's like . . . if the TPS would stop or something and I get stopped in a car I would be there [deported to El Salvador]. Or if something went wrong or something, I'd end up over there." Marisol Sanabria, who was undocumented and who said that she felt that she was from California, was not able to characterize herself as a quasi-citizen, saying only, "I think I do consider myself something here, you know." Despite having a biography that, she felt, placed her in Los Angeles, Marisol could not name the status that she had achieved.

As noted above, even though they had similar biographies, interviewees held different legal statuses. Some were born in the United States and therefore were U.S. citizens. Others, who emigrated at quite young ages and who were in other respects similar to those born in the United States, had to traverse a complex immigration process in order to obtain citizenship. At the time of their interviews with me, some had successfully done so; others had become LPRs through a variety of mechanisms, most commonly through parents who participated in the 1986 legalization program, filed a family visa petition for them, obtained employment-based legal status, or qualified for residency through the Nicaraguan Adjustment and Central American Relief Act (NACARA); others had TPS or a pending asylum application; still others were undocumented; and some had been deported to El Salvador.

In addition to these varied outcomes, most interviewees had had multiple statuses during their lives, and they often aspired to change their statuses in the future. In this sense, their paths toward legalization were fragmented and multidirectional, much as are the journeys of unauthorized migrants (Collyer 2010). Some had obtained work permits (and temporary permission to remain in the country) through a parent's case, only to lose it again if the parent was unsuccessful. Those who held TPS or were LPRs had often been undocumented when they were younger. Individuals who naturalized or who had residency might have been undocumented or had only temporary status earlier. And many of the lawful permanent residents I interviewed were planning to eventually naturalize, while those who were undocumented or who held TPS were seeking ways to gain residency. Moreover, this variation characterized not only my interview sample, but also some interviewees' own families. William Campos was a U.S. citizen, his mother and one brother were LPRs, another brother was a U.S. citizen, a sister was still awaiting a visa, and one brother was undocumented.

The reasons for these varying outcomes and histories among similarly situated people shed light on the vagaries of U.S. immigration law. For example, Rodolfo Martinez and William Martinez could have become LPRs or even naturalized but had only TPS at the time of our interview. These two brothers immigrated to the United States in the late 1980s. In 1991, their mother applied for TPS, but she left them out of her application, hoping to protect them from deportation in the event that TPS was not extended beyond the original eighteen-month period of validity. As a result, while their mother was eventually able to apply for residency under NACARA, Rodolfo and William remained undocumented until 2001, when a second opportunity to apply for TPS came about due to the Salvadoran earthquakes. At the time of our interview, their only hope for residency was through a family visa petition that their mother had filed for them. In the meantime, they could not marry because they had to be single in order to maintain eligibility for the family visa petition.

In contrast, Juana Rocio immigrated only a few years after William and Rodolfo, in 1991, at the age of three, but instead of holding TPS while waiting for a family visa petition to come through, she was in removal proceedings, fighting deportation. Juana's family had immigrated to the United States after her family suffered persecution in El Salvador. Juana told me that her family had applied for political asylum and NACARA and that she had obtained a work permit at a very young age. However, when her family was called for an interview on their NACARA case, they were told that they didn't qualify, because they had not applied for asylum prior to the cut-off date for the program. Their asylum claim was referred to immigration court, where they continued to fight it, which drained the family's resources. Juana said that the judge appeared to be sympathetic to their case and had granted multiple extensions. When I met her for a re-interview a year and a half later, her case was still pending but she hoped to be able to retroactively obtain TPS or to qualify for status through the DREAM Act, in the event that it passed.

Juan José Olvera Saldivar had yet a different experience. He immigrated to the United States at the age of six in 1993, two years after Juana. His father, a union member, had been threatened and had immigrated to the United States earlier. Juan José and his sister flew to the United States by plane, using other children's passports. Juan José was not sure how he and his family obtained status, but he told me that he had had a work permit through TPS or NACARA and then became a resident in 2004. Seemingly, his father's earlier entry date, timely TPS or asylum application, and inclusion of Juan José on the application enabled Juan José to qualify for residency, whereas Juana, William, and Rodolfo, who had immigrated earlier, did not. Children's entry dates, dependence on parents, and family circumstances influenced their abilities to obtain legal status more than did substantive factors, such as the violence that they had experienced in El Salvador or their acculturation to the United States.

Interviewees' experiences of the legalization process also shed light on what it was like to be an unrecognized or not fully recognized child subject of the United States. Due to a shortage of qualified, low-cost immigration attorneys, many depended on unscrupulous or inept service providers. David Zavala recalled that his mother had applied for a work permit through an organization that he chose not to name and that submitted an asylum application on her behalf. He said that the government sent his mother a letter asking for more documentation. When she brought this letter to the organization, she was told, "Oh, don't send anything, they just want money." Then, David related, "The latest letter came. [It said,] 'You know what, everything is denied. We asked you for more stuff and you didn't send any.'" Similarly, Manuel Cañas's mother had immigrated in the early 1980s, obtained status through the 1986 legalization program, and attempted to apply for Manuel as well. However, as he explained, "The lady who was handling our case took off with all of the paperwork and she took off with the money." The cost of immigration procedures also led to missed opportunities, when individuals did not have the funds to pay the costs of application fees.

Even when interviewees qualified for particular statuses, they had to contend with procedural issues. These procedural challenges have an extralegal character that likely reflects tensions—between service and suspicion, discretion and accountability—within the administrative apparatus of U.S. immigration law. A common problem for TPS recipients was any gap in documentation occasioned by delays in receiving their renewed work permits. TPS is authorized for a particular period of time, usually eighteen months, so TPS holders' work permits reflect this expiration date. TPS holders cannot apply to renew their work permits until there is an announcement that TPS status for their country is extended for another eighteen-month period. The timing of these announcements and renewals sometimes leads to periods when TPS holders lack evidence of work authorization, through no fault of their own. To address this problem, U.S. immigration authorities often announce that the expired work permits are officially extended for three months past their stated expiration dates; however, employers do not always accept this notice, which can be downloaded and printed out from the U.S. Citizenship and Immigration Services website, as proof of work eligibility. As William Martinez related, "I remember one of my employers, he read it, but he wasn't that confident. He thought that I was lying or that there was something behind it. It was kind of weird."

In addition to losing job opportunities due to such delays, noncitizens are adversely affected when immigration officials make errors in their cases. Julian Becerra told me that he once received a "totally false" letter of deportation, which he was able to correct, while Monica Ramirez's mother's TPS application was inexplicably denied. When Monica investigated, she discovered that "they had sent out a letter saying that she needed to have more proofs. But we never received that letter. And then I took the initiative and I called them and they didn't have any record of when the letter was sent out. So then we went to the lawyer, we filed a petition, and then they just sent it to her. And we went through this whole program and then they approved it." Though her mother prevailed, she and Monica had to go to considerable effort and presumably expense to correct what seems to have been a mistake made by U.S. immigration officials, a process that contradicts norms of legal accountability.

Even as immigration procedures subjected noncitizens to unqualified service providers, delays, occasional errors, and political scrutiny, so too did the partial statuses that noncitizens obtained have particular shortcomings. Of course, the most challenging status was that of being undocumented. Most significantly, perhaps, was the stigmatization that undocumented youths experienced (Abrego 2011). Bayardo Morazan described this in eloquent terms: "You just felt this sense of the dread that you—kind of like it's an underlying sense that you always have, you know, that someone is going to find you out. You know, it's something that I think that permeates—you may not be thinking about it consciously, I think, but it's just there constantly when you, you know, when you are undocumented." This stigma extended to some interviewees who held TPS or were LPRs. Jessica Morales, who had become a U.S. citizen, recalled, "I think growing up when I was a resident . . . to me it was something shameful. And I remember when I was in junior high I think somebody was talking about being a citizen and they said, 'Oh, but you were born here, right? You're a citizen?' And I lied and I said, 'Yes,' because I was ashamed that I wasn't." William Martinez, who had TPS, told me, "I feel uncomfortable showing my TPS, my work permit. I would like just to go there and just, you know, be like one of those citizens that when you go there you say, 'You know what? I can give my Social and that will do it.'" The very documents—a green card, a work permit—that provided status were simultaneously markers of not being citizens.

TPS recipients faced a unique set of constraints due to the liminal status that they held (Hallet 2014). TPS recipients were protected from removal and granted work authorization as long as their status did not expire, but they were unable to reenter the country if they left without permission and had no pathway to residency or citizenship. When asked about the shortcomings of this status, interviewees mentioned a number of practical issues: curtailed job opportunities, inability to serve in the armed forces, limited access to financial aid, the inability to travel internationally, and limitations on political expression due to the need to avoid being arrested during a protest. Uncertainty about the future loomed large in the minds of numerous interviewees who held TPS.

When asked if she worried about TPS being extended, Monica Ramirez commented, "I *am* worried about it [heightened tone]. Because of school mainly. And, because that would take away a lot of the things that, my job, and my driver's license, you know, things that I need to survive." Manuel Cañas felt that, with rising anti-immigrant sentiment, he had to be on the lookout for opportunities to change his status. He commented, "Because the way that I see it now is that Temporary Protected Status is not always going to be there."

The continued vulnerability associated with temporary statuses is conveyed by the experiences of Araceli Muñoz and Tomás Marino Vegas, both of whom had TPS and were interviewed before and after the 2008 recession. When I first met Araceli in January 2008, she was attending community college with a goal of completing a nursing program and then transferring to a four-year institution in order to get her bachelor's degree. Her future looked quite bright. When we next met, in July 2010, her fortunes had changed, due to the economy, her legal status, and her mother's health. Her mother, a housecleaner, had been injured. Araceli and her mother lacked health insurance, so they had to cover the bills for physical therapy, but her mother could not work much, so Araceli took a job at a fast food restaurant to earn the money for the medical expenses. Araceli had finished her two-year degree at her community college but needed to retake one course, which, due to budget cutbacks, was over-inscribed, so she had been unable to reenroll, despite multiple attempts. While waiting, she had begun to think that it would be too hard for her to go back to school anyway. If she qualified for student loans and financial aid, then she might have been able to do so, but at the time of our interview, she could not afford to go to school full-time in any case. Sounding frustrated, Araceli wondered if she would ever be able to achieve her educational goals.

Tomás Marino Vegas's experiences were similar. When I first met him in April 2008, he was working part-time, while attending a local California State campus where he was majoring in business administration. When I met him again, two years later, he had experienced major setbacks and had had to withdraw from school. With the economic downturn, the company that he worked for failed. He found a new job quickly, but, unfortunately, his work permit was about to expire and there was no word about whether or not TPS would be extended. He therefore had to present his company with a work permit that was only valid for approximately another month, and then as soon as word of the extension came out, he had to go to great lengths to get proof that would satisfy his employer. Unfortunately, given his temporary unemployment and the cost of renewing his work permit, he was not able to cover his tuition and had to withdraw from school. Additionally, his new job was not as flexible. He was contemplating turning to a for-profit university that would enable him to take classes online. Tomás told me, "I've put my life, like, on hold" until being able to gain residency. He was pinning his hopes on the fact that he had lived in the United States for many years, worked, paid taxes, gone to school, and never committed crimes. But, in the meantime, as a TPS recipient who continued to have to renew his work permit, he was vulnerable to the vicissitudes of the economy.

Despite such shortcomings, interviewees who had obtained temporary status were generally appreciative of the opportunities that these statuses provided. William Martinez described TPS as "a blessing from heaven" in that it had enabled his parents to qualify for better jobs. Bayardo Morazan got temporary residency through a late amnesty case; he said, "I felt like I had been like underground and I finally came out for light. That I was able to, you know—you know, just be real, I guess, you know, so. So definitely I think it was a big relief; definitely hope. . . . It was just this sense of just feeling normal." Numerous TPS recipients stressed that they felt a sense of comfort and safety knowing that they had status, albeit a temporary one.

Regardless of their immigration status, interviewees' relationships to the United States were shaped by the ways that others perceived them, as shown by Sandra Mejillas's experience being questioned by an immigration official on the train home from San Diego. Like Sandra, many noted the ways that, despite being LPRs or U.S. citizens, they were defined as "different" due to their race, gender, and/or class. Marta Dominguez, who had naturalized for the sake of a relative for whom she was petitioning, commented, "For me to say I'm just American [it]'d be a lie because society doesn't see me as just American. They see me as, first, as a woman, and as a woman of color, and as a Salvadoran woman." Other interviewees who had been born in the United States remarked that they nonetheless shared certain immigrant experiences, such as being placed in English as a second language classes due to coming from monolingual Spanish homes. And still others focused on class differences that were associated with race. Marisol Sanabria was shocked when she moved into a dorm on her college campus, only to discover that there were no Latino students. As she struggled to afford tuition without access to financial aid or work authorization, her roommate seemingly took for granted having grown up in a big house with a pool. Interviewees also noted the popular and media stereotypes of Salvadorans that they had to contend with: images of sexualized women, maids, gang members, criminals, and, after 9/11, terrorists. Julian Becerra felt that immigration policies blamed all Latinos for the bad actions of a few, while Monica Ramirez and Araceli Muñoz were particularly troubled by others' perceptions that they could have legalized, if only they had tried—that they were somehow at fault for not being residents or citizens.

Clearly, as unrecognized child subjects of the United States, Salvadoran youths faced challenges. The biggest challenge, perhaps, was vulnerability to removal as, in some instances, national security discourses were superimposed on their biographies.

Reinserted Subjects

In the case of 1.5-generation immigrants who were deported, the lack of acknowledgment experienced by unrecognized child migrants became an explicit disavowal from the "parent" nation. As a *legal* process, then, being reinserted in El Salvador as Salvadoran citizens was also coupled with being (re)inserted into the status of undocumented aliens in the United States. The term *reinsertion* (or *reinserción*) has been used by immigration scholars, social scientists, and policy makers to refer to efforts to reintegrate migrants into their countries of origin, following a lengthy period of absence (e.g., Diatta and Mbow 1999; Dustmann, Bentolila, and Faini 1996; Entzinger 1985; Hammond 1999). I use the term *reinsertion* here in a somewhat different fashion, to denote the ways that removal both reinserted migrants within an alien status vis-à-vis the United States and also placed them physically within Salvadoran territory. Chapter 4 provided an overview of this process, focusing on the history that left them vulnerable to deportation, the ties they forged to U.S. communities, the process through which they were deported, and the alienation that they experienced in El Salvador.[6] I now return to this process with a particular focus on the connections between being an unrecognized child subject in the United States and becoming a reinserted subject of El Salvador. To examine these connections, I focus here on (a) the legal snares through which interviewees were "reinserted" within the status of unauthorized alien in the United States, and (b) the meanings of being a "reinserted subject" in El Salvador, as demonstrated by deportees' sources of support, accounts of their arrival, and understandings of their citizenship status. Together, this material suggests that, legally, reinserted subjects and unrecognized subjects had much in common: both experienced the law's failure to live up to its promise of justice. In both countries, this failure was brought about by superimposing national narratives about security risks on the biographies that individual deportees argued ought to determine their belonging.

In the case at hand, reinsertion began when, despite having grown up in the United States, 1.5-generation noncitizens found themselves entangled in legal snares that irrevocably redefined them as a criminal threat. The notion that immigrants are a security risk has led to what some scholars have termed *crimmigration*, that is, "the criminalization of immigration law" (Stumpf 2006:373).[7] Such criminalization was brought about by the 1996 immigration reforms and other measures that expanded the definition of "aggravated felony" for the purposes of immigration law, eliminated waivers that had permitted noncitizens with criminal convictions to ask judges to allow them to remain in the United States, deployed police in immigration enforcement efforts (Decker, Lewis, Provine, and Varsanyi 2009), and created Secure Communities programs that gave Immigration and Customs Enforcement (ICE) officials access to individuals in U.S. prisons and jails (Gill 2013).[8] These measures focused enforcement attention on criminal issues to the exclusion of other aspects of individuals' biographies, coordinated record-keeping systems such that individuals' immigration status and prior convictions were apparent to a range of enforcement officials, and treated both statuses and offenses as categorical matters in which there is little room for discretion. For noncitizens convicted of what immigration law defines as an aggravated felony or of two or more crimes of moral turpitude, detention is mandatory and relief from removal is unavailable, with the exception of extreme circumstances in which an individual is more likely than not to face torture in his or her country of origin (see Zilberg 2011 for a discussion of one such case). One of the few ways to avoid removal is to seek to reopen and overturn or reduce the sentence for a criminal conviction—a challenging process that few are able to successfully pursue (Kanstroom 2012; Moore 2007–2008).

Numerous interviewees who had been deported described being caught up in these legal developments. For example, Norberto Manzano, who immigrated to the United States in 1988 and was deported ten years later, had been convicted of possessing a firearm and of multiple DUIs. After fifteen days in jail, he paid a fine and was released. He was supposed to continue making payments on his fine but did not do so. In what he characterized as a "trick," he received a paper telling him to present himself to Immigration for an interview. He went to the interview, thinking that it would result in "some solution for my well-being." Instead, he was handcuffed, detained, and, six months later, deported.

Herbert Osorio immigrated later, in 1997. He applied for political asylum but was ordered deported in absentia after he missed his last court hearing. In 2004, he was stopped by police due to having a broken gas tank, and when the police "put [him] in the computer," they discovered two outstanding traffic tickets that had been issued in another state. He was sentenced to twenty-four hours of community service for the tickets and was released, but two days later, he said, immigration officials picked him up in order to execute the old deportation order. Francisco Ramirez was deported because "all these little things had followed me." Francisco had been found with marijuana in his car, for which he was given probation and his license was suspended. Then, while driving without a license, he was pulled over again, and he pretended to be his brother, who in fact had a license. Francisco was later charged with the crime of giving false information. He also had an arrest for disorderly conduct on his record for an occasion when he and his brothers had been drinking and were noisy. Although his drug charges were misdemeanors, Francisco explained, "After your first one, they consider that an aggravated felony. So they got me for aggravated felony." Of course, some interviewees were convicted of more serious offenses, including homicide. Nonetheless, deportation is a harsh consequence for traffic tickets, DUIs, disorderly conduct, and minor drug charges, given that citizens convicted of such offenses commonly face fines, probation, or short jail or prison terms. In these interviewees' cases, their history of convictions or of a missed immigration hearing extinguished any status that they may have had in the United States and led seemingly irrevocably to removal.

Interviewees were reinserted in the status of undocumented aliens not only through their criminal and immigration records but also through a series of procedural challenges that seemed to them to violate principles on which U.S. law is based. Many lacked resources to hire immigration attorneys, so, without any right to state-appointed counsel in immigration proceedings (Kaufman 2008), they were unable to fight their cases. Those who did obtain attorneys or who sought to represent themselves sometimes found that procedural compliance was prioritized over substantive justice. For example, Lorenzo Gómez told me that, according to his own legal research while in detention, the fact that he was detained in 1996, before the immigration reforms were passed, made him eligible to apply for a 212(c) waiver of deportation. However, he discovered that, unbeknownst to him, he had been ordered deported in absentia due to failing to attend an immigration hearing that he had received no notice of. He tried to file a habeas corpus petition but was told by the Ninth Circuit that his petition was untimely, as more than a year had passed since the deportation order had been issued. Lorenzo complained that the issue of timeliness had trumped his eligibility for this form of relief: "I was eligible for it, and I'm still eligible for it, but I'm untimely now."

Deportees, much like unauthorized child migrants, were also hampered by faulty advice and insufficient legal knowledge. Francisco Ramirez was told that he should sign deportation papers in order to get his residency back more quickly, whereas Frank Sandoval's attorney told him that, after being deported, "possibly you'll still be a resident." In fact, individuals' abilities to fight their cases are better if they remain in the United States (see Kanstroom 2012) and those who are deported will lose any residency that they obtained. Many interviewees insisted that they had accepted plea bargains without understanding the immigration consequences of pleading guilty. Being held in detention, where some complained of being subjected to physical and verbal abuse while being told by guards that they had no hope of obtaining relief, further eroded their willingness to fight against deportation. Perhaps most appalling to deportees were some judges' comments that appeared callous and unconcerned with equity or justice. For instance, Cesar Rojas reported with some horror that his judge had said, "I don't care if they are going to kill you when you get off the plane, you are still going back," while Jorge Rodríguez said that he was told that if he appealed, "Washington's gonna tell you, 'You know what? You gotta go. If you're gonna get killed, get tortured, or get, you know, whatever's gonna happen to you, that's your business.'" Such comments appear to counter legal principles that prohibit deporting individuals to places where they would face persecution.

Interviewees who had been deported complained that U.S. immigration authorities had failed to fully evaluate their character and U.S. histories before ordering them removed. Marcus Lopez commented, "It's really sad because they do not have the time to look into your history and to say, 'Okay, you are a real criminal and you should go back.'" Likewise, Carlos Alas felt that deportation ignored his life in the United States: "I tried to tell them, 'Look, I've been here all my life, I've studied here. I want to continue studying, go to college.' We all have our ups and downs and we make mistakes and we try to correct them. But they weren't willing to give me that opportunity." Some argued that it was illegal for the United States to deport them. Four interviewees (roughly 10 percent of the deportee interview sample) told me that they believed they had become U.S. citizens through their parents when they were children, and they therefore believed they had been deported erroneously.[9] As described in chapter 4, many of the deportees whom I interviewed argued that growing up in the United States meant that they were from there, regardless of their formal, legal status. Strikingly, deportees often used the same nomenclature as their non-deported peers. Both Edgar Ramirez and Francisco Ramirez (no relation) told me, "I'm Salvadoran, but I was raised in Los Angeles." Some interviewees had been close to naturalizing at earlier points in their lives. David Mardoqueo had actually completed a naturalization form and set aside the money for the application fee, but he never mailed in the application. Numerous interviewees cited their willingness to enlist in the U.S. armed forces, join the National Guard, or serve in the Gulf War as evidence of their commitment to the United States. One interviewee had actually been in the U.S. military and stationed in El Salvador prior to being deported. Deportation, interviewees argued, ignored these histories, commitments, and relationships.

Interviewees found the uprooting associated with reinsertion to be emotionally, financially, and physically devastating. As Butler (2003:12) describes, those who "are dispossessed from a place, or a community," also find their senses of selves destroyed along with the very terms of their relationship to the place or community. Interviewees felt like they were trash, something to be thrown out or discarded, "disposable," to use the term that Melissa Wright (2006) employs to describe low-skilled global workers (see also de Genova 2002). Interviewees' terms are equally evocative: "I came emotionally broken" (Norberto Manzano); "I felt alone, abandoned, destroyed" (Edgar Ramirez); "I was just thrown over here" (Frank Sandoval); they "discard you" (Mervyn Velasquez and Ed Casals); "from there, hell started" (Jorge Rodríguez); and "I felt like my life was shattered" (Diego Aguilar). These strong terms convey the despair individuals felt on learning that they would be deported, the feeling that their lives were completely upended, and the destructive impact of deportation. Frank described how, on the day that he expected to be released from prison, he learned that he was instead being transferred to immigration detention:

So the day of my release [from prison] where everybody exits to go home, I remember there is a line of guys, you know, ready to go home. And they are calling, you know, here and there. And they are going out a gate. And I'm looking around and I see a few people and there's only like maybe three of us. And I start, you know, determining, well, he looks like he's from Honduras, he looks like he's from Guatemala, he looks like he's Salvadorian. You know, and all of a sudden, the big crowd decreased and we just started talking. You know, the new guys that I met. So, all of a sudden, they come to inform us that I am being picked up by INS. That was a total shock to me. I was, I really, I mean, I, I, I held, you know, tears because my parent was expecting to see me that day.

Frank's account conveys the shock of his almost unbelievable realization that he was caught in an immigration proceeding and would continue to be confined.

Legally, "reinserting" 1.5-generation migrants through removal reconstitutes them not only as alien subjects of the United States but also as suspect citizens of El Salvador. Focusing on what happens to those who are forcibly returned is relatively new within work on immigrant integration, which has tended to focus on the ways that migrants establish ties in their countries of new residence, rather than on what happens if they return or are returned to their countries of origin (Dingeman-Cerda 2014). Two assumptions are behind this focus: first, that, with the exception of cyclical migration, the direction of migration is generally from the country of origin to the country of migration, rather than the reverse; second, that migrants have already adapted to their countries of origin, but how well they will adapt to their countries of new settlement is an open question (Kearney 1995; Massey, Durand, and Malone 2002; Portes and Rumbaut 2006). With the rise of deportation studies (e.g., de Genova 2002; Dreby 2012, 2013; Ellerman 2009; Peutz and de Genova 2010), both of these assumptions have come into question. The massive upsurge in deportation that has accompanied the securitization of immigration policies in numerous nations means that a massive, albeit forced, movement from "receiving" countries to countries of origin is under way, and within these return flows are many migrants who have acculturated to their countries of settlement. While, ultimately, some deportees may become reintegrated into their countries of origin (Dingeman-Cerda 2014), this outcome is impacted by the legally violent process of removal that they undergo.

In El Salvador, concern over the need to support reinsertion grew in the late 1990s as, following the 1996 immigration reforms, numbers of deportees and the frequency of deportations escalated rapidly, and the challenges associated with receiving these citizens, especially in the cases of those who had lived outside the country for much of their lives, also grew (Funes 2008). I recall encountering this term in El Salvador in the early 2000s, during meetings with U.S. and Salvadoran officials as well as with nongovernmental organization (NGO) members who worked with a Salvadoran government program, "Bienvenidos a Casa" or "Welcome Home," designed to provide orientation, transportation assistance, temporary housing, medical attention, and, in some cases, job training to deportees recently arriving from the United States (see Coutin 2007). As a U.S. official told me during a 2001 interview at the U.S. embassy in San Salvador,

> It's essential to reintegrate returnees, regardless of the reason that they are returning. It is in the interests of the receiving country too. Otherwise, they will just turn around and go back again, and they will face enormous risks on the way. There are lots of dangers in traveling to the United States illegally. This is a very important issue, particularly for returnees who left El Salvador at a young age and their rootedness in El Salvador is attenuated. (Coutin 2007:36)

When they reentered El Salvador, deportees acquired a new relationship with a government that, at the time of my research, appeared to view them with a high degree of suspicion. In 2008, when I interviewed Salvadoran deportees, the conservative Alianza Republicana Nacionalista (Republican Nationalist Alliance, ARENA) party held the Salvadoran presidency, and the Saca administration had implemented a series of security measures known as "super mano dura," or "very heavy hand." Based on the conclusion that gangs were a national security threat, these measures criminalized gang involvement, defined tattoos and throwing signs as evidence of gang membership, deployed the National Guard along with the police in the fight against gangs, and relied on repressive tactics such as apprehension and incarceration, more than on social programs, to eliminate gangs (Funes 2008; Moodie 2011; Zilberg 2011). Many of these laws were declared unconstitutional by the Salvadoran courts, on the grounds that they violated civil liberties and punished people for who they were rather than what they did (Coutin 2007). Deportees from the United States were nonetheless received by El Salvador as potential criminals and gang members. Human rights group members told me that when deportees arrived at the airport, police photographed them, inspected their bodies and made records of any tattoos, questioned them about their criminal histories, and took down their names, addresses, and personal information. Some interviewees felt threatened by such procedures. Jorge Rodriguez told me, "Once you get to El Salvador [at the] airport they give you a list. There's a picture. You have [a] picture and you got to tell them who you are, what is your address, where you live, what's your phone number where you live. From there they used to give facts to people who want to execute you." Numerous interviewees reported being physically inspected by security guards, harassed by police, and repeatedly incarcerated for seventy-two hours—the period of time that someone can be held without being formally charged—on pretexts. A Salvadoran human rights attorney whom I interviewed told me that the police felt free to question anyone about potential gang membership, on the grounds that gang members could be disguised as non–gang members.

In this securitized context, institutional support for deportees' reintegration was limited. Organizations that made up the Mesa Permanente de la Procuraduría para la Defensa de los Derechos Humanos para las Personas Migrantes (Permanent Board of the Ombudsman for the Defense of the Human Rights for Migrant Persons) had produced a document entitled the "Plataforma Mínima de los Derechos de las Personas Migrantes" (Minimum platform of the rights of migrant persons), which included sections on deportation to El Salvador and about reception and reinsertion of migrants who return or are returned. Members of the Mesa Permanente, many of whom had previously been involved in Bienvenidos a Casa before control of the program was transferred to other entities, conducted monitoring at the airport in order to ensure that deportees' human rights were being respected. Monitors were not allowed to observe the Bienvenidos a Casa program itself; rather, they had to stand outside, in the sun, and question deportees as they left the airport. The organization Homies Unidos, a transnational gang violence prevention program, also supported deportees, helping them to obtain jobs and identity documents. However, Homies Unidos staff told me that they had been accused of being part of organized criminal rings and that they had not been permitted to become formally recognized as a nonprofit within El Salvador. The director of another NGO that worked with youths (including some deportees) who were in or at risk of joining gangs told me that such work was dangerous because security forces viewed anyone who associated with gangs as a gang sympathizer. Lastly, some religious organizations provided food, shelter, support groups, tattoo removal, and drug and alcohol rehabilitation for deportees, as they did for other individuals in need.

Further evidence of what it meant to be a reinserted subject is provided by deportees' "arrival stories," that is, their accounts of their first moments in El Salvador following removal. Significantly, in these first moments, many deportees relied largely on informal sources of support, namely, their own families and friends, for transportation, housing, financial support, and advice. When Francisco Ramirez arrived, he was terrified that he would be kidnapped or killed as soon as he left the airport. Instead of being killed, he was met by relatives who took him to their house. Deris Posada had an even more positive experience. He told the story of his joyous reencounter with his mother. With tears in his eyes, he said, "She saw me like, she even cried, she said, 'The best thing that could have happened in my life is for you to have come!' She cried! She said, 'Te amo, te quiero!' [I love you.] She had never said that to me. And when you hear that, you feel like there is a reason for you to live." Jorge Ramirez was at a complete loss when he arrived. He told me, "I didn't know nothing about here, you know? It was just like I was in the jungle, you know? Like, 'Wow, man. Where am I? What am I gonna do?'" Fortunately, his U.S. relatives had made arrangements for his arrival. Jorge explained, "So like my mom told me, 'Once you get to the airport the address you give at the airport, they're gonna take you to the house. You know, you're gonna go home and you're just there. You'll meet your family and just, you know, you call me when you get there.' So that's why—that's why—I had money so to get a taxi to get all the way from the airport to here." Reynaldo Rivas, a former member of the U.S. military, was unique among interviewees in that after spending "five nights running the streets, getting wet," he turned to a Salvadoran police sergeant who gave him money and took him to a shelter.

The support that deportees received, however, paled in contrast to the challenges they faced due to others' suspicions that they were members of criminal gangs and to their sorrow at being separated from lives and loved ones in the United States. Moreover, not all were well received by relatives in El Salvador, either due to relatives' lack of resources or the fear that deportees were gang members. Further, the limited nature of institutional support available to them indicates that deportees were incomplete legal subjects in El Salvador, just as they had been previously in the United States, but that the nature of this incomplete relationship was inverted. In the United States, they felt like quasi-U.S. citizens but lacked full legal recognition, whereas, in El Salvador, they had legal citizenship but found social recognition difficult to attain.

In addition to demonstrating the informal nature of deportees' social support, arrival stories indicate how out of place deportees felt in El Salvador—a feeling that, as we shall see, was in some ways echoed by U.S.-based interviewees who traveled to the country for short visits. Carlos Alas, a deportee, recounted his first experience eating *pupusas*, a thick tortilla filled with cheese, beans, or meat and topped with a pickled cabbage, carrot, and onion slaw:

I stepped off the plane and everything. I saw my aunts, and my mom was here. And my brother was here. They were all like, "What do you want to eat? It's up to you?" "Whatever, man. What do y'all want to eat?" They all wanted to satisfy me, because I had just arrived. My mom said, "What do you want to eat? Whatever you want to eat, we'll eat today!" So I'm like, "Let's eat some *pupusas*." I hadn't ate *pupusas* in years!

So we went to the restaurant, we were right there in Santa Tecla, and they bring out the *pupusas* and everything. And I seen my cousin and my aunt, they grabbing them with their hands, right? And my brother's next to me. And I'm like, "Say, brother, where're the utensils at? The forks and knives." And he's like, "Naw, fool! You eat that shit with your hands! You eat *pupusas* with your hands!" And I'm like, "Yeah, that's right." I'm tripping. "Every time we ate *pupusas*—" I'm thinking, say, in the past, now, "Oh yeah, we did eat them with our hands. It would have been stupid of me to eat them with a fork. It's just the culture, already." So I started eating them with my hands, but I kind of felt awkward, because I was so used to eating with a fork and stuff.

This story is emblematic of the complex relationship that deportees had with El Salvador. When Carlos arrived, he responded to his family's generous attempt to make him feel better by proposing to eat *pupusas*, something of a national dish. But when he ate them, he could not remember how. When his brother explained, Carlos found himself "tripping" at the sudden memory of his own past experience eating *pupusas* with his hands. But when he did so, he felt awkward at what had now become an unfamiliar approach to food. Clearly, return is an embodied experience, one that entails "remaking" the self (see Berg 2015).

Enrique Lemus told a similar story of his own arrival:

My uncle was here—he came, because there was no one here to pick me up from the airport. . . . As we were on the way, he was like, "What do you want to do?" I was like [sad tone of voice], "All I want to do is just go find a bed, and relax." . . . [Kindly tone of voice.] "Oh, yeah! There's a bed waiting for you!" And I'm thinking of my bed! You know, a big, queen-sized bed, with big pillows. I get to my grandmother's house, and she had one of those, uh, what are they called? . . . A little *colchoneta* [mat]. And my grandpa goes, "I bought this 'specially for you, so you'd be comfortable!" And I'm over here, "Dang! Are you serious?" And I'm like, "For real?" I was like, "What about a pillow?" "Oh, we'll buy one for you!" I was like, "Man!" And all I had was two pairs of shorts, three pants, four shirts. And my shoes. And next thing you know, "Oh, oh oh! You can't wear those shoes!" And I'm like, "What?" I had some Nike Cortezes, fool! And I'm like, "Man! I haven't even been here for an hour, and I can't wear shoes?" Because they were gang-related shoes. At least to the people here.

As in Carlos's story, Enrique describes the familiar yet alienating encounter with what would be his new life. He was among relatives who were attempting to help him feel at home, yet far from making him comfortable, the mattress they purchased for him was nothing like the luxurious bed he had had in the United States. Furthermore, he had to give up his shoes, a popular brand of Nikes and perhaps a connection to his earlier life, because in El Salvador, they would make people think he was a gang member.

Perhaps not surprisingly, then, when asked whether or not they considered themselves Salvadoran citizens, deportees' answers were mixed. Some insisted that, because they had thought of themselves as citizens of the United States, they did not consider themselves to be citizens of El Salvador. Such individuals also tended to have negative impressions of El Salvador, remarking on their shock at seeing children trying to earn pennies washing car windows, for example. Others saw their Salvadoran citizenship as externally determined. Norberto Manzano told me, "I'm Salvadoran, according to my documents. I have them here." Showing me a Salvadoran ID, Norberto explained that he carried it with him at all times, to avoid being detained as an undocumented immigrant from another Central American country. Manuel Urquilla said that he had "no choice" but to think of himself as Salvadoran, while Roberto Orellana commented, "They reminded me of that when they deported me. 'Don't forget. You're Salvadoran.'" Remarking on how different he and other deportees were from Salvadoran citizens, Amilcar Mejía pointed out, "You never saw a cow before. You were used to the city. 'Wait a minute, what's this?' You're scared of a cow!" And a small number of interviewees commented positively about their connections with El Salvador. Deris Posada, who had once dreamed of being adopted by the United States, recalled that when he was deported, "I said to myself, 'I am Salvadoran. I also have suffered and am going to *salir adelante* [get ahead, move forward]. I landed here. I'm Salvadoran and this country has suffered like me. We are the same.' I had come to my home, and no one was going to kick me out. So I came here to live my life."

Deportees' experiences of becoming reinserted subjects demonstrate the power and limitations of legal definitions of belonging. Though some, such as Deris, seemed to welcome the opportunity to create a new life and others were able to obtain jobs, form families, and achieve a degree of resolution in El Salvador, many 1.5-generation deportees, at least at the time of our interviews, deeply identified as being from the United States and felt alienated from El Salvador. As we saw in the last chapter, a number of deportees attempt to return illicitly to the United States, where they face potential incarceration in the country that may have previously granted them temporary status or lawful residency. Indeed, while their lives in the United States may have (in their eyes) defined them as belonging, their *legal records* there kept them out. Thus, after they were deported, they *had* a legal relationship to the United States, but it was one that forbade their presence, whereas before they ever immigrated, they had no particular legal relationship at all. In that sense, rather than merely being "aliens," they were "reinserted subjects," individuals whose legal history in the United States now excluded them from U.S. territory.

Likewise, deportees' legal relationship to El Salvador underwent qualitative changes over the course of their lives, though, technically, it remained constant. When they were children, they had to flee the country, because despite being citizens, their families were unable to enjoy the safety and economic well-being that they desired. While living in the United States, they remained "technically" Salvadoran citizens, though many came to understand their Salvadoranness as an ethnicity or nationality more than a legal relationship. Then, when they were deported, their earlier legal relationship was resumed, but with the caveat that their histories in the United States now made them suspect, thus potentially subjecting them to harassment, interrogation, and apprehension on the part of Salvadoran authorities and (potentially) ostracization or even violence from "fellow" citizens. "Reinsertion" therefore proved to be a complex and even violent process.

Deportees were not the only 1.5-generation Salvadorans drawn to El Salvador. In addition, interviewees who continued to live in the United States found that the country loomed large in both their histories and imaginations.

Diasporic Citizens

If the United States appeared to some interviewees as a foster or adoptive parent who had not fully recognized or had even abandoned its immigrant offspring, then, continuing this analogy, El Salvador was like these interviewees' birth parent. Indeed, as we saw in chapter 2, William Martinez, a TPS holder, compared his desire for knowledge of El Salvador to when "you realize that you're adopted. And then you want—'you know what I would like to know is who is my real dad or who is my real mom.'" In William's powerful analogy, birth in El Salvador creates both a relationship and a mystery—what is the country where William and other interviewees were born like? How did it shape them? Why did they have to leave? And who would they have been if they had not?

Such questions, which resonate deeply with those posed by adoptees, colonial subjects, and subjugated and displaced persons more generally (Axel 2004; Bhabha 1994; Yngvesson 2010), reveal the law's power and its evisceration in the lives of what Lok Siu (2005:4) refers to as "diasporic citizens": individuals who navigate belonging while also developing "a consciousness, a positioning, a subjective expression of living at the intersection of different cultural-national formations." Law is at play within these intersections in that law fixes origin by taking legal cognizance of the fact of birth (Shachar 2009) even as, in the eyes of many interviewees, their Salvadoran citizenship became more of an ethnicity, an identity, or a product of family history than a legal status (Baker-Cristales 2004b). At the same time, immigration status in the United States influenced interviewees' senses of connection to El Salvador. Ironically, it was TPS holders and undocumented immigrants, whose status in the United States was most tenuous, who were least able to travel to El Salvador, while U.S. citizens and LPRs, whose ability to remain in the United States was more secure, were more able to visit there. Regardless of their immigration status, however, many U.S. interviewees described being pulled to their origins in El Salvador, a place that, for many, had become "saturate[d] . . . with social meaning" (Micieli-Voutsinas 2013:31), as they attempted to overcome the dis/memberment associated with wartime emigration. Adelmo Umanzor, for example, told me, "I always go back. There's something there that no other place has." Interviewees thus developed what Patricia Zavella (2011) has referred to as the "peripheral vision" associated with a transnational imaginary, that is, a continual envisioning of and comparison to life in the country from which they had been displaced. Importantly, for diasporic citizens, homeland can be not only a physical place but also "a concept and a desire—a place to return to through the imagination" (Espiritu and Tran 2002:369).

While deportees were pulled back to El Salvador by law, U.S.-based interviewees often went or sought to go there for nonlegal reasons (though some did return as young children with their parents, to obtain a visa at the U.S. embassy and then to return to the United States as LPRs). Consistent with their understandings of themselves as "technically Salvadoran but basically from the U.S.," U.S.-based interviewees' responses to my question about whether they considered themselves Salvadoran citizens were mixed. While some immediately replied that they did, others put forward substantive definitions of citizenship according to which being a Salvadoran citizen would require living in El Salvador, contributing to the country, participating in activities there, or having an impact. Saying that he was of Salvadoran descent but did not feel like a citizen, Tomás Marino Vegas told me, "I was born there and that would make me a citizen, but I've never lived there." Julian Becerra was uncertain of his status in El Salvador: "Do I even exist over there? You know, it's like am I even registered over there? [Be]cause like I don't even know. Like I have a birth certificate from over there, [but] it's so long ago, 1989, and they've never seen me, you know. They just saw me when I was born, and you know that's it." According to Julian, having a birth certificate from El Salvador might not be enough to still be "registered" in a country where, according to him, he had never been seen. And still other interviewees were stumped by the question, as in the following exchange with Guillermo Arguelles, who, at the time, was an LPR:

SUSAN: Do you think of yourself as a Salvadoran citizen?
GUILLERMO: I've never considered it.
SUSAN: Never considered?
GUILLERMO: No.

Guillermo's response is revealing. He did not *have* to consider whether he was a Salvadoran citizen. Being legal citizens of El Salvador was legally irrelevant to most interviewees' lives in the United States, with the exception of proving eligibility for a nationally specific immigration process (such as TPS or NACARA) or retrieving a legal record, such as a birth certificate or passport. Though interviewees were continually asked where they were from and many were proud to be Salvadoran, they were rarely asked to demonstrate their Salvadoran *citizenship* as a legal status. It was their status in the United States, rather than in El Salvador, that was at issue.

Although its legal significance may have been less consequential to U.S.-based interviewees, origin in El Salvador nonetheless led many—but not all!—U.S. interviewees to desire a deeper knowledge of Salvadoran history and culture. As Padilla notes, "For 1.5 and second-generation Salvadorans whose contact with El Salvador has been limited or is nonexistent, establishing a connection with the country from which their parents migrated, including its indigenous roots, and understanding the past of war that prompted such moves are necessary steps in their process of self-individuation as Salvadoran-Americans, and to a larger extent as Latina/os of Central American descent" (2012:8). Many interviewees were troubled by what they perceived as a disconnection between their origins in El Salvador and their memories of the country (see also Behar 2007). Marisol Sanabria, who was undocumented and therefore unable to travel legally at the times of our interviews, was disturbed that she knew "nothing" of El Salvador. She feared that until she could travel there, she would feel an "emptiness." Walter Olivar wanted to go to El Salvador "to remember those things, you know. To remember where I grew up; where, you know, I was there—I did this during that time; the moments that I lived." Julian Becerra told me that, in the absence of knowledge of El Salvador, he had developed a stock answer to others' questions about what the country was like: "I'll be like, 'It's hot.' Because that's what they told me." Many hoped to perform service for El Salvador, by working with schools there, creating a clinic, or doing volunteer work. A few interviewees, in contrast, were so disturbed by experiences or stories of wartime violence that they feared traveling to El Salvador. One interviewee, who did plan to travel there, said that he was nonetheless resistant to "revisiting . . . memories of war." Finally, a few interviewees were simply uninterested in traveling to El Salvador, explaining that they had lived in the United States for a long time, that their families were in the U.S., and that they had no reason to go to El Salvador. One interviewee felt that what he characterized as "the fervor of going, wanting to just know, or just to smell and see the ocean over there; the mountains; volcanoes" was part of an earlier life stage that he had left behind when he turned thirty.

U.S.-based interviewees' sense that traveling to El Salvador would enable them to revisit their origins suggests that immigration creates a complex temporality, according to which the past exists *simultaneously with* and even *can come after* the present. In other words, if the past was still accessible in El Salvador, then individuals who were living in the United States right now could go there to experience it in the future. This sense that the past was not "over with" but rather still evolving was conveyed by Milda Escobar's insistence that "we are part of the 1980s; we are connected to the civil war." As well, Ernesto Duran argued that knowing the past was key to understanding the present, that there were layers hidden underneath present surfaces. He explained:

> In El Salvador particularly I would like to go to the U.S. embassy. . . . I know it was built on an archaeological site. . . . I want to just see that area . . . , you know, just in my head what it was back then and what it is now— particularly, a U.S. embassy on top of land was historically, you know—like basically could have been excavated for archaeology stuff. . . . Different areas that have been established as areas of civil war kind of battles. I know that

there was one area that they massacred a lot of people which—El Mozote, El Mozote—I want to go there. I just, I want to go everywhere.

Other interviewees described uncanny recognitions, in which individuals who had known them *before* they immigrated suddenly connected that memory to their current selves. Mauricio Nuñez Arellano told me that when he went to El Salvador for the first time, "I didn't remember anything from there. But my cousins remembered me. 'Oh, yeah, you're the little kid that would like ran'—his cousin over. Because all the cousins were the mischievous ones? So we would like beat up my little cousins. They're like, 'That was like you.'" In this comment, Mauricio discovered his past self in his cousins' memory. Other interviewees sought to interview grandparents or other relatives about historically significant events. Cecilia Molina wanted to learn about the expropriation of family land by one of El Salvador's ruling families, the founding of the San Miguel carnival, and an important teachers' strike in 1969 or 1970. Conveying her sense that history was very much alive, she commented, "This stuff, when you read about it, it doesn't go back that far. It really doesn't go back that far."

Note that, in striking contrast to such comments, deportees rarely described returning to El Salvador as an opportunity to revisit their pasts, though as Carlos Alas's story of eating *pupusas* demonstrates, sometimes they did relive earlier moments. For them, El Salvador was much more a present reality, and the past that they longed to revisit was in the United States. Recall Francisco Ramirez's's comment, quoted in chapter 4: "It's a Tuesday, just like any other Tuesday. One more day to get through, that we have to be here." This contrast indicates that part of the desire for the past comes from a cut-off (whether through emigration or deportation) that separated it from present existence.

Linked to this understanding of the past as somehow continuing alongside or beneath the present were some interviewees' sense of alternative realities, the shadow selves they would have become if they had not immigrated. As noted above, Marta Dominguez felt that when U.S. policies forced her family out of El Salvador, she was "robbed of a different life" and that returning to El Salvador was like becoming a child again. Milda Escobar felt that connecting with current Salvadoran youths made it possible to understand the lives that "youth who were taken out" might have lived. For some interviewees, alternative realities were terrifying. Mauricio Nuñez Arellano and Cecilia Molina both commented that if their families had stayed in El Salvador, their fathers would have been killed, while Eduardo Sanchez remarked that if he had grown up in El Salvador, he could "have been shot as a little kid in the street by the

National Guard in El Salvador" or "been murdered as a kid, you know. We know people who have been bombed or threatened around that time." Other interviewees stressed that they would have experienced poverty or been unable to go to college. Being conscious of those alternatives, Graciela Nuñez said, makes her realize that her current problems are not so bad. Some interviewees compared their current lives to those of friends and relatives who had remained in El Salvador. Rafael Espinoza said that some of his former friends had grown up to be gangsters so that might have been his fate, while Juana Rocio more optimistically noted that one of her cousins was becoming a dentist, so she might have done something similar.

Diasporic citizenship has gendered dimensions, as women commented on the ways that they might have been constrained, had they stayed in El Salvador, by gender conventions requiring them to marry young, have children, and serve their husbands. Women also noted that during visits to El Salvador, relatives there criticized them for dressing too provocatively, staying out late, or drinking in public. One interviewee, who had returned to El Salvador to live when she was a teenager, said that her grandmother burned her clothes and sent her to cosmetology school. Likewise, interviewees who were gay worried about encountering homophobia. One interviewee commented, "The other thing, I guess, for me, is that I'm gay and I felt, 'I'm out.' Here [in Los Angeles] I feel comfortable and I don't know how comfortable I would have felt with that over there [in El Salvador]. So even though there are some organizations now and there's more support, I think that there's also [more discrimination]."

The desire to understand their pasts shaped what interviewees who traveled to El Salvador did during their time there. Many wanted to visit family members, see historical sites, experience Salvadoran culture, and become familiar with the landscape—goals that, with the exception of visiting family, are not unlike those most tourists might have. Yet, for some interviewees, such visits were something of a personal quest. Juana Rocio, who was fighting removal, told me that she "would love to go on vacation" in El Salvador, and that if she did, she would "go look over like what the places were my mom has told me, learn about the culture. Meet some of the family my mom has over there in El Salvador, . . . go to like the main places, . . . compare and contrast El Salvador to here, like what's the big differences. . . . Visit like where they have their government offices. You know, go to the landmark places. To the beaches. Learn about maybe their educational system." Juana's description of her "vacation" sounds like a research trip. Indeed, those who traveled on student-led delegations took something of a "social consciousness" tour of the country, and thus they sought to overcome official silences over past injustices, including massacres of the indigenous population in 1932 and the 1980–1992 Salvadoran civil war (see DeLugan 2012).[10] In addition to seeing relatives and going to lakes and the beach, they visited such places as the church where the Salvadoran archbishop Oscar Romero (a martyr of the civil war) was buried, Tazumal (an archaeological site), the Museo de la Revolución (Museum of the Revolution, which houses artifacts from the Salvadoran civil war), the grave of Farabundo Martí (the leader of the 1932 peasant uprising that is known as "La Matanza," or "the Slaughter," due to the brutality with which it was repressed; the Salvadoran guerrilla forces were named after him), and Intipucá (a city known for the impact of migrant remittances on the local economy—see Pedersen 2002). Additionally, they sought to understand the social landscape by exploring rural communities, meeting with government officials, going to a mall to observe who was shopping there, speaking with politically progressive groups about their ongoing projects, and listening to stories about the war and social life. While traveling, they received some attention. One delegation was able to participate in radio interviews in which people called in from as far away as Australia, while another was invited to the inauguration of the Salvadoran president, Mauricio Funes. These experiences contrasted sharply with the rejection that deportees had encountered.

Whether traveling individually or as part of a delegation, U.S.-based interviewees' trips to El Salvador could be transformational or unsettling. For many, being in El Salvador was an encounter with an authentic self, a place where there was a unique fit between who they were and their surroundings. Rosa Hernández struggled to put this feeling into words:

> I feel like free. It's just something like, as soon as I go in, I mean, I feel the heat, you know, and sometimes it's kind of hard, you know? You just feel it hit you, and stuff? But then it's like I could breathe! It's so hard to explain! Like I try to explain it to my husband too, and I'm like, "I don't know, it's just, it's like a feeling or something." It's probably nothing, really? But it's just me, maybe. But I just feel so like relieved or something. It feels weird! It's just, I mean, it's weird. And just to think about it. Like, I don't know. It feels good, I guess.

At the same time, such visceral experiences of place (see also Hayes-Conroy and Hayes-Conroy 2010) were coupled with evidence of being out of place. Despite Rosa's profound feeling of belonging, she was called a "gringa" by others. Veronica Reina spent most of her time with cousins because others might consider her "spoiled" simply due to being from the United States, and Marta Rodriguez found herself tongue-tied linguistically: "They make fun of me a lot. . . . I feel like I'm stuck between two languages. Because, for me, I feel like I feel that I think in Spanish, but I speak English." Juan José expected to feel "comfortable" when he returned to El Salvador, but instead he found that people mistook him for a drug dealer due to being overly friendly. The essential ambivalence of his position there was demonstrated by his cousin's praise for participating in the same activities as everyone else: "You know what, I thought you were going to be different. That you were going to be this kid that didn't want to go out, very careful what he ate." Juan José was proud to have defied this expectation, but at the same time, the notion that he would be "different" othered him in the first place.

Whether transformational, troubling, or both, the significance of U.S-based interviewees' return trips to El Salvador is shown by the fact that some tried to document their experiences (including by participating in interviews with me). Many seemed to see such trips as an opportunity to learn, either by asking relatives about family history, becoming better acquainted with the country's past, or talking with others. Marilyn Funes said that to overcome her family's silences, she had to do her own research.

> Like I told this kid, I said, "Look, start asking questions. Start going to the books and learn. Read about El Salvador. You know, go into websites and . . . read how everything is going there. Go into independent, you know, media and find out how everything is going out in El Salvador. So pretty much do your own self-history because you can't depend on the family. You know, the family is not going to give you." Up till this day my parents really haven't told me a lot, you know, that I should know. And I've actually found out from different people. And when I tell them, they're, "How do you know? How did you, you know, figure it out?" And I think that's—that's, you know, doing your own—you know, your own history, learning, going—going back, learning how to—how everything started. Um, that's—that's basically what I did.

Many who went on delegations documented their experiences through photography and videography, which they planned to post on websites, disseminate through public radio, or incorporate into workshops and presentations on their campuses.[11]

By traveling to El Salvador, some found that being "technically" from El Salvador became real. These trips, combined with noncitizen youths' efforts to secure formal recognition from the United States and deportees' quests for acceptance in El Salvador and the ability to return to the United States, constituted efforts to re/member, to weave together history and biography in ways that generated belonging in both the United States and El Salvador.

Conclusion

Interviewees' accounts of their relationships to the United States and El Salvador re/member such that individual biographies can be integrated into, rather than disconnected from, national history. Thus, 1.5-generation noncitizens seek recognition of their multiple origins as "Salvadorans raised in Los Angeles"; deportees reject being inserted in an alien status vis-à-vis both the United States and El Salvador; and U.S.-based interviewees who returned to El Salvador sought to overcome the lacuna in knowledge, memory, and relationships created through their original expulsion by wartime violence and economic exploitation. In short, youths sought to re/member, to recuperate biographies submerged by national narratives about the Latino threat (Chavez 2008), criminal aliens (Inda 2006), deported gang members (Zilberg 2011), and the perception that youths raised in the United States were "different" Salvadorans. In overcoming these narratives through recourse to their own and others' histories, 1.5-generation and second-generation Salvadorans pursued novel forms of membership, according to which substantive ties outweighed legal technicalities (Bosniak 2006), and multiple origins "elsewhere" could be seen as strengthening rather than weakening the nation-state. Re/membered nations could be simultaneously whole and partial, spilling over their own boundaries yet incomplete. By affirming rather than rejecting such contradictions, interviewees gestured toward forms of memory and membership consistent with the realities of their lives.

Interviewees' efforts to place their lives within national histories shed light on the temporality of memory. Memories are something to which one returns. They can be vivid, haunting, fleeting, impossible to escape, or dreamlike, as in Araceli Muñoz's memories of her babyhood in El Salvador prior to immigrating: "I have like bits and pieces and they mostly seem like dreams. Because . . . like I would tell my mother, I remember such and such things and she said, 'No, that's probably real because that was there.' And I said, 'Oh, well, I thought it was a dream, you know.'" Memories of events that actually occurred are sometimes contrasted with imagination, which entails invention (Loftus 1993). Yet there is a *selectivity* to memory—individuals do not remember everything; therefore that which they do recall must serve some purpose (Micieli-Voutsinas 2013). In this sense, there is a connection between imagination and memory, one that overcomes the accuracy/invention binary: both memories and imaginings develop out of perhaps infinite possibilities and are formed in relation to present realities. In this sense, interviewees' memories of the past are connected to imagined futures that they seek to bring into being or to avoid. As Jacque Micieli-Voutsinas (2013:31–32) notes, diasporic memory "unleashes and recalls a series of past-present connections, thus blurring the distinction between past and present time-spaces, however momentary, and potentially changing future meanings altogether." When noncitizens who are in the United States remember their biographies there, they are doing so to claim a future in which they would actually be granted legal recognition such that their abilities to remain in the country would be secure. When deportees remember their lives in the United States they seek an imagined future in which they could return to those lives. Likewise, when U.S.-based interviewees traveled to El Salvador in order to revisit the past, they simultaneously sought more just futures in which they and their family members would not be separated, in which child poverty could be overcome, in which the violence that pushed their families from El Salvador would be acknowledged and perhaps even redressed. Re/membering thus seeks to align the past with a desired future. To paraphrase Coddington (2011:753), pasts that haunt call out for justice.

Likewise, the accounts analyzed here shed light on the geography of memory. Re/membering entails traveling not only in time but also through space. Consider, for example, this account provided by Jorge Rodríguez, who had immigrated to the United States at the age of six and was eventually deported:

> I've been here [in El Salvador] for a year and a half already and I'm already kinda—I'm still—half of my mind is still in the United States and the other half is here, you know? I feel sometimes like I—I feel like I'm over there, you know? I'm driving or I'm sitting in a car and my mind is over there, I'm in the freeway or somewhere, you know? Or I'm on the beach or I'm somewhere over there. But at the end I'm not over there, I'm over here, you know? So I'm over there and at the same time I'm over here. So it's really—it's *hard*, you know?

As Jorge relates, his memory of the United States is so powerful that his mind is still "over there" such that the landscapes that he has occupied seem to intermingle, placing him in the United States and El Salvador at the same time, even though, as he explained, in the end, he is in El Salvador, not the United

States. Similarly, when Marta Dominguez, a naturalized U.S. citizen, felt "stuck between two languages," it was as though Marta could not fully be in either El Salvador or in the United States, as part of her (linguistically) was in the other place all of the time. Such comments suggest that as individuals revisit the pasts, they simultaneously keep the places that they previously occupied alive in the present, almost enabling these landscapes to move *with them* when they themselves travel. In this sense, migrants become nodes through which national territories become interspersed.

The temporality and geography of re/membering are also closely linked to the legal subjects created through transnational securityscapes (Zilberg 2011). As noted previously, interviewees' legal statuses varied tremendously and included U.S. citizenship, LPR, TPS, having a pending application for asylum, undocumented, and having been deported. Most interviewees were also Salvadoran citizens by birth or potential Salvadoran citizens through their parents. Yet, despite this legal diversity, interviewees' positions as legal subjects had certain commonalities. Many were subject to procedural challenges that placed them in a situation of immigration dependency (for example, delays in receiving a renewed work permit could result in loss of employment), they often lacked access to affordable and competent legal counsel in immigration proceedings, they were potentially subject to punitive state actions (including detention and removal), they experienced discrimination and social exclusion (sometimes in both countries), their right to be present in the United States was questioned (as experienced by Sandra Mejillas), and their sense of Salvadoran citizenship as a legal status was attenuated in comparison to the legal significance of U.S. citizenship. Thus, as individuals who were legally and socially suspect, and in multiple countries, interviewees found that their origins elsewhere (whether birth in El Salvador or having been raised in the United States) continued to define their presents and potentially shape their futures (see also Menjívar 2006). Law could pull migrants back to their countries of origin, whether through deportation or even the requirement to go to the U.S. embassy in El Salvador as part of the family visa petition process. At the same time, in the United States, social exclusion positioned undocumented and liminal migrants "elsewhere," thus creating "holes" through which "foreign territories" could enter U.S. landscapes.

These temporalities, geographies, and legalities also shaped the forms of justice that interviewees sought in relation to the legal and physical violence that they had experienced earlier in their lives. Running through their narratives were references to the "real" and the "fictive": for example, being "basically" from the United States, but "technically" from El Salvador, or the notion that the United States was like an adoptive or foster parent, in contrast to their "birth" or "real" parent, El Salvador. What is considered "real" shifts in these comparisons: from the United States to El Salvador, from biography to origins. The point of such shifts is that *origins and biography are both real and fictional* in that individuals can have multiple origins, live with and reassume alternative versions of themselves, and be members of multiple states and localities (note that many interviewees stressed that they were from L.A., not the United States).[12] Social justice then would be achieved by enabling these seeming contradictions to be true simultaneously. In other words, if submerged histories — the impacts of the Salvadoran civil war on civilian populations, the role that the United States played in the civil conflict, the denial of refugee status to Salvadoran immigrants who came to the United States, the lack of services provided to these arriving migrants, the criminalization and marginalization of Central American immigrant populations — could be officially acknowledged, then remedies could be created for atrocities, legal violence, social exclusions, deportation policies, and the "othering" of expatriate citizens. Re/membering biographies and nations calls for accountability, which is not only an end, but also a beginning (Nelson 2009).

JULY 2008. While in El Salvador conducting interviewees with deportees, I visited the El Mozote memorial for the first time. El Mozote was one of the most infamous massacres of the Salvadoran civil war. In 1981, the Atlacatl battalion of the Salvadoran Armed Forces entered the village of El Mozote; separated the men, women, and children; and killed almost everyone. The memorial site has become a key stop in "war-related tourism" (Johnson 2007). Also, interviewees who described themselves as "conscious" had made a point of visiting this site either individually or as part of delegations through which they explored El Salvador's history, particularly the civil war period. I decided that I had to make this trek myself and that, if possible, I would try to do so as part of an organized group.

So, one weekend, I found myself on a Centro de Intercambio y Solidaridad (Center of Exchange and Solidarity, or CIS) van with CIS volunteers from the United States, Canada, and the United Kingdom, who were a bit perplexed about who I was and what I was doing there. "I'm a professor," I kept explaining. After a five-hour drive into the mountains, and a visit to the Museo de la Revolución, we reached the memorial. This was something that I had to make

FIGURE 5.1 El Mozote memorial. Photo by author.

FIGURE 5.2 Church at El Mozote. Photo by author.

myself do. I dreaded actually being at the site. I had seen a reenactment of the massacre in the film *Homeland*, made by deported gang members; had read accounts of the massacre and of the exhumations of the victims; and had been deeply disturbed.

We gathered around the memorial, a silhouette of a family in front of a wall where the names of the victims were inscribed. A community member who had fled El Mozote prior to the massacre and then returned when the village was repopulated spoke to us. She had learned what had happened directly from Rufina Amaya, the sole survivor, who had fallen to the ground and pretended to be dead and then had escaped by hiding among some cattle.

In El Mozote, the ground itself bore the marks of the massacre. The community member took us around, showing us the ruins of buildings in which people had been killed. We could see bullet holes in the walls that still stood. We climbed over a barbed-wire fence into a cluster of trees where there were still bits of fabric from the clothing people had been wearing. Some group members reached out to touch the clothing. Outside of the church there were bricks that, we were told, still bore the stains of children's blood. And then there were the marks that had been made as part of the memorial: silhouettes of a family, happy images of children rising upward on the church wall. Along the bottom of the church wall was a listing of the children who had been killed, grouped by their ages.

Before leaving, a number of us purchased literature and crafts from the bookstore in the church. As we drove away, one volunteer turned immediately to reading Rufina Amaya's published testimony, asking several of us for help translating difficult terms and phrases. As we explained points of grammar, the text circulated within the van and beyond, as we re/membered this testimony and our visit to El Mozote.

CONCLUSION
Re/membering Exiled Homes

If state and society are to remedy injustices from the
past, honor lives lost, and embrace an inclusive society,
the process will require remembering together.
— DELUGAN 2012:128

JULY 3, 2014. A headline in the *Los Angeles Times* read "Desperate to Go North: More Than Rumors Drive Central American Youths." The article described the journeys of two Guatemalan sisters who attempted to join their mother in the United States but were caught in Mexico and sent back. In recent weeks, the news had been filled with similar stories about the rising numbers of Central American children immigrating to the United States and of the humanitarian challenge posed by the young detainees. On July 2, busloads of children heading to a Border Patrol processing center in Murietta, California, were blocked by anti-immigrant protesters concerned about the new arrivals' impacts on their communities. One protester was quoted as vowing that if buses returned, "We're going to be there to do the same thing" (Esquivel, Linthicum, and Simon 2014). On list-servs in which I participated, scholars suggested that asylum might be an appropriate response, given that many of these children were fleeing gang violence or domestic abuse. During a conference call I had with Central American leaders and advocates, someone observed that the dominant logic of the response to date had been to view immigrants as a security issue and to adopt punitive policies, including sending children back to their home countries before they encounter legal assistance. Indeed, earlier that week, President Obama announced plans to expedite processing of these youths so that they could be deported quickly, and he asked Congress to appropriate funding for a "surge" in border enforcement. Some advocates argued that the mass exodus of Central American children was a crisis akin to the emigration of Central American refugees during the 1980s. One advocate suggested that, in response to this crisis, the solidarity movement of the 1980s needed to be reactivated.

This recent movement of Central American children bears much in common with the experiences of the youths who are the subject of this book. Like these new arrivals (J. Bhabha 2014; Terrio 2015; Zatz and Rodriguez 2015), many interviewees and their families fled violence in their countries of origin, traveled without authorization, suffered hardships while en route to the United States, were denied asylum or other forms of legal recognition, struggled to overcome lengthy separations from family members, and were at risk of being deported or else were actually removed. In both cases, dominant narratives of such experiences failed to recount the deeper histories in which decisions to migrate were made. During the civil war in El Salvador, U.S. authorities treated Salvadoran asylum seekers as economic migrants, in search of jobs rather than safety. And in 2014, unaccompanied minors from Central America were described as children who, enticed by the myth that they would be granted permission to remain in the United States, were seeking to escape poverty and violence in their homelands. The first of these narratives ignored the widespread political violence in El Salvador, as well as U.S. involvement in that violence (Hull 1985; C. Smith 1996). Likewise, the second narrative ignores U.S. involvement in the history that produced poverty and high crime in El Salvador, Guatemala, and Honduras (Abrego 2014a; Menjívar 2011a; Menjívar and Abrego 2012; Perla 2014; Pine 2008). Indeed, the exoduses of wartime refugees and of current unaccompanied children are not merely historical parallels; in fact, the social, legal, and political violence of the civil war period helped to create the conditions that have led Salvadoran children, teenagers, and families to continue to migrate. The continued violence in El Salvador, where the homicide rate exceeds that of the civil war, suggests that the "post" in "postwar" is a bit of a misnomer (see also Nelson 2009). Yet, if perpetrators of wartime violence had been held accountable, if the United States had granted asylum to refugees in a timely fashion, and if the United States had recognized its historical responsibility to victims of this crisis, whether they remained in El Salvador or emigrated, then perhaps Salvadoran children would not be migrating in such high numbers today.[1] Perhaps, if migrant populations could be granted status, thus recognizing their biographies and histories, then this cycle of violence could be broken.

In this book, I have argued that, rather than simply being the movement of a person or family from one country to another, immigration can involve violent dismembering, such that individuals are excluded from their countries of origin and destination, which in turn are transformed as they are populated by individuals who are regarded as nonmembers (in the case of countries of destination) or depopulated when their citizens and longtime residents are re-located elsewhere (in the case of countries of origin). I have further argued that membership and memory are interconnected in that social, legal, and physical exclusion disconnects individuals from national histories such that accounts of the processes that led to and followed their migration or displacement can be submerged, denied, or ignored. Based on analyses of 1.5-generation and second-generation Salvadoran migrants' life histories, I have suggested that such dismemberment can be countered by re/membering, by recuperating and recognizing submerged histories as bases for inclusion in migrants' countries of origin and residence. In fact, re/membering troubles distinctions between origin and destination as it revisits the past in order to account for the present and to advocate for more just and inclusive futures. Likewise, re/membering also interweaves spaces as migrants come to define current locations in relation to past and potentially future homes. Temporal, spatial, and legal disruptions are particularly pronounced in the case of child migrants, who may lack both memories of their countries of origin and membership in their countries of residence. Therefore, examining their efforts to re/member, whether through activism or through their personal lives, sheds light on the new social realities that are created in the wake of war and economic injustice.

To make this argument, I have brought readers along the paths traveled by Central American child migrants who, at the time of my interviews with them, had become adults living in, between, and outside of the United States and/or El Salvador. Their accounts of their families' departures from their countries of origin demonstrate how the violence of the Salvadoran civil war became the violence of immigrating without authorization and then of being denied asylum in the United States (Menjívar and Abrego 2012). Michael Collyer's comment that the situation of undocumented migrants might best be understood as "a failure of protection, rather than a failure of control," is apt in relation to their circumstances (2010:275). Interviewees' descriptions of their childhoods in the United States speak to the ways that the disjunctures that they experienced between law and illegality, past and present, and El Salvador and the United States were sites of not only marginalization but also opportunity, as, in these liminal spaces, interviewees forged their own understandings of identity, belonging, and deservingness. Some interviewees built on these understandings by seeking justice for undocumented students, forming new Central American student organizations on their campuses, and producing literature about their experiences. Other interviewees underwent criminalization and illegalization as their origins outside of the United States pulled them back to El Salvador, where they were also regarded as foreigners. Whether in the United States or in El Salvador, interviewees had complex relationships with the nations where they had been born and/or grew up. U.S.-based noncitizen interviewees sought legal recognition from the United States, those who had been deported sought the right to return, and those who returned to El Salvador to visit family members or as part of student delegations sought to revisit their own pasts. Through such practices, 1.5-generation and second-generation Salvadorans sought to re/member, to gain recognition of the complex lives that they had lived and to be accepted as members of the multiple countries to which, they argued, they had pledged allegiance. If successful, youths would not only overcome and make sense of the disjunctures that they and their families had experienced, but also help to make the nations that they were part of whole. It is this effort to overcome disjunctures by reassembling nations, persons, and histories that I have termed re/membering.

Re/membering is also a strategy for addressing the global insecurities that gave rise to both the increased emigration of Central American children in 2014 and the earlier migrations experienced by the individuals interviewed for this manuscript. Such insecurities have more typically been addressed through legal and militaristic security measures. Thus, unauthorized border crossings are typically defined as a law enforcement problem, one that necessitates stiffened border controls, rather than as evidence of dire living conditions that demand a humanitarian response. Likewise, the unauthorized immigrant population in the United States has been considered—particularly by restrictionists—as a sign that legal controls are ineffective rather than as the product of exclusionary measures that produce illegality, as described in chapter 4. Whether through the "war on crime" in the United States (Simon 2007), "mano dura" gang-repression strategies in El Salvador (Coutin 2007; McGuire 2011; Zilberg

2011), or detention and deportation strategies that transcend countries, the process of securitization has treated phenomena such as poverty, crime, gangs, violence, and illegality as matters that require military or law enforcement interventions (Caldeira 2000). This dynamic has persisted even though one lesson of the histories recounted here is that securitization contributes to insecurity by exacerbating social exclusions. Thus, undocumented students who are denied legal status and work authorization must resort to working in the informal economy and driving without authorization, while deported youths may resort to returning to the United States illicitly, at great personal risk. In contrast, re/membering promotes both inclusion and accountability in ways that, as I outline below, can reduce rather than exacerbate global insecurities.

Why Does Re/membering Matter?

Re/membering matters for both practical and analytical reasons. Practically speaking, nations that have dismembered populations face a number of challenges. In receiving countries, having substantial noncitizen populations undermines democracy in that noncitizens are usually unable to participate in the formal political process, due to lack of voting rights (Benhabib 2004; Bosniak 2006), even though they can participate in other ways (Nicholls 2013). Noncitizen residents may not be able to achieve their full potential, due both to their immigration status and to living with uncertainty about their futures (Mountz, Wright, Miyares, and Bailey 2002). If such individuals are ultimately deported, they likely will leave behind relatives who are citizens, thus further disrupting families, communities, and the nation (Kanstroom 2007, 2012).[2] Undocumented and temporarily authorized residents may be barred from performing national service, such as serving in the military (Kerwin and Stock 2007). As well, emigrant citizens may be disenfranchised in their countries of origin, though increasingly voting rights are being extended to citizens living outside of national territories (Marcin 2013). Relatives in emigrants' home countries experience the effects of divided families, which can lead to increased insecurity and continued emigration (Abrego 2014b). Failure to welcome returnees may lead them to re-emigrate or to turn to illicit activities, thus further increasing crime. For both sending and receiving states, then, these challenges could be addressed by granting legal recognition to long-term noncitizen residents and by devising a means of more fully incorporating migrant citizens, whether they live outside of or within national territories. For these reasons, sending nations have reached out to citizens living abroad (Basch, Glick Schiller, and

Szanton Blanc 1994; Coutin 2007; Mahler 2000; Rivas 2014), though they have generally been less quick to incorporate deportees (Zilberg 2011). Coupling the social inclusion of migrant populations with policies to encourage the social well-being of nonmigrants would also potentially reduce motivations to migrate, thus stemming unauthorized immigration.

As well, re/membering has practical implications for migrants themselves. Migrants who lack full legal recognition in their countries of residence face challenges moving forward with their educational and career plans. Without U.S. citizenship or lawful permanent residency, migrants cannot petition for their immediate family members to immigrate legally. If family members nonetheless emigrate, they face the hazards of unauthorized movement. Without the right to reenter the United States after going abroad, unauthorized or temporarily authorized migrants cannot visit family members in their countries of origin. Without such visits, the emotional effects of parental absences are exacerbated (Abrego 2014b). Migrants who lack citizenship are at risk of deportation. Without full social recognition in their countries of origin, returnees may be treated as foreigners, passed over for job opportunities, and subjected to police harassment. Re/membering would grant recognition to the multiple origins of those who have moved between countries, thus connecting individuals' lives to the complex histories that lead to and result from emigration. Improved knowledge of the connections between structural conditions, national histories, and individual lives provides rationales for social inclusion and thus undergirds "strong frameworks of belonging" (C. Rodriguez 2008:1111).

In addition to these practical considerations, as an analytical concept, re/membering advances theory regarding violence, memory, membership, and law. First, regarding violence, the notion of re/membering challenges distinctions that have sometimes been drawn between deserving and undeserving victims of violence. For example, U.S. asylum law distinguishes sharply between political and other forms of violence, such as economic suffering or criminal victimization (Harris 1993). Such distinctions can create hierarchies of deservingness by suggesting that physical violence is more significant than psychological suffering (Jenkins 1996, 1998), that those who are directly targeted for persecution are more deserving of refuge than are those who are at risk of generalized violence (Hull 1985), or that individuals who are targeted by death squads are at greater risk than those targeted by gang members (Lister 2007; Wilkinson 2010). Violence has also been conceptualized as an action rather than a condition, which makes it difficult to secure legal recognition of structural and nonagentive forms of violence that may continue over time, result from policies, and therefore lack clearly identifiable perpetrators (Kleinman, Das, and Locke 1997; Scheper-Hughes 1993). For instance, Operation Gatekeeper, which increased border patrol presence in key sectors of the U.S.-Mexico border, led to increased border deaths, as migrants attempted to cross in more remote areas (Nevins 2002). Drawing distinctions between forms of violence makes it difficult to see the ways that violence can be transformed over time, such that the violence of the Salvadoran civil war gave rise to the violence of traveling without authorization and to the legal violence of being denied asylum in the United States (Menjívar and Abrego 2012). Delays in granting legal protections to Salvadorans who immigrated during the civil war left many 1.5-generation youths without U.S. citizenship and therefore vulnerable to deportation, which in turn has produced a new wave of family separations as deportees leave behind parents, siblings, spouses, partners, and children in the United States.

The concept of re/membering challenges scholars to overcome such distinctions by examining the connections between forms of violence and across historical moments. Poverty, political violence, and crime may all be life-threatening. Therefore, to treat only some victims of these phenomena as deserving of refuge is, in and of itself, a form of dismemberment. Likewise, re/membering connects seemingly nonagentive forms of violence, such as border deaths, to the structural and political conditions that produce them. Such connections demonstrate the ways that violence travels over time, such that violent historical, structural, and geopolitical processes at one moment may be connected to emigration, deportability, and other social traumas at another.

Second, the concept of re/membering contributes to understanding both the temporality and geography of memory. A rich anthropological literature has challenged the limitations of linear notions of time, according to which the passage of time is construed as a chronology, with the past preceding the present and being followed by the future. Alternative conceptualizations of temporality include cyclical time (e.g., a ritual cycle, which repeats); nostalgia, which "constructs a dialectic between the past and the present" (Cavanaugh 2004); punctuated time, that is, "signal event moments in near-future time at which the whole world could change" (Guyer 2007:417); and time-space compression, or the speeding up of communication and production associated with the Internet and globalization (Harvey 2005), among others. Each of these alternative conceptions disrupts notions of linearity, by emphasizing repetition, dialectic, turning points (which disrupt the even flow of time), and simultaneity.

My contribution to these alternative interpretations is to suggest that re/membering entails revisiting the past in light of the present, a process in which the past is returned to (rather than repeated) in order to reincorporate a past "signal event," namely, migration, and to deepen understandings of the present in ways that will authorize more just futures.[3] Unlike linear notions of time, then, re/membering populates the past with visitors from the present, enabling individuals to encounter shadow lives that might have been, alternative realities to which they could perhaps actually return, and futures that could yet be realized. Re/membering is thus temporally complex in that "people emerge from and as the products of their stories about themselves as much as their stories emerge from their lives" and that "the meaning of any past event may change as the larger, continuing story lengthens and grows in complexity" (Antze and Lambek 1996:xviii–xix).

This understanding of temporality, in which the relationships among past, present, and future become multidirectional, also has spatial implications in that revisiting the past, whether through travel, memory, uncovering historical accounts, or re-creating a past life, simultaneously takes individuals to other places, enabling territories to become interspersed. Thus, in contrast to Cartesian understandings of space (Gupta and Ferguson 1997), according to which spaces are inert and territories can be mapped, re/membering suggests that territories can "move" with people and that individuals who are socially excluded can be located "elsewhere," in a nonspace, or what I have termed a "space of nonexistence" (Coutin 2000). These nonspaces both transcend and are located within the nation-state. In other words, individuals who are defined as unauthorized are removed through practices of social exclusion, even as they continue to reside within U.S. territory. Their physical presence is therefore simultaneously a "hole," a conduit, a pocket of absence that permits "foreignness" or "alienage" to enter the United States. Likewise, deportation extends U.S. places of confinement to El Salvador where deportees may experience their presence there and their prohibition on reentry as extensions of their previous detention or incarceration. Re/membering such gaps or nonspaces, which are produced by yet fall outside of known grids, suggests that they are sites of both marginalization and creativity. Furthermore, attending to the geography of memory contributes to work on transnationalism by pointing out that the nonspaces that migrants occupy both transcend and are within particular national territories.

Third, re/membering emphasizes the importance of substantive forms of belonging in determinations of membership. Immigration scholars have noted that the mass population displacements associated with globalization and geopolitical conflict have created sharp distinctions between individuals who are full, legal citizens of the countries where they live and those who may have substantive ties but who lack formal, legal recognition (Bosniak 2006; Hammar 1990; Motomura 2014; Shachar 2009). The concept of re/membering contributes to this work by noting the ways that substantive ties denaturalize immigration categories. Individuals are not intrinsically undocumented or deportable any more than they are intrinsically citizens or lawful residents; rather, they are historically constituted as such (de Genova 2004; Ngai 2004; Peutz and de Genova 2010). As they come to occupy local spaces within their new countries of residence, they transform these spaces through their presences, reconfiguring existing landscapes and institutions. As a result, migrants become part of the very contexts that receive them. Likewise, confronted with existing definitions of race and ethnicity, definitions in which they may be either invisible or stereotyped, migrants invent their own categories, such as, for instance, "Salvadoran from L.A." At the same time, interviewees' understandings of themselves as *legally* Salvadoran were, in many cases, weakened, making migrants' "Salvadoranness" more an ethnicity or nationality than a legal relationship to the Salvadoran state. Such definitions mark interviewees' presence in space, naming their multiple origins—El Salvador, L.A.—while simultaneously suggesting that they occupy a new sort of space that transcends national distinctions. Similarly, deportees who insisted that they "could be American" highlighted the importance of their own biographies in and substantive ties to the United States. Linking membership and memory in these ways challenges the authoritativeness of formal legal categories.

Fourth, the concept of re/membering sheds light on new forms of legal subjectivity being created by current global processes and enforcement regimes. In contrast to the autonomous, rights-bearing citizen that was the hallmark of liberal law (Collier, Maurer, and Suarez-Navaz 1996), those who migrate without authorization or who are subsequently removed enjoy, in practice, only an attenuated set of legal rights (Johnson 1996). In the United States, unauthorized migrants are subject to administrative procedures that do not include the right to state-appointed counsel. They can be detained without bond, they can be ordered deported in absentia, and they act in a legal field in which affordable, qualified attorneys are hard to come by and in which nonprofits that can provide such services are overwhelmed. Through the removal process, noncitizens can be stripped of any legal status that they may have attained and, in this sense, noncitizens who are potentially subject to removal and noncitizens who are actually being removed share a common legal position. Despite these attenuated rights, noncitizen interviewees sought to invoke the obligations that an adoptive, foster, or natural parent has to a fictive or illegitimate child. In this relationship, the parent/nation has the discretion to decide whether to fulfill its parental responsibilities, even though the parent-child/migrant-state relationship is made "real" by the substantive relationship that exists and the role that the United States (in this case) played in contributing to the conditions that led individuals to emigrate. By focusing attention on differences between the forms of membership that law recognizes and that migrants seek, re/membering demonstrates that, in the new global era, law's power derives in part from its departure from the very principles (equity, proportionality, due process) that give it force.

Fifth, and finally, by contributing to understandings of violence, memory, membership, and law, re/membering promotes accountability. The term *accountability* encompasses multiple meanings, including justice (i.e., holding individuals or entities accountable for past actions); finance, as in calculating a balance, determining what is owed; and narrative, as when individuals produce an account (Nelson 2009). The migrant youths interviewed for this project invoked such notions as they recounted their own life histories, explicated their understandings of the way that U.S. law ought to work, and sought justice in the future. In particular, youths who were activists drew on traditions of *testimonio* and of memorialization, which deploy accounts of social injustice, victimization, or sacrifice in seeking to shape the future (Nance 2006). They spoke of the past, for example, to document an injustice that should be overcome, to call for policy changes, to challenge official accounts, or to commemorate an event that, it was hoped, would never be repeated. Testimony and memorialization therefore both produce and intervene in history. At the same time, U.S. immigration processes often solicit individual biographies—birthplaces, ages at time of entry, criminal records, achievements, victimization, experiences of persecution—even as they use this biographical information to predict future behavior (likelihood of future persecution, good moral character, credibility). By citing such facts within their own narratives, noncitizen interviewees emulated these criteria, suggesting that they deserved legal recognition. In other words, retelling one's own life history and situating this story within historical time *are* ways of demanding social justice, in this case, recognition of youths' multiple origins, unique identities, and (trans)national ties. When youth activists sought to recuperate historical memory by returning to El Salvador, the notion of what was "real" and what was merely a "technical" relationship shifted, as in one interviewee's comment that being able to travel to El Salvador would be like an adoptee seeking information about his or her birth parent. Likewise, if official histories are reifications that entail forgetting, then re/membering is a way to both recuperate and challenge the "real" (see also Antze and Lambek 1996). Such shifts raise questions about the relationship between knowledge and re/membering.

Can Ethnographies Re/member?

Though they are different practices—re/membering is a quest for self-knowledge, historical memory, and legal recognition, and ethnography produces academic knowledge—re/membering bears numerous resemblances to ethnography. While it does not strive to overcome violent disjuncture, as does re/membering, ethnography often *does* attempt to bridge differences between multiple social worlds. Historically, U.S. and European anthropologists employed ethnography to study small-scale non-Western societies, while sociologists conducted fieldwork to examine the lives of the urban poor (Emerson 2001). Today, anthropologists do not necessarily write about "faraway" places (Darian-Smith 2004); in fact, ethnographic research is now often conducted "at home," even in ethnographers' own institutions (e.g., Lederman 2006), while the field of anthropology has spread far beyond the United States and Europe. But the element of cultural translation remains core to the ethnography, as ethnographers attempt to make the worlds of physicists, law schools, financial institutions, United Nations personnel, and many other groups discernible to readers from potentially very different walks of life (Maurer 2006; Merry 2009; Mertz 2007; Traweek 2009).

Such efforts to bridge worlds employ the same sorts of temporal and spatial shifts that are key to re/membering. Marilyn Strathern (1999:1) writes that ethnographic practice "has always had a double location, both in . . . 'the field' and in the study, at the desk or on the lap." As Strathern explains, when ethnographers are in "the field," they are anticipating the later moment of writing, and when they are in the study, they reinhabit the field through the notes that they have taken. Ethnography therefore also employs multiple temporalities: it is "anticipatory" (9) but also backward-looking: "The writing only works, as the student discovers, as an imaginative re-creation of some of the effects of fieldwork itself" (1). This double location and multiple temporality are reminiscent of the conditions experienced by interviewees. Recall David Zavala's comment that "it's like I'm half here and half there and in between two worlds," or Jorge Rodríguez's remark that, even a year and a half after being deported, "Half of my mind is still in the United States and the other half is here, you know? I feel sometimes like I—I feel like I'm over there, you know?" Both re/membering and ethnography thus blur past and present, here and elsewhere, as they attempt to bridge gulfs created by violence or by social distances.

Through such temporal and spatial movements, origins take unanticipated forms, both for ethnographers and for those who re/member. Interviewees stressed the multiplicity of their origins. They were "Salvadorans from L.A.," "technically Salvadoran" but, "basically, U.S. citizens." According to such formulations, the significance of origin shifted over time. Being "technically Salvadoran" could turn out to be tremendously important, and being a "Salvadoran from L.A." meant that the initial origin of being born in El Salvador became something else (at a minimum, incomplete) in relation to a subsequent origin in the United States. Likewise, for ethnographers, origins are not always clear at the moment that they occur. To again turn to Strathern, "The would-be ethnographer gathers material whose use cannot be foreseen, facts and issues collected with little knowledge as to their connections. The result is a 'field' of information to which it is possible to return, intellectually speaking, in order to ask questions about subsequent developments whose trajectory was not evident at the outset" (9). In contrast to deductive sciences, in which research is conducted to confirm or disprove previously formulated hypotheses, ethnography proceeds inductively, with the analytical significance of facts, objects, and observations emerging over time. Much as the meaning of an origin in El Salvador is redefined in light of interviewees' present circumstances, so too do the importance and meaning of any particular piece of "data" only become fully apparent when the data are being employed in an ethnographic product, such as an article or book manuscript. Origins are thus simultaneously destinations to which one returns.

As the meanings of origin shift within both re/membering and ethnography, so too do the accounts that each produces simultaneously become both whole and partial. Re/membering seeks to piece together submerged histories, thus relocating individual biographies within national trajectories. In doing so it relies on, among other things, *testimonio*, according to which accounts of individual experiences are taken simultaneously as evidence of collective histories (Arias 2001). Thus, when student activist Pedro Marroquín trusted in "the power of personal narrative. . . . And using stories, I guess, as a tool to bring about change," he assumed that personal stories would be received and interpreted as instances of broader migrant experiences. Similarly, when ethnographers rely on interview material to illustrate broader social processes, they treat individual accounts as social narratives. The resulting account is simultaneously whole and partial. Ethnographers are well aware that knowledge is situated (Haraway 1988) and that accounts are produced from particular subject positions (Clifford 1988; Clifford and Marcus 1986). But at the same time, as I have written elsewhere, through a process of substitution, individual accounts are made to stand in for a whole: "A particular subset of informants is made to stand in for a society, a particular informant is made to stand in for this subset, an interview with this informant is made to stand in for the informant, a transcript or notes are made to stand in for the interview, and a quote from these notes is made to stand in for the entire interview" (Coutin 2005a:203). In this way, ethnographic truths are conveyed by assembling the record that makes them evident, just as re/membered accounts revisit the past in order to encounter and explain present realities.

Both ethnography and re/membering are thus committed to explication of the real, even as the incompleteness of any given account fuels a search for more knowledge. In seeking to uncover and publicize submerged histories, denied realities, and hidden truths, interviewees strived to overcome, rather than perpetuate, biases and silences. They were committed to documenting and disseminating the knowledge they hoped to acquire and convey, whether through poetry, narrative, research, journalism, or documentary filmmaking. When Marilyn Funes was confronted by her parents' silence about the reasons her family had come to the United States, she concluded, "I'm going to have to do my own—my own research." At the same time, these were also personal quests, informed by subjective experiences of trauma or by the desire to formulate better answers to the perennial questions "Who are you?" and "Where are you from?" Given the profundity of these questions, no answer could be complete. Likewise, anthropologists have been motivated by perspectivalism, "the late modern conception that all phenomena are infinitely complex and that all perspectives are only partial because the same information can be seen differently from another point of view" (Riles 2000:18). If knowledge is always partial, then more complete knowledge can be produced by adopting another perspective, changing scale, or moving to another vantage point. At the same time, in that it brings a field into being, each ethnography is complete in and of itself, and in fact, the very selection of a particular topic for ethnographic inquiry can be a form of claims making. As Carol Greenhouse (2011b) has documented, during the 1990s, as neoliberal political ideologies challenged the significance of social analysis and collective rights, U.S. ethnographers turned to studying communities in ways that amplified marginalized voices, insisted on the vitality of social life, and critiqued state policies (see, e.g., Bourgois 2003).

The understanding of particular accounts as simultaneously whole yet partial suggests that fact and fiction, science and subjectivity, are false dichotomies. Recall that for a number of interviewees, the "real" and the "fictive" shifted. As individuals who were raised in the United States, they felt that they had "real," substantive ties to and claims on the U.S. state, yet at the same time, many also described their relation to the United States as unreal or fictive, as like adoption, a fostering relationship, or illegitimacy. The reality of being from El Salvador also shifted. Recall that asylum applicant Juana Rocio, who was fighting removal, commented, "It's as if I was born here [in the United States]!" Similarly, if ethnographic truths are conveyed by assembling the record (interview excerpts, examples from fieldnotes) that makes them evident, then ethnographies are both accurate—the goal of such an account, as noted above, is to re-create the effects of the fieldwork experience—and inventions on the part of the ethnographer (Visweswaran 1994). Just as, within quantum physics, the act of measurement selects among multiple paths that a photon has actually taken (Greene 2004), so too do "ethnographic accounts retroactively instantiate realities that potentially existed all along" (Yngvesson and Coutin 2008:63). For these reasons, anthropology has been characterized as "the most disorderly and interdisciplinary of disciplines" within the social sciences (Marcus and Fischer 1986:22; see also Coutin and Fortin 2015).

How, then, to understand the present account? I would argue that this book in some ways participates in and reproduces the very practices of re/membering that it recounts. That is, I deliberately have sought to overcome disjunctures by narrating migrants' journeys, examining connections between multiple forms of violence, explicating what happens in gaps between the United States and El Salvador, recounting the experiences of deportees and continued U.S. residents in one book, and including snippets of my own experiences. As Paul Farmer (2004:309) notes, "richly socialized accounts," accounts populated with complex persons that are located historically and geographically, can challenge the silences that enable structural violence. Yet my claim to participate in re/membering is somewhat fraudulent in that the histories that the book re/members are not my own. I am not young, Salvadoran, undocumented, deported, or forbidden to travel internationally. So, in the end, all that my ethnography can do is to exist alongside the accounts produced by 1.5-generation and second-generation Salvadorans themselves. Yet, in some limited sense this account *is* my story, in that I was mobilized as an academic by Salvadorans who founded and participated in the solidarity movement of the 1980s. By "mobilized," I mean that I was drawn to the sanctuary movement as an object of ethnographic inquiry, and, since the 1980s, I have continued to study, write about, and engage in political and legal advocacy by and on behalf of Central Americans who immigrated to the United States during the Salvadoran civil war. I do worry that by making violence the origin point of my account, I have deemphasized other important aspects of interviewees' lives, such as parties, friendships, family relationships, or the richness of their lives. At the same time, I was compelled to write about the accounts that were entrusted to me. I recall the words of Rodolfo Martínez, a Temporary Protected Status (TPS) recipient who was working in construction and as a truck driver when I first met him. As our interview concluded, he commented:

> You know if one day you ever get to publish or, you know, bring all of these comments to life, you know, people will realize that, "Hey, look, we have history, you know. We—we, um," you know what I'm saying? I mean we came to this country, but, ah, I came as a child, but, I mean, um, I—I think I have a voice, you know, I mean.

I hope that this book *does* re/member and "bring all of these comments to life," that is, that it provides a detailed and accurate account of events that led interviewees to migrate, of their lives in the United States, of their returns to El Salvador, and of the continued significance (or, in some cases, insignificance; following the above comment, Rodolfo returned to an interview theme, telling me that "Salvadoran" was "just a name") of both countries in individuals' lives. I hope as well that, in providing this account, I simultaneously convey the nature of the membership claims that many interviewees sought to stake in the United States, El Salvador, or both countries.

What Are the Policy Implications of Re/membering?

Re/membering has clear policy implications: namely, to develop and support policies that recognize and take responsibility for historical inequities, promote inclusion, unite families, and foster conditions that would enable individuals to thrive within their countries of origin and destination. I therefore conclude by detailing specific policy objectives that would further these goals. I focus particularly on policies and policy-making principles that could be adopted in the United States. While these principles may be somewhat utopian, clear and practical policy implications can be derived from them. As well, circumstances can change so that what is unthinkable at one moment becomes viable in the next. A case in point is the passage of the Nicaraguan Adjustment and Central American Relief Act (NACARA), discussed in chapters 1 and 4. After the Illegal Immigration Reform and Immigrant Responsibility Act became law in 1996, Central American advocates were advised that the political situation was so strongly restrictionist that it was pointless to seek relief for Central Americans with pending asylum applications. Advocates ignored this advice and moved forward anyway, forging an alliance with beneficiaries of the Nicaraguan Review Program. As a result, NACARA was approved in 1997. The policy recommendations that I outline below could likewise gain traction in the future.

1. Recognize and promote accountability for multiple forms of violence. Recognizing, instead of downplaying, human rights abuses being perpetrated by the Salvadoran government during the civil war ought to have required the United States to withdraw its support for Salvadoran authorities. According to a number of analysts (e.g., Byrne 1996; DeLugan 2012:3; Montgomery 1995), such a withdrawal of support would likely have meant that the war would have ended more quickly. The United States has recognized that it has a particular responsibility to the victims of the Central American civil wars; this was one reason for awarding TPS to Salvadorans in 1990 and passing NACARA in 1997. However, delays in creating these remedies meant that many Salvadorans were left without protection for years. Furthermore, earlier destabilization in these countries has resulted in continued violence, now of a "criminal" rather than explicitly "political" nature, to the degree that such a distinction can be drawn. To avoid repeating the exclusions of the war years, it is important to consider expanding the grounds for asylum such that victims of multiple forms of violence could be acknowledged. Individuals who are being targeted for gang recruitment could be recognized as a social group, and, of course, they would have to meet the stringent requirements needed to win asylum. Given the current volume of unaccompanied minors from Central America, a more efficient alternative might simply be to grant TPS to these new arrivals.

Violence and accountability could also be promoted through the U.S. educational system. Recall interviewees' complaints that no one, including themselves, really knew about their own histories and that teachers rarely spoke of the civil war. U.S. textbooks could be revised to include detailed accounts of the Central American civil wars, U.S. involvement in these conflicts, and the causes of Central American immigration to the United States. At the college level, universities could support multi-ethnic, multicampus, transnational student organizations and writing collectives in order to enable Central Americans and other groups to explore their own histories. To further acknowledge U.S. involvement in the civil conflicts in Central America and to promote historical memory, a national memorial could be constructed, with input from Central Americans who live within the United States. Such a memorial would build on the more limited forms of recognition that already exist, such as the stone placed in Arlington National Cemetery to acknowledge U.S. soldiers who died in El Salvador or the statue of Archbishop Romero in MacArthur Park in Los Angeles.

2. *Foster inclusion by giving weight to substantive ties.* Re/membering also suggests the importance of granting legal recognition to the substantive ties that immigrants, particularly those who arrive as children, develop in the United States. Of course, there has been some recent movement in that direction, with the creation of the Deferred Action for Childhood Arrivals (DACA) program in 2012. Furthermore, U.S. immigration law has long given special consideration to children, through provisions designed to promote family unity (e.g., adults are often able to include their minor children in their own immigration cases), through case law granting children the right to attend public schools regardless of immigration status, and through exemptions for undocumented children under the age of eighteen so that they do not accrue an "unlawful presence" in the United States. Yet, as the interview material analyzed in this book indicates, such provisions do not go far enough. To further recognize the substantive ties to the United States that immigrant children develop, I suggest that those who arrive at young ages—say, under the age of sixteen, to use DACA's definition of childhood arrivals—and live in the United States continuously for a specified period of time, such as five years, could be regarded as de facto lawful permanent residents for immigration purposes (Trager and Coutin n.d.). While the details of such a proposal would need to be determined, such a designation would ideally formalize the de facto residency of childhood arrivals by granting them green cards, employment authorization, the ability to reenter the United States after departing, and eligibility to naturalize after five years of a formalized status. Such an approach would build on legal doctrines, such as those underlying adverse possession and common-law marriage, that allow for the formalization of relationships (ownership, marriage) that have existed publicly for an extended period of time but have not been legally acknowledged.

Short of formalizing de facto residency, several other measures would give greater legal weight to the substantive ties to the United States that child migrants develop. Most prominently, passage of the DREAM Act, an explicit goal of a number of interviewees, would enable undocumented students to regularize their status based on their age at time of immigration, the number of years lived within the United States, and educational or military service accomplishments. Inclusion could also be promoted by legislation that would automatically grant TPS holders the right to adjust their status after a specified period of time, say, five years. Such legislation would eliminate the legal uncertainty that many TPS recipients currently experience. The social inclusion of noncitizens with criminal convictions could be promoted by restoring their eligibility for 212(c) waivers for discretionary relief from deportation or removal—these waivers were eliminated by immigration reforms adopted in 1996. Prior to 1996, to obtain a 212(c) waiver, a noncitizen who had been convicted of crimes and who was in deportation proceedings went before an immigration judge, who had the discretion to assess whether the respondent's equities in the United States outweighed the harm associated with the respondent's criminal or immigration offense. If it was determined that they did not, then the respondent would be deported, but if they did, then the waiver would be issued. Such an approach would ensure that those who are being deported do not belong in the United States and would be an improvement on the overly inclusive categorical approach being used currently.

3. *Enable international travel.* There are three international travel challenges faced by dismembered populations. The first is the challenge of traveling without authorization. To address this challenge, the United States could adopt sustainable immigration procedures that meet the nation's labor needs, while also prioritizing family reunification and humanitarian concerns. I am not advocating that the United States admit everyone who desires to enter; however, there clearly is a discrepancy between the targets currently set for labor, family, and refugee migration, and the reality that greater numbers of individuals are entering the country to work, join family members, or seek safety than these targets would allow. It is time to bring these targets and needs into sync so that family members can be together, labor needs can be met, and those in harm's way can find safety, all without exposing individuals to the trauma of unauthorized migration. These goals can be met by reducing wait times for family visa petitions, more closely adjusting employment-related immigration to current labor needs, and ensuring that refugee admissions remain robust. I therefore concur with the legal scholar Hiroshi Motomura's (2010) call for strengthening our existing admissions programs in ways that are more attentive to current immigration-related priorities. Noting that one-time legalization programs are

backward-looking and do little to fix future immigration challenges, Motomura has suggested several measures, including (1) restoring 245(i), the section of the Immigration and Nationality Act that allows individuals to adjust their status in the United States instead of returning to their countries of origin and thus triggering bars to reentry; (2) restoring discretionary relief from removal, as I advocated above; and (3) reworking admissions categories to admit more unskilled laborers and "to relax or repeal numerical limits that currently cap immigrant admissions in many categories on a country-by-country basis" (231).[4]

The second international travel challenge is experienced by temporarily authorized individuals, such as TPS holders, who cannot reenter the United States legally after traveling outside the country, unless they first obtain advance parole from immigration officials. Numerous interviewees spoke of the hardships associated with lengthy separations from family members. These hardships could be mitigated by granting TPS recipients travel authorization. They then would not be trapped within U.S. borders.

The third international travel challenge is faced by deportees who are prohibited from reentering the United States. This challenge could be addressed by making humanitarian travel visas available to deportees who had family members in the United States and who could provide evidence that they were likely to comply with the terms of their visas. Such evidence might include steady employment in their country of origin, law-abidingness for a specified period of time, character references, evidence of rehabilitation (if appropriate), or even posting a financial deposit that they could reclaim upon returning after the expiration of their visas. Permitting such visits would help to address the emotional consequences of family separations for deportees and their children who do not qualify for 212(c) waivers. Taken together, reforms that enable international travel would reduce both the harms associated with unauthorized movement and the illicit economies of gangs, traffickers, and smugglers that facilitate such movement.

4. *Support the "right not to emigrate."* Over the past decade, immigrant rights advocates in El Salvador have begun to advocate for *el derecho de no emigrar*, or the right not to emigrate. By advocating for the right not to emigrate, activists seek to mobilize state and nonstate entities to foster conditions that enable citizens to thrive within their countries of origin. These conditions include the ability to work, go to school, have a family, be involved in civic issues, and move about in safety. To quote the 2010 report of the United Nations Global Forum on Migration and Development:

Participants at this session [regarding joint strategies to address irregular migration] recognized the lack of development in the countries of origin as one of the causes of irregular migration. Therefore, many delegates also stressed the need for sustainable development in the countries of origin, including decent labour conditions, as a way of giving people the right to not migrate. It was also suggested that it is important to overcome the economic imbalances between countries. (22)

While the best way to promote sustainable development is open to debate, the United States could adopt a more holistic approach to immigration policy, one that evaluates U.S. economic and foreign policies in relation to their potential to foster education, job opportunities, and security within individuals' home communities. Policies such as the Central America Free Trade Agreement, for example, have been criticized for provoking the current influx of unaccompanied children from Central America (Perla 2014).

If some subset of these policy recommendations were adopted, then perhaps there would be a new origin point, one that would give rise to an era in which immigration policies cease to be hot-button political issues because fewer people feel compelled to leave their countries of origin, and countries, families, and persons are not dismembered. Only the passage of time will reveal whether or not this is possible. And, of course, origins often only become apparent after the fact.

SPRING 1982. I sat at a table in the dining room of what was then called the Ridge Project Co-op, at the University of California in Berkeley, where I was an undergraduate student. As I ate cereal and milk before rushing off to class, I read the *San Francisco Chronicle*. Headlines about death-squad killings in El Salvador leapt out at me. How, I wondered, could people be so cruel to each other? I then headed off to class, not yet able to see my future self: marching through the streets of San Francisco during a protest focusing on U.S. Central American policy, joining an (at the time, dwindling) student action group at Stanford, making the sanctuary movement the subject of my dissertation research, sorting donated clothing in the basement of a Northern California sanctuary congregation, helping to complete asylum applications for ABC class members, sitting with activists in a restaurant in El Salvador while flashes of lightning illuminated volcanoes hidden by the darkness, attending an immigrant rights rally in Washington D.C., accompanying members of a nongovernmental organization who delivered earthquake relief to devastated villages in the Salvadoran countryside, eating *pupusas* in Los Angeles with student activists, munching on chicken wings in San Salvador with young men who had been deported from the United States, and much more. In 1982, while some of the people I would eventually interview for this book were already making their way to the United States, I did not yet know the degree to which I would be shaped by events that this conflict set into motion. Nor can I now predict what the future holds. All I can do is re/member.

"Central American-American" by Maya Chinchilla

Centralamerican   American
does that come with a hyphen?
a space?
Central   America
America
América
Las Américas

Español chapín
black beans and white rice
tortillas de maiz almost an inch thick
refugees and exiles
as playmates
movies with trembling
mountains, bombs and
gunfire raging in my heart.
black lists and secrets.
Huipiles and mysterious people
passing through my home.

Where is the center of America, anyway?
Are there flowers on a volcano?

You can find the center in my heart
where I imagine the flowers never die

But today the volcano explodes in the way
it has every day for 30 years.
No it is not a sacrifice it desires,
for we already have sacrificed too much.

They want us out of this country
they say we don't belong here
vamos pa' el norte
they tell us the American dream is the truth
but that our stories of escape from horror are not.
When can we rest from running?
When will the explosions in my heart stop
and show me where my home is?

Are there flowers on a volcano?
am I a CENTRAL
American?
Where is the center of America?

Reprinted with the permission of Maya Chinchilla. "Central American-American" appeared in
La Revista (University of Santa Cruz, 1999) and has also been published in Maya Chinchilla, *The
Cha Cha Files: A Chapina Poética* (San Francisco: Kórima Press, 2014), and in *Desde el EpiCentro:
An Anthology of U.S. Central American Poetry and Art*, edited by Maya Chinchilla and Karina
Oliva-Alvarado (Los Angeles: Epicentro, 2007).

"hybrideities" by GusTavo Guerra Vásquez

Kukulcán
Quetzalcoatl
hybrid names for a hybrid god

Our next millennium
brings in its basket of goodies
more hybrid names
for bridges
people of hope:

GuateMayAngelino
GuanaMex
Guanachapín
GuanaChapílena
GuanaChapiMex
ChapiCano
GuanaCatraChapicana

GuaNiCatraChapicano
TicoGuanaCatraChapicanAngelina

and the list continues . . .
as does our struggle
and our hope.

"hibrideidades" by GusTavo Guerra Vásquez

Quetzalcoatl
Kukulcán

nombres híbridos
deidad híbrida

el próximo milenio
trae en su costal
más nombres híbridos
para gente especial
puentes de esperanza
entre nuestra comunidad

GuateMayAngelino
GuanaMex
Guanachapín
GuanaChapílena
GuanaChapiMex
ChapiCano
GuanaCatraChapicana
GuaNiCatraChapicano
TicoGuanaCatraChapicanAngelina

y la lista continua
igual que la lucha
y la esperanza

Reprinted with the permission of GusTavo Guerra Vásquez. "hybrideities" and "hibrideidades" were published in *Desde el EpiCentro: An Anthology of U.S. Central American Poetry and Art*, edited by Maya Chinchilla and Karina Oliva-Alvarado (Los Angeles: Epicentro, 2007).

Introduction

1. An image of dismemberment—a hand that is missing two fingers—has also been used in images commemorating the 9/11 destruction of the Twin Towers (Micieli-Voutsinas 2010).

2. As Farmer (2004:308) notes, "Erasure or distortion of history is perhaps the most common explanatory sleight-of-hand relied upon by the architects of structural violence." See also Hall 1996; Thompson 1975; Williams 1977; Zúñiga Núñez 2010.

3. Examples include Coutin and Hirsch 1998; Deloria 1969; DeLugan 2012; Hamber and Wilson 2002; Moodie 2011; and Taylor 1997.

4. Analyses of such scapegoating include Chavez 2001, 2003, 2008; Higham 2002; Perea 1997; and Suárez-Orozco and Suárez-Orozco 1995.

5. Relatedly, Johnson (1996:268) notes that "the term alien masks the privilege of citizenship and helps to justify the legal status quo."

6. I do not mean to imply that emigration necessarily or naturally creates deep schisms. Rather, I join Jansen and Löfving in calling for study of "the unequal, differential, and contested processes by which persons come to be (dis)associated—and (dis) associate themselves—with or from place" (2009:6).

7. Depoliticization and discursive transformation are analyzed in Anker 1992; Godoy 2002, 2005; Goldstein 2010; and Moodie 2006.

8. For accounts of such "returns," see Hondagneu-Sotelo and Ávila 1997; Yngvesson and Coutin 2006; and Zavella 2011.

9. These ambiguous or liminal zones are discussed in Bauböck 1994; Bosniak 2006; Chavez 1992; Hammar 1990; and Menjívar 2006.

10. *American Baptist Churches v. Thornburgh*, 760 F. Supp. 796 (N.D. Cal. 1991).

11. And, of course, not all ethnographers agree that it is possible to arrive at "truth"—see Clifford 1986.

12. Note that Golash-Boza and Hondagneu-Sotelo (2013) estimate that 85 percent of individuals who are deported from the United States are male.

13. As Ruth Behar (1993:271) notes, "any ethnographic representation . . . inevitably includes a self-representation."

14. For a discussion of the role of personal narratives within social science research, see Maynes, Pierce, and Laslett 2008.

15. I thank William Flores for sharing the script of *De la locura a la esperanza*. This quotation comes from the testimony of Rufina Amaya, in Amaya, Danner, and Henríquez Consalvi 2008:20. Translation by author.

16. The song "Que canten los niños" was written by José Luis Perales. The complete lyrics are available at www.musica.com/letras.asp?letra=84753. Translation by author.

17. This quotation is taken from the script, but it also echoes the conclusion of Rufina Amaya's testimony, in Amaya, Danner, and Henríquez Consalvi 2008. Translation by author.

1. Violence and Silence

1. By the late 1980s, the civil conflict had reached a stalemate until, in November 1989, the guerrilla forces entered San Salvador in what came to be known as the *ofensiva final* (the final offensive). During this final offensive, the Salvadoran military also assassinated six Jesuit priests, their housekeeper, and the housekeeper's daughter.

2. See Farmer 1996, 2004, 2005; Greenhouse 2011a; Kleinman, Das, and Lock 1997; Menjívar 2011a; and Scheper-Hughes 1993.

3. Work that theorizes and problematizes distinctions between legal and other forms of violence includes Benjamin 1978; Cover 1986; Jansen and Löfving 2009; Sarat 2014; and Sarat and Kearns 1995.

4. U.S. asylum law is more likely to recognize violence that is physical, politically motivated, and directly inflicted by a clearly identifiable perpetrator than that which is psychological, criminal or economic, indirect, and structural or nonagentive. An example of the former would be a government detaining and torturing a well-known political dissident. An example of the latter would include feeling terrified due to living in a village that was bombed on a regular basis.

5. Silences regarding the Salvadoran civil war are discussed in Churgin 1996; Hamilton and Chinchilla 1991; Menjívar 2000; and Zolberg 1990. For silences within other national contexts, see Cho 2008 and Raj 2000.

6. Of course, this particular erasure and dismemberment is only one in a long line of erasures. Equally, the 1932 *matanza*, in which indigenous peasants were killed throughout El Salvador, could be traced as an origin point. See DeLugan 2012 for a discussion of recent commemorations of that period of Salvadoran history, and see Taylor and Vanden 1982 for an analysis of the connections between the *matanza* and the Salvadoran civil war.

7. According to international human rights law, governments are responsible for guaranteeing the rights of their citizens; when that does not occur or, worse yet, when the

government of a particular country violates its own citizens' human rights, then such a government simultaneously defines those who are targeted as outside the boundaries of the nation. Note that chapter 1, article 1, of the 1967 United Nations Convention Relating to the Status of Refugees defines a refugee, in part, as an individual who "owing to well-founded fear of being persecuted for reasons of race, religion, nationality, membership of a particular social group or political opinion, is outside the country of his nationality and is unable or, owing to such fear, is unwilling *to avail himself of the protection of that country*" (see unhcr.org/3b66c2aa10.html; emphasis added).

8. The FMLN was made up of five organizations: the FPL (Fuerzas Populares de Liberación; Popular Forces of Liberation), the ERP (Ejército Revolucionario del Pueblo; Revolutionary Army of the People), the FARN (Fuerzas Armadas de la Resistencia Nacional; Armed Forces of National Resistance), the PCS (Partido Comunista de El Salvador; Communist Party of El Salvador), and the PRTC (Partido Revolucionario de los Trabajadores Centroamericanos; Revolutionary Party of Central American Workers). See Brockett 2005; Byrne 1996; and Montgomery 1995.

9. The original quotation is "las heridas creadas en un momento histórico específico, donde las relaciones sociales han cristalizado de una forma determinada."

10. For a complex account of migrant smuggling, see Spener 2009.

11. See U.S. Citizenship and Immigration Services, "Temporary Protected Status Extended for Salvadorans," www.uscis.gov and http://www.uscis.gov/humanitarian /temporary-protected-status/temporary-protected-status-designated-country-el -salvador.

12. Identifying details have been changed in order to maintain the interviewee's confidentiality.

13. You can lose your LPR status if you "remain outside of the United States for more than 1 year without obtaining a reentry permit or returning resident visa. However, in determining whether your status has been abandoned, any length of absence from the United States may be considered, even if less than 1 year." See U.S. Citizenship and Immigration Services, "Maintaining Permanent Residence," www.uscis.gov.

2. Living in the Gap

1. My concept of social history, by which I mean a history of the day-to-day lives of ordinary people—in contrast to historical accounts that focus on central events and major political figures—derives from my reading of E. P. Thompson's work (1963, 1975). It also owes something to Latin American traditions of *testimonio* and to the influence of one of my mentors, Renato Rosaldo, who advocated that anthropologists attend to history (1980).

2. Of course, the literature on immigrant incorporation does recognize that the existence of co-ethnics as well as immigrant-founded businesses and services that cater to new arrivals can facilitate incorporation.

3. In 2013, this largely Latino and low-income school was ranked at 3 on a 10-point scale. See http://school-ratings.com/school_details/19647336058341.html.

4. Suárez-Orozco and Suárez-Orozco (1995) also found that new immigrants who are adolescents are generally committed to education, have positive impressions of their schools, and achieve at high rates.

5. Che Guevara was an Argentine activist known for his involvement in the revolutionary movement in Cuba.

6. Roque Dalton was a Salvadoran poet who was also involved in the Salvadoran left.

7. *Raza* literally means "race" and is a short-hand way of referring to those of Latino descent.

8. Indeed, when I have met first-generation Salvadoran immigrants for interviews, I have sometimes been told that it was the first time that they had spoken to a white person.

9. Cruz Salazar (2011:152) observes, "La manera en que la representación de México—'país latinoamericano vanguardista en el aspecto económico'—frente a la representación de los países centroamericanos—'las naciones menos desarrolladas de todo el continente'—incide significativamente en las relaciones sociales, en particular, en las formas de identificar y tratar a las centroamericanas migrantes en la frontera sur mexicana." [Translation: The way in which the representation of Mexico—"a vanguard Latin American country in economic aspects"—contrasted with the representation of the Central American countries—"the least developed nations in the whole continent"—significantly influences social relations, in particular, in the ways of identifying and treating Central American migrants on the Southern Mexican border.]

10. To give another example, Juan José told me, "I meet somebody—I've probably known them for a while, maybe they're not my friend, just somebody I know from school, and I've known them for a couple of quarters. And, you know, they're okay with me. You know, they seemed like a cool person and everything. And then they ask me, 'Oh, where are you from?' And then I tell them I'm Salvadoran. And then they start—they start saying—they start talking the slang of Salvadorans. Or, you know, mocking me or something. I'm like what's—what's going on? You know I find *that* very uncomfortable. I—I—and they start like . . . , 'Oh *vos*, and la, la.' And I'm like oh my gosh. You know like why did you have to do this? I don't like you anymore."

11. If Central Americans successfully "passed" as Mexican, then they would only be deported to Mexico instead of all the way to Central America, thus making their return journeys easier.

12. *Vos* is a way to say "you" that is common in El Salvador, but that is generally not used in Mexico.

13. Such creative alternatives are reminiscent of the Third Culture Kids movement, made up of "people who have spent a portion of their formative childhood years (0–18) in a culture different than their parents" (see www.denizenmag.com/third-culture-kid/). I thank Keramet Reiter for bringing this connection to my attention.

3. Dreams

1. Betancur and Garcia's analysis creatively combines resource mobilization theory, poor people's movements theory, and new movement theory (Jiménez 2011; McCarthy and Zald 1977; Piven and Cloward 1977; Tilly 1979).

2. Gonzalez links the marches to a history of Latino activism, a history that includes the 1970s Chicano movement, the 1980s Central American solidarity movement, and the 1990s protests against California Proposition 187, which would have required

various service providers to check the immigration status of their clients. See Abrego 2008; R. Gonzalez 2008; and Martin 1995 for details.

3. On generational differences between immigrant parents and children more generally, see Suárez-Orozco and Suárez-Orozco 1995.

4. On Salvadoran immigrant youths' desire to give back, see Súarez-Orozco 1987.

5. Beth Baker-Cristales (2004b:16) argues that, in El Salvador, first-generation migrants had "class-based notions of collectivity" but that, in the United States, they developed "national-ethnic forms of social identity."

6. King and Punti found that undocumented youths "experience their immigration status not as an administrative or bureaucratic obstacle, but as essential to their experience and enmeshed with their racial identity" (2012:246).

7. There is, in fact, a rich literature both about Central America and produced by Central Americans in the United States, so this complaint reflects not a lack of literature, but possibly that some interviewees' educational experiences had not exposed them sufficiently to it.

8. On the benefits of Chicano studies courses in creating a supportive atmosphere and positive student-university relationships, see Nuñez 2011.

9. According to the UCLA USEU website (http://www.studentgroups.ucla.edu/home /index.php/clubs/clubslist?withcat=27): "The purpose of 'la Union Salvadorena de Estudiantes Universitarios' is to empower the Salvadoran student community through the promotion of higher education by: (1) Developing an interest towards higher education amongst the Salvadoran community; (2) Developing an awareness of cultural, political, and economic issues that directly affect the Salvadoran community; (3) Preserving the historical and cultural identity of El Salvador; (4) Mobilizing the Salvadoran student population to take action through higher education. The purpose of the national governing board is to coordinate and direct USEU activity throughout the Nation."

10. For an example of an anthology focused on the narratives of Asian American students, see Garrod and Kilkenny 2007.

11. In discussing the work of emerging Central American artists and writers, I wish neither to imply homogeneity of thought nor to ignore other U.S. Central American writers and scholars, who have been producing important work for some time. My account is necessarily incomplete, as I only encountered some of these new writers.

12. Its website describes Epicentro as follows: "From the center of America erupts Epicentro: an organic literary collective straddling performance, spoken word and testimonial artforms, composed of inter-generational community-minded cultural activists of Central American extraction that write to resurrect memory and inspire action." See http://epicentroamerica.blogspot.com/2007/09/desde-el-epicentro .html (accessed August 30, 2012).

13. Some details in this account have been changed to protect confidentiality.

4. Exiled Home through Deportation

1. I do not have sufficient information or the legal expertise to evaluate their chances of qualifying for a waiver. However, a guide prepared by Boston College's Post-deportation Human Rights Project warns, "If you have been ordered removed and

have left the U.S., it will probably be extremely difficult to obtain permission to permanently return. In order to do so, you will need two things: an approved visa petition, and a waiver of inadmissibility. If you are applying to return to the United States permanently, you will be applying for an immigrant visa (this is the same thing as a green card). People who have been removed from the United States have unique challenges to overcome before they can get an immigrant visa" (6). Available at www .bc.edu/content/dam/files/centers/humanrights/pdf/Returning%20to%20the%20 US%20AFter%20Deportation-%20self-assmt%20guide_UPD.pdf (accessed October 2, 2014).

2. U.S. Department of Homeland Security 2006.

3. U.S. Immigration and Customs Enforcement 2013.

4. U.S. Immigration and Customs Enforcement 2013.

5. Sally Merry defines the archaeology of law as a "historical analysis of layers of legality and the historical contexts of their deposition." She further notes "the archeology metaphor suggests simple contiguity in chronological order, but in practice each system affects the operation of the others" (2004:570).

6. In contrast, Janis Jenkins notes that "the systematic deployment of terror as a means of coercion defies distinction between actual violence and the threat of immanent violence. Is not the display of mutilated bodies more than the result of violence or the threat of violence, but a form of violence itself?" (1998:124).

7. As a Congressional Research Service report explains, "In 1987, Attorney General Edwin Meese initiated a Nicaraguan Review Program (NRP) that required extended review of deportation orders issued against Nicaraguans. Thereafter, few deportable Nicaraguans were actually removed, and those who remained were allowed to work" (Eig 1998:1).

8. The complexity of the settlement agreement, which required sending particular notices to applicants, made ABC asylum petitions a lower priority for the asylum unit than non-ABC cases. Additionally, there was some expectation on the part of both the ABC class counsel and at least some immigration officials that an alternative remedy would be created for ABC class members, making adjudication of their claims unnecessary.

9. The IIRIRA provisions adversely affected not only Salvadoran and Guatemalan ABC class members but also Nicaraguans, who had been permitted to remain in the United States without a permanent status even if they were denied asylum. Salvadorans, Guatemalans, and Nicaraguans joined forces to request relief, and the Central American governments, concerned about reduced remittances and the impact of deportations, pressured the U.S. government to assist their nationals. The Clinton administration responded favorably to these governments' concerns. At a May 1997 summit meeting, Bill Clinton told the Central American presidents that it would be problematic for the United States to deport Central Americans who had lengthy ties to the United States and who supported their countries through family remittances. In addition, at least some U.S. immigration officials supported restoring suspension eligibility to ABC class members and NRP participants. Tellingly, this act was originally called the Victims of Communism Relief Act.

10. "Continuous presence" has been given a precise legal meaning in that brief, casual,

and innocent absences totaling less than 180 days are not considered an interruption. "Presence" is a legal construct in that, historically, individuals who were paroled into the United States without going through a formal admission (for example, in the case of a delayed entry inspection) were deemed to be outside of the country, seeking admission (and therefore were subject to exclusion rather than to deportation). Legal presence can also be produced through territorial rituals. For example, individuals who are in the United States and who become eligible to adjust their status to that of permanent residents (through a family visa petition) have usually had to return to their country of origin to secure a visa before reentering the United States with their new status. Similarly, during the *bracero* program, U.S. officials legalized or "dried out" undocumented workers by bringing them across the U.S.-Mexico border and then issuing them a permit to reenter the country legally (Calavita 1992; de Genova 2004). Enforcement tactics have also taken territorial forms, in that immigrant-receiving countries have treated particular spaces as being "outside" of national territories for immigration purposes (Hyndman and Mountz 2008).

11. The trace that remains behind evokes the hip hop video for "They Can't Deport All of Us" by Chingo Bling, which, as Kurt Newman points out in his blog post "The Not-All, Revisited (Chingo Bling and the Politics of Interruption, Part III)," could mean either that it is impossible for everyone to be deported or that if someone *is* deported, not all of the person disappears (http://s-usih.org/2014/03/the-not-all-revisited-chingo-bling-and-the-politics-of-interruption-part-iii.html).

12. As an extreme example of unreality, see Délano and Nienass 2014 for an analysis of the invisibility of undocumented immigrants who are presumed to have died during the 9/11 attacks on the World Trade Center. Due to their immigration status, there was insufficient evidence of their presence to acknowledge them in the 9/11 memorial.

13. The Migration Policy Institute reported that the number of immigration detainees per day averaged 6,785 in 1994, and that in 2008, this figure had grown to 33,400 per day. This report also details the amount of time individuals spend in detention (Kerwin and Lin 2009).

14. Such differences in legal rights may be a key factor in why U.S. authorities sometimes charge noncitizens with immigration violations instead of with crimes (Cole and Dempsey 2006; Eagly 2010).

15. See Rivas 2014 for an analysis of Salvadoran call centers' willingness to hire deportees. She writes, "Speaking English 'like a native,' often perceived as a sign of integration into mainstream society in the United States, becomes entangled with a history of deportation from the United States" (111).

5. Biographies and Nations

1. Indeed, the emotional power of this narrative exceeds my analysis here.

2. In this sense, migrant youth can also feel both countryless and that they have "too much country" (Behar 1996:142).

3. The sense of illegitimacy, of being somehow outside of the law, was also conveyed by Julian Becerra, who told me that he wanted to legalize in the United States, but "there's no law that covers" him beyond TPS.

4. As has long been noted, kinship and national belonging intersect in that citizenship can be passed on through filiation, the idea of a *patria*, fatherland, or motherland defines a nation's citizens or subjects as its children; and membership in a nation is thought to be a natural or ascribed quality, part of one's "blood" (Anderson 1983; Collier and Yanagisako 1983; Gellner 1983; Schneider 1968). Cho (2008:194–195) also notes that "the ties that bind are not confined to those of family or nation but are formed by a kinship of trauma and its uncertainties."

5. The U.S. Citizenship and Immigration Services website (www.uscis.gov/forms /n-600-application-certificate-citizenship-frequently-asked-questions; accessed August 6, 2014) explains these requirements as follows:

If you are claiming U.S. citizenship after birth, your birth out of wedlock may affect your ability to acquire citizenship through your mother depending on when you turned 18 years of age.

- If you were over 18 years of age on February 27, 2001, and you were born out of wedlock, you generally could only acquire citizenship after birth through your mother if your paternity had not been established by legitimation.
- If you were under 18 years of age on February 27, 2001, or were born after that date, you can acquire U.S. citizenship through your U.S. citizen mother regardless of whether you were born out of wedlock if, before you turn 18, your mother is a citizen and you are residing in the U.S. based on a lawful admission for permanent residence in the legal and physical custody of your U.S. citizen mother.

I am claiming U.S. citizenship through my father. My parents were not married at the time of my birth. Does this affect whether I automatically acquired citizenship? It may. If you were born out of wedlock, are claiming that you acquired U.S. citizenship at the time of your birth, and you were born after November 14, 1986, you must demonstrate:

- That your father was physically present in the United States for 5 years, at least 2 of which were after 14 years of age;
- A blood relationship with your father by clear and convincing evidence;
- That your father was a U.S. citizen at the time of your birth;
- That your father (unless deceased) has agreed in writing to provide financial support for you until you reach 18 years of age; *and*
- While you are under 18 years of age
  ◦ You are legitimated under the law of your residence or domicile;
  ◦ Your father acknowledges paternity of you in writing under oath; *or*
  ◦ Your paternity is established by a court.

If you were born out of wedlock, are claiming that you acquired U.S. citizenship at the time of your birth, and you were born between January 13, 1941, and November 14, 1986, you must establish that your paternity was established by legitimation while you were under the age of 21.

6. Of course, the deported population includes many individuals who are not 1.5-generation migrants. In an interview with a high-level official in the Salvadoran General Directorate of Immigration (Dirección General de Migración y Extranjería),

I was told that 38.6 percent of deportees were ages 18–25, 33 percent were 26–33, 19 percent were 34–41, 6 percent were 42–49, and 3 percent were "other." I was also informed that, in a recent period, 724 people who were deported had been captured crossing the border, 542 had lived in the United States for 1–8 years, 222 had lived there for 9–16 years, and 130 had lived in the United States for 16–24 years. In my sample, the average number of years that individuals had lived outside of El Salvador was 16.17.

7. For discussions of criminal and immigration law, see Chacón 2007; Eagly 2010; and Velloso 2013.

8. President Obama's announcement of executive relief in November 2014 replaced Secure Communities with the Priority Enforcement Program, which is intended to be more targeted in focusing immigration law enforcement against individuals who have been convicted of crimes and/or fall into key priority areas. For an explanation of the differences between Secure Communities and the Priority Enforcement Program, see National Immigration Law Center 2014.

9. Unfortunately, I cannot evaluate whether or not they are correct. However, there have been documented instances in which U.S. citizens have been deported. See *Orange County Register* 2007.

10. Moreover, as "museum-going is connected to civilizing practices that produce national subjects" (DeLugan 2012:109), youths' participation in delegations, which also visited other sites, potentially produced alternative versions of such subjects.

11. In fact, a film, *Children of the Diaspora: For Peace and Democracy*, was made by Jennifer Cárcamo (see www.facebook.com/ChildrenoftheDiaspora).

12. Interestingly, interviewees' repeated instances that they were from Los Angeles, a city, may reflect ambivalence about claiming to be "American." Similarly, in their ethnographic research about 1.5-generation and second-generation immigrants in New York, Kasinitz, Mollenk and Waters (2004:17) found that "many respondents sidestepped this ambivalent understanding of the meaning of being American by describing themselves as 'New Yorkers.'"

Conclusion

1. Menjívar (2011a:41, emphasis in the original) points out that gang activity has flourished, particularly in the Central American countries "with a recent history of *state* violence (not just political conflict) that targeted their own people."

2. Butler (2003, 2009) notes the importance of attending to which lives and which losses are grievable. In this sense, if the nation fails to grieve over the losses of those who are deported, then the nation itself is harmed as a result.

3. Coddington (2011:752) argues that "haunting collapses time, bringing the past into and thereby permanently altering the present."

4. The other measures that Motomura proposes are (4) international economic development programs to reduce demand for immigration, (5) investing more deeply in education in the United States, and (6) continuing to focus on immigration law enforcement.

REFERENCES

Abrego, Leisy. 2008. "Legitimacy, Social Identity, and the Mobilization of Law: The Effects of Assembly Bill 540 on Undocumented Students in California." *Law and Social Inquiry* 33(3): 709–734.

———. 2009. "Economic Well-Being in Salvadoran Transnational Families: How Gender Affects Remittance Practices." *Journal of Marriage and Family* 71(4): 1070–1085.

———. 2011. "Legal Consciousness of Undocumented Latinos: Fear and Stigma as Barriers to Claims-Making for First-and 1.5-Generation Immigrants." *Law and Society Review* 45(2): 337–370.

———. 2014a. "Rejecting Obama's Deportation and Drug War Surge on Central American Kids." *Huffington Post,* July 9. Available at www.huffingtonpost.com/leisy-j -abrego/. Accessed September 24, 2014.

———. 2014b. *Sacrificing Families: Navigating Laws, Labor, and Love across Borders.* Stanford, CA: Stanford University Press.

Abrego, Leisy J., and Roberto G. Gonzales 2010. "Blocked Paths, Uncertain Futures: The Postsecondary Education and Labor Market Prospects of Undocumented Latino Youth." *Journal of Education for Students Placed at Risk* 15(1–2): 144–157.

Aguilera Peralta, Gabriel Edgardo, Ricardo Córdova Macías, and Francisco López Rodríguez. 1988. *El Salvador: Límites y alcances de una pacificación negociada.* No. 11. Mexico City, Mexico: Centro de Investigación y Acción Social (CINAS).

Amaya, Rufina, Mark Danner, and Carlos Henríquez Consalvi. 2008. *Luciérnagas en El Mozote.* 8th ed. San Salvador: Museo de la Palabra y la Imagen.

Amnesty International. 2008, March 28. "The Missing Children of El Salvador." Available at www.amnesty.org. Accessed September 19, 2011.

Anderson, Benedict. 1983. *Imagined Communities: Reflections on the Origin and Spread of Nationalism.* London: Verso.

Andreas, Peter. 2012. *Border Games: Policing the U.S.-Mexico Divide.* Ithaca, NY: Cornell University Press.

Anker, Deborah E. 1992. "Determining Asylum Claims in the United States: A Case Study on the Implementation of Legal Norms in an Unstructured Adjudicatory Environment." *New York University Review of Law and Social Change* 19(3): 433–528.

Antze, Paul, and Michael Lambek, eds. 1996. *Tense Past: Cultural Essays in Trauma and Memory.* New York: Routledge.

Anzaldúa, Gloria. 1987. *Borderlands: La Frontera = The New Mestiza.* San Francisco: Aunt Lute.

Arias, Arturo, ed. 2001. *The Rigoberta Menchú Controversy.* Minneapolis: University of Minnesota Press.

———. 2012. "EpiCentro: The Emergence of a New Central American-American Literature." *Comparative Literature* 64(3): 300–315.

Arias, Enrique Desmond, and Daniel M. Goldstein, eds. 2010. *Violent Democracies in Latin America.* Durham, NC: Duke University Press.

Axel, Brian Keith. 2002. "The Diasporic Imaginary." *Public Culture* 14(2): 411–428.

———. 2004. "The Context of Diaspora." *Cultural Anthropology* 19(1): 26–60.

Baker-Cristales, Beth. 2004a. *Salvadoran Migration to Southern California: Redefining El Hermano Lejano.* Gainesville: University Press of Florida.

———. 2004b. "Salvadoran Transformations: Class Consciousness and Ethnic Identity in a Transnational Milieu." *Latin American Perspectives* 31(5): 15–33.

Basch, Linda, Nina Glick Schiller, and Cristina Szanton Blanc. 1994. *Nations Unbound: Transnational Projects, Postcolonial Predicaments, and Deterritorialized Nation-States.* New York: Routledge.

Bauböck, Rainer, ed. 1994. *From Aliens to Citizens: Redefining the Status of Immigrants in Europe.* Aldershot, UK: Avebury.

Bauman, Richard, and Charles L. Briggs. 1990. "Poetics and Performances as Critical Perspectives on Language and Social Life." *Annual Review of Anthropology* 19: 59–88.

Beccaria, Cesare. 1963. *On Crimes and Punishments.* Indianapolis: Bobbs-Merrill.

Behar, Ruth. 1993 (2003). *Translated Woman: Tenth Anniversary Edition.* Boston: Beacon Press.

———. 1996. *The Vulnerable Observer: Anthropology That Breaks Your Heart.* Boston: Beacon Press.

———. 2007. *An Island Called Home: Returning to Jewish Cuba.* New Brunswick, NJ: Rutgers University Press.

Benhabib, Seyla. 2004. *The Rights of Others: Aliens, Residents, and Citizens.* Cambridge: Cambridge University Press.

Benjamin, Walter. 1978. "Critique of Violence." In *Reflections: Essays, Aphorisms, Autobiographical Writings,* trans. Edmund Jephcott, 277–300. New York: Harcourt Brace Jovanovich.

Berdahl, Daphne. 1999. "'(N)Ostalgie' for the Present: Memory, Longing, and East German Things." *Ethnos* 64(2): 192–211.

Berg, Ulla. 2015. *Mobile Selves: Race, Migration, and Belonging in Peru and the U.S.* New York: New York University Press.

Betancur, John J., and Maricela Garcia. 2011. "The 2006–2007 Immigration Mobilizations and Community Capacity: The Experience of Chicago." *Latino Studies* 9(1): 10–37.

Beverley, John. 2004. *Testimonio: On the Politics of Truth*. Minneapolis: University of Minnesota Press.

Bhabha, Homi K. 1994. *The Location of Culture*. New York: Routledge.

Bhabha, Jacqueline. 2014. *Child Migration and Human Rights in a Global Age*. Princeton: Princeton University Press.

Binford, Leigh. 1996. *The El Mozote Massacre: Anthropology and Human Rights*. Tucson: University of Arizona Press.

Bissell, W. C. 2005. "Engaging Colonial Nostalgia." *Cultural Anthropology* 20(2): 215–248.

Bloemraad, Irene, Kim Voss, and Taeku Lee. 2011. "The Protests of 2006: What Were They, How Do We Understand Them, Where Do We Go?" In *Rallying for Immigrant Rights*, edited by K. Voss and I. Bloemraad. Berkeley: University of California Press.

Blum, Carolyn Patty. 1991. "Settlement of *American Baptist Churches v. Thornburgh*: Landmark Victory for Central American Asylum-Seekers." *International Journal of Refugee Law* 3(2): 347–356.

Boehm, Deborah A. 2011. "Here/Not Here: Contingent Citizenship and Transnational Mexican Children." In *Everyday Ruptures: Children, Youth, and Migration in Global Perspective*, edited by Cati Coe, Rachel R. Reynolds, Deborah A. Boehm, Julia Meredith Hess, and Heather Rae-Espinoza, 171–173. Nashville, TN: Vanderbilt University Press.

———. 2012. *Intimate Migrations: Gender, Family, and Illegality among Transnational Mexicans*. New York: New York University Press.

Boehm, Deborah A., Julia Meredith Hess, Cati Coe, Heather Rae-Espinoza, and Rachel R. Reynolds. 2011. "Introduction: Children, Youth, and the Everyday Ruptures of Migration." In *Everyday Ruptures: Children, Youth, and Migration in Global Perspective*, edited by Cati Coe, Rachel R. Reynolds, Deborah A. Boehm, Julia Meredith Hess, and Heather Rae-Espinoza, 1–19. Nashville, TN: Vanderbilt University Press.

Bohmer, Carol, and Amy Shuman. 2008. *Rejecting Refugees: Political Asylum in the 21st Century*. New York: Routledge.

Bonilla-Silva, Eduardo. 2014. *Racism without Racists: Color-Blind Racism and the Persistence of Racial Inequality in America*. Lanham, MD: Rowman and Littlefield.

Bosniak, Linda. 2006. *The Citizen and the Alien: Dilemmas of Contemporary Membership*. Princeton: Princeton University Press.

Boston College, Center for Human Rights and International Justice. Post-deportation Human Rights Project. 2011. *Returning to the United States after Deportation: A Guide to Assess Your Eligibility*. Newton, MA: Boston College. Available at www.bc.edu /centers/humanrights/projects/deportation.html. Accessed October 2, 2014.

Bourgois, Philippe. 2003. *In Search of Respect: Selling Crack in El Barrio*. 2nd ed. Cambridge: Cambridge University Press.

Brettell, Caroline B., ed. 2007. *Constructing Borders/Crossing Boundaries: Race, Ethnicity, and Immigration*. Lanham, MD: Lexington.

Brettell, Caroline B., and Faith Nibbs. 2009. "Lived Hybridity: Second-Generation

Identity Construction through College Festival." *Identities: Global Studies in Culture and Power* 16(6): 678–699.

Brockett, Charles. 2005. *Political Movements and Violence in Central America*. New York: Cambridge University Press.

Butler, Judith. 1993. *Bodies That Matter: On the Discursive Limits of "Sex."* New York: Routledge.

———. 2003. "Violence, Mourning, Politics." *Studies in Gender and Sexuality*, 4(1): 9–37.

———. 2009. *Frames of War: When Is Life Grievable?* London: Verso.

Byrne, Hugh. 1996. *El Salvador's Civil War: A Study of Revolution*. Boulder, CO: Lynne Rienner.

Cabot, Heath. 2013. "The Social Aesthetics of Eligibility: NGO Aid and Indeterminacy in the Greek Asylum Process." *American Ethnologist* 40(3): 452–466.

Calavita, Kitty. 1992. *Inside the State: The Bracero Program, Immigration, and the I.N.S.* New York: Routledge.

———. 1996. "The New Politics of Immigration: 'Balanced-Budget Conservatism' and the Symbolism of Proposition 187." *Social Problems* 43(3): 284–305.

Caldeira, Teresa Pires do Rio. 2000. *City of Walls: Crime, Segregation, and Citizenship in São Paulo*. Berkeley: University of California Press.

Carranza, Mirna E. 2007. "Building Resilience and Resistance against Racism and Discrimination among Salvadorian Female Youth in Canada." *Child and Family Social Work* 12: 390–398.

Cavanaugh, Jillian R. 2004. "Remembering and Forgetting: Ideologies of Language Loss in a Northern Italian Town." *Journal of Linguistic Anthropology* 14(1): 24–38.

Chacón, Jennifer M. 2007. "Unsecured Borders: Immigration Restrictions, Crime Control, and National Security." *Connecticut Law Review* 39: 1827–1891.

Chavez, Leo R. 1992. *Shadowed Lives: Undocumented Immigrants in American Society*. Fort Worth, TX: Harcourt Brace Jovanovich.

———. 2001. *Covering Immigration: Popular Images and the Politics of the Nation*. Berkeley: University of California Press.

———. 2003. "Immigration Reform and Nativism: The Nationalist Response to the Transnationalist Challenge." In *Perspectives on Las Américas: A Reader in Culture, History and Representation*, edited by Matthew C. Gutmann, Felix V. Matos-Rodriquez, Lynn Stephen, and Patricia Zavella, 418–429. New York: Wiley-Blackwell.

———. 2008. *The Latino Threat: Constructing Immigrants, Citizens, and the Nation*. Stanford, CA: Stanford University Press.

Chinchilla, Maya. 2007. "Desde el Epicentro." http://epicentroamerica.blogspot.com /2007/09/desde-el-epicentro.html. Accessed June 14, 2013.

———. 2014. *The Cha Cha Files: A Chapina Poética*. San Francisco: Kórima.

Chinchilla, Maya, and Karina Oliva Alvarado, eds. 2007. *Desde el EpiCentro: An Anthology of U.S. Central American Poetry and Art*. Los Angeles: Epicentro.

Cho, Grace M. 2008. *Haunting the Korean Diaspora: Shame, Secrecy, and the Forgotten War*. Minneapolis: University of Minnesota Press.

Churgin, Michael J. 1996. "Mass Exoduses: The Response of the United States." *International Migration Review* 30(1): 310–324.

Clifford, James. 1986. "Introduction: Partial Truths." In *Writing Culture: The Poetics and Politics of Ethnography*, edited by James Clifford and George E. Marcus, 1–26. Berkeley: University of California Press.

———. 1988. *The Predicament of Culture: Twentieth-Century Ethnography, Literature and Art.* Cambridge, MA: Harvard University Press.

Clifford, James, and George E. Marcus, eds. 1986. *Writing Culture: The Poetics and Politics of Ethnography.* Berkeley: University of California Press.

Coddington, Kate Shipley. 2011. "Spectral Geographies: Haunting and Everyday State Practices in Colonial and Present-Day Alaska." *Social and Cultural Geography* 12(7): 743–756.

Coe, Cati, Rachel R. Reynolds, Deborah A. Boehm, Julia Meredith Hess, and Heather Rae-Espinoza, eds. 2011. *Everyday Ruptures: Children, Youth, and Migration in Global Perspective.* Nashville, TN: Vanderbilt University Press.

Cole, David, and James X. Dempsey. 2006. *Terrorism and the Constitution: Sacrificing Civil Liberties in the Name of National Security.* New York: New Press.

Coleman, Mathew. 2007. "A Geopolitics of Engagement: Neoliberalism, the War on Terrorism, and the Reconfiguration of U.S. Immigration Enforcement." *Geopolitics* 12(4): 607–634.

Collier, Jane, and Sylvia Yanagisako, eds. 1983. *Gender and Kinship: Essays toward a Unified Analysis.* Stanford, CA: Stanford University Press.

Collier, Jane F., Bill Maurer, and Liliana Suárez-Navaz. 1996. "Sanctioned Identities: Legal Constructions of Modern Personhood." *Identities: Global Studies in Culture and Power* 2(1–2): 1–27.

Collyer, Michael. 2010. "Stranded Migrants and the Fragmented Journey." *Journal of Refugee Studies* 23(3): 273–293.

Comaroff, John L., and Jean Comaroff. 2009. *Ethnicity, Inc.* Chicago: University of Chicago Press.

Comfort, Megan. 2009. *Doing Time Together: Love and Family in the Shadow of the Prison.* Chicago: University of Chicago Press.

Contreras, Frances. 2009. "Sin papeles y rompiendo barreras: Latino Students and the Challenges of Persisting in College." *Harvard Educational Review* 79(4): 610–631.

Córdova Macías, Ricardo. 1993. *El Salvador: Las negociaciones de paz y los retos de la postguerra.* San Salvador: Instituto de Estudios Latino Americanos.

Cornelius, Wayne A., Philip L. Martin, and James F. Hollifield, eds. 1994. *Controlling Immigration: A Global Perspective.* Stanford, CA: Stanford University Press.

Corrunker, Laura. 2012. "'Coming out of the Shadows': DREAM Act Activism in the Context of Global Anti-Deportation Activism." *Indiana Journal of Global Legal Studies* 19(1): 143–168.

Corsín Jiménez, Alberto, and Rane Willerslev. 2007. "'An Anthropological Concept of the Concept': Reversibility among the Siberian Yukaghirs." *Journal of the Royal Anthropological Institute* 13: 527–544.

Coutin, Susan Bibler. 1993. *The Culture of Protest: Religious Activism and the U.S. Sanctuary Movement.* Boulder, CO: Westview.

———. 2000. *Legalizing Moves: Salvadoran Immigrants' Struggle for U.S. Residency.* Ann Arbor: University of Michigan Press.

———. 2001. "The Oppressed, the Suspect, and the Citizen: Subjectivity in Competing Accounts of Political Violence." *Law and Social Inquiry* 26(1): 63–94.

———. 2003. "Suspension of Deportation Hearings: Racialization, Immigration, and 'Americanness.'" *Journal of Latin American Anthropology* 8(2): 58–95.

———. 2005a. "Being en Route." *American Anthropologist*, 107(2): 195–206.

———. 2005b. "The Formation and Transformation of Central American Community Organizations in Los Angeles." In *Latino Los Angeles: Transformations, Communities, and Activism*, edited by Gilda Ochoa and Enrique Ochoa, 155–177. Tucson: University of Arizona Press.

———. 2007. *Nations of Emigrants: Shifting Boundaries of Citizenship in El Salvador and the United States*. Ithaca, NY: Cornell University Press.

———. 2011. "The Rights of Noncitizens in the United States." *Annual Review of Law and Social Science* 7: 289–308.

———. 2013. "In the Breach: Citizenship and Its Approximations." *Indiana Journal of Global Legal Studies* 20(1): 109–140.

Coutin, Susan Bibler, and Véronique Fortin. 2015. "Legal Ethnographies and Ethnographic Law." In *The Handbook of Law and Society*, edited by Austin Sarat and Patty Ewick, 71–84. Oxford: Wiley Blackwell.

Coutin, Susan Bibler, and Susan F. Hirsch. 1998. "Naming Resistance: Ethnographers, Dissidents, and States." *Anthropological Quarterly* 71(1): 1–17.

Coutin, Susan Bibler, Bill Maurer, and Barbara Yngvesson. 2002. "In the Mirror: The Legitimation Work of Globalization." *Law and Social Inquiry* 27(4): 801–843.

Cover, Robert M. 1986. "Violence and the Word." *Yale Law Journal* 95(8): 1601–1629.

Cruz Salazar, Tania. 2011. "Racismo cultural y representaciones de inmigrantes centroamericanas en Chiapas." *Migraciones Internacionales* 6(2): 133–157.

Darian-Smith, Eve. 2004. "Ethnographies of Law." In *The Blackwell Companion to Law and Society*, edited by Austin Sarat, 545–568. Malden, MA: Blackwell.

———. 2007. "Precedents of Injustice: Thinking about History in Law and Society Scholarship." *Studies in Law, Politics, and Society* 41: 61–81.

Dauvergne, Catherine. 2008. *Making People Illegal: What Globalization Means for Migration and Law*. Cambridge: Cambridge University Press.

de Certeau, Michel, Fredric Jameson, and Carl Lovitt. 1980. "On the Oppositional Practices of Everyday Life." *Social Text* 3(Autumn): 3–43.

Decker, Scott H., Paul G. Lewis, Doris M. Provine, and Monica W. Varsanyi. 2009. "On the Frontier of Local Law Enforcement: Local Police and Federal Immigration Law." *Sociology of Crime, Law, and Deviance* 13: 261–276.

de Genova, Nicholas P. 2002. "Migrant 'Illegality' and Deportability in Everyday Life." *Annual Review of Anthropology* 31: 419–447.

———. 2004. "The Legal Production of Mexican/Migrant 'Illegality.'" *Latino Studies* 2(2): 160–185.

de Genova, Nicholas, and Ana Y. Ramos-Zayas. 2003. *Latino Crossings: Mexicans, Puerto Ricans, and the Politics of Race and Citizenship*. New York: Routledge.

Délano, Alexandra, and Benjamin Nienass. 2014. "Invisible Victims: Undocumented Migrants and the Aftermath of September 11." *Politics and Society* 42(3): 399–421.

Deloria, Vine. 1969. *Custer Died for Your Sins: An Indian Manifesto*. Norman: University of Oklahoma Press.

DeLugan, Robin Maria. 2010. "Indigeneity across Borders: Hemispheric Migrations and Cosmopolitan Encounters." *American Ethnologist* 37(1): 83–97.

———. 2012. *Reimagining National Belonging: Post–Civil War El Salvador in a Global Context*. Tucson: University of Arizona Press.

Derrida, Jacques. 1992. "Force of Law: The 'Mystical Foundation of Authority.'" In *Deconstruction and the Possibility of Justice*, edited by Drucilla Cornell, Michel Rosenfeld, and David Gray Carlson, 3–67. New York: Routledge.

DeShazer, Mary K. 1994. *A Poetics of Resistance: Women Writing in El Salvador, South Africa, and the United States*. Ann Arbor: University of Michigan Press.

DeWind, Josh, and Philip Kasinitz. 1997. "Everything Old Is New Again? Processes and Theories of Immigrant Incorporation." *International Migration Review* 31(4): 1096–1111.

Diatta, M. A., and N. Mbow. 1999. "Releasing the Development Potential of Return Migration: The Case of Senegal." *International Migration*, 37: 243–266.

Dickson-Gómez, Julia. 2002. "The Sound of Barking Dogs: Violence and Terror among Salvadoran Families in the Postwar." *Medical Anthropology Quarterly* 16(4): 415–438.

———. 2003. "Growing Up in Guerrilla Camp: The Long-Term Impact of Being a Child Soldier in El Salvador's Civil War." *Ethos* 30(4): 327–356.

———. 2009. "Child Soldiers." In *Cultures of Fear: A Critical Reader*, edited by U. Linke and D. T. Smith. London: Pluto.

Dingeman-Cerda, Katie. 2014. "Bienvenidos a Casa? Deportation and the Making of Home in the U.S.-El Salvador Transnation." Doctoral dissertation, Department of Sociology, University of California, Irvine.

Dingeman-Cerda, Katie, and Susan Bibler Coutin. 2012. "The Ruptures of Return: Deportation's Confounding Effects." In *Punishing Immigrants: Policy, Politics and Injustice*, edited by Charis M. Kubrin, Marjorie S. Zatz, and Ramiro Martinez Jr., 113–137. New York: New York University Press.

Dowling, Julie, and Jonathan Inda, eds. 2013. *Governing Immigration through Crime: A Reader*. Stanford, CA: Stanford University Press.

Dreby, Joanna. 2012. "The Burden of Deportation on Children in Mexican Immigrant Families." *Journal of Marriage and Family* 74(4): 829–845.

———. 2013. "The Modern Deportation Regime and Mexican Families." In *Constructing Immigrant "Illegality": Critiques, Experiences, and Responses*, edited by Cecilia Menjívar and Daniel Kanstroom, 181–202. Cambridge: Cambridge University Press.

———. 2015. *Everyday Illegal: When Policies Undermine Immigrant Families*. Oakland, CA: University of California Press.

Duncombe, Stephen. 2007. *Dream: Re-Imagining Progressive Politics in an Age of Fantasy*. New York: New Press.

Dustmann, Christian, Samuel Bentolila, and Riccardo Faini. 1996. "Return Migration: The European Experience." *Economic Policy* 11(22): 213–250.

Eagly, Ingrid V. 2010. "Prosecuting Immigration." *Northwestern University Law Review* 104: 1281–1360.

Eig, Larry M. 1998. *The Nicaraguan Adjustment and Central American Relief Act: Hardship Relief and Long-Term Illegal Aliens.* Washington, DC: Congressional Research Service.

Ellermann, Antje. 2009. *States against Migrants: Deportation in Germany and the United States.* Cambridge: Cambridge University Press.

Emerson, Robert M., ed. 2001. *Contemporary Field Research: Perspectives and Formulations.* 2nd ed. Prospect Heights, IL: Waveland.

Entzinger, Han. 1985. "Return Migration in Western Europe." *International Migration* 23(2): 263–290.

Escobar, Mario. 2012. *Paciente 1980.* Turlock, CA: Orbis.

Espiritu, Yen Le, and Thom Tran. 2002. "'Viet Nam, Nuoc Toi' (Vietnam, My Country): Vietnamese Americans and Transnationalism." In *The Changing Face of Home: The Transnational Lives of the Second Generation,* edited by Peggy Levitt and Mary C. Waters. 367–398. New York: Russell Sage Foundation.

Esquivel, Paloma, Kate Linthicum, and Richard Simon. 2014, July 3. "New Flood of Immigrants Unsettles Some U.S. Towns." *Los Angeles Times,* pp. A1, A12.

Eyerman, Ron, and Bryan S. Turner. 1998. "Outline of a Theory of Generations." *European Journal of Social Theory* 1: 91–106.

Farmer, Paul. 1996. "On Suffering and Structural Violence: A View from Below." *Daedalus* 125(1): 261–283.

———. 2004. "An Anthropology of Structural Violence." *Current Anthropology* 45(3): 305–325.

———. 2005. *Pathologies of Power: Health, Human Rights, and the New War on the Poor.* Berkeley: University of California Press.

Farrell, Jeffry. 1995. "Culture, Crime, and Cultural Criminology." *Journal of Criminal Justice and Popular Culture* 3(2): 25–42.

Fassin, Didier. 2011. "Policing Borders, Producing Boundaries. The Governmentality of Immigration in Dark Times." *Annual Review of Anthropology* 40: 213–226.

Fix, Michael, and Wendy Zimmerman. 2001. "All under One Roof: Mixed-Status Families in an Era of Reform." *International Migration Review* 35: 397–419.

Flores, Araceli, and Christina M. Rodriguez. 2006. "University Faculty Attitudes on Affirmative Action Principles toward Faculty and Students." *Equity and Excellence in Education* 39(4): 303–312.

Foner, Nancy, and Joanna Dreby. 2011. "Relations between the Generations in Immigrant Families." *Annual Review of Sociology* 37: 545–564.

Funes, F. 2008. "Removal of Central American Gang Members: How Immigration Laws Fail to Reflect Global Reality." *University of Miami Law Review* 63: 301–337.

García, Angela S. 2014. "Hidden in Plain Sight: How Unauthorised Migrants Strategically Assimilate in Restrictive Localities in California." *Journal of Ethnic and Migration Studies* 40(12): 1895–1914.

García, María Cristina. 2006. *Seeking Refuge: Central American Migration to Mexico, the United States, and Canada.* Berkeley: University of California Press.

Gardner, Katy. 2012. "Transnational Migration and the Study of Children: An Introduction." *Journal of Ethnic and Migration Studies* 38(6): 889–912.

Garrod, Andrew, and Robert Kilkenny, eds. 2007. *Balancing Two Worlds: Asian American College Students Tell Their Life Stories.* Ithaca, NY: Cornell University Press.

Garrod, Andrew, Robert Kilkenny, and Christina Gómez, eds. 2007. *Mi voz, mi vida: Latino College Students Tell Their Life Stories.* Ithaca, NY: Cornell University Press.

Gellner, Ernst. 1983. *Nations and Nationalism.* Oxford: Blackwell.

Getrich, Christina M. 2008. "Negotiating Boundaries of Social Belonging: Second-Generation Mexican Youth and the Immigrant Rights Protests of 2006." *American Behavioral Scientist* 52(2): 533–556.

Gilad, Lisa. 1990. *The Northern Route: An Ethnography of Refugee Experiences.* St. John's, NL: Institute of Social and Economic Research, Memorial University of Newfoundland.

Gill, Lindsey J. 2013. "Secure Communities: Burdening Local Law Enforcement and Undermining the U Visa." *William and Mary Law Review* 54(6): 2055–2085.

Ginther, Donna K., et al. 2011. "Race, Ethnicity, and NIH Research Awards." *Science* 333(6045): 1015–1019.

Glick Schiller, Nina, Linda Basch, and Cristina Szanton Blanc. 1995. "From Immigrant to Transmigrant: Theorizing Transnational Migration." *Anthropological Quarterly* 61(1): 48–63.

Godoy, Angelina Snodgrass. 2002. "Lynchings and the Democratization of Terror in Postwar Guatemala: Implications for Human Rights." *Human Rights Quarterly* 24: 640–661.

———. 2005. "La Muchacha Respondona: Reflections on the Razor's Edge between Crime and Human Rights." *Human Rights Quarterly* 27(2): 597–624.

Golash-Boza, Tanya, and Pierrette Hondagneu-Sotelo. 2013. "Latino Immigrant Men and the Deportation Crisis: A Gendered Racial Removal Program." *Latino Studies* 11(3): 271–292.

Goldstein, Daniel. 2010. "Toward a Critical Anthropology of Security." *Current Anthropology* 51(4): 487–517.

Gómez, Laura E. 2012. "Looking for Race in All the Wrong Places." *Law and Society Review* 46(2): 221–245.

Gonzalez, Alfonso. 2009. "The 2006 Mega Marchas in Greater Los Angeles: Counter-Hegemonic Moment and the Future of El Migrante Struggle." *Latino Studies* 7: 30–59.

Gonzales, Roberto G. 2008. "Left Out but Not Shut Down: Political Activism and the Undocumented Student Movement." *Northwestern Journal of Law and Social Policy* 3(2): 219–239.

———. 2011. "Learning to Be Illegal: Undocumented Youth and Shifting Legal Contexts in the Transition to Adulthood." *American Sociological Review* 76(4): 602–619.

Gonzales, Roberto G., and Leo R. Chavez 2012. "Awakening to a Nightmare." *Current Anthropology* 53(3): 255–281.

Gooding-Williams, R., ed. 1993. *Reading Rodney King: Reading Urban Uprising.* New York: Routledge.

Goodwin, Jeff, James M. Jasper, and Francesca Polletta. 2000. "The Return of the Repressed: The Rise and Fall of Emotions in Social Movement Theory." *Mobilization: An International Journal* 5(1): 65–83.

Gordon, Avery F. 1997. *Ghostly Matters: Haunting and the Sociological Imagination.* Minneapolis: University of Minnesota Press.

Greene, Brian. 2004. *The Fabric of the Cosmos: Space, Time, and the Texture of Reality.* New York: Vintage.

Greenhouse, Carol J. 1996. *A Moment's Notice: Time Politics across Cultures*. Ithaca, NY: Cornell University Press.

———. 2008. "Life Stories, Law's Stories: Subjectivity and Responsibility in the Politicization of the Discourse of Identity." *PoLAR: Political and Legal Anthropology Review* 31(1): 79–95.

———, ed. 2011a. *Ethnographies of Neoliberalism*. Philadelphia: University of Pennsylvania Press.

———. 2011b. *The Paradox of Relevance: Ethnography and Citizenship in the United States*. Philadelphia: University of Pennsylvania Press.

Gupta, Akhil, and James Ferguson, eds. 1997. *Anthropological Locations: Boundaries and Grounds of a Field Science*. Berkeley: University of California Press.

Gurrola, María, Cecilia Ayón, and Lorraine Moya Salas. 2013. "Mexican Adolescents' Education and Hopes in an Anti-Immigrant Environment: The Perspectives of First- and Second-Generation Youth and Parents." *Journal of Family Issues*.

Guyer, Jane I. 2007. "Prophecy and the Near Future: Thoughts on Macroeconomic, Evangelical, and Punctuated Time." *American Ethnologist* 34(3): 409–421.

Halbwachs, Maurice. 1992. *On Collective Memory*. Edited and tranlsated by Lewis A. Coser. Chicago: University of Chicago Press.

Hall, Stuart. 1996. "Gramsci's Relevance for the Study of Race and Ethnicity." In *Stuart Hall: Critical Dialogues in Cultural Studies*, edited by David Morley and Kuan-Hsing Chen, 411–440. London: Routledge.

Haller, William, and Patricia Landolt. 2005. "The Transnational Dimensions of Identity Formation: Adult Children of Immigrants in Miami." *Ethnic and Racial Studies* 28(6): 1182–1214.

Hallett, Miranda Cady. 2014. "Temporary Protection, Enduring Contradiction: The Contested and Contradictory Meanings of Temporary Immigration Status." *Law and Social Inquiry* 39(3): 621–642.

Halliday, Terence, and Bruce Carruthers. 2007. "The Recursivity of Law: Global Norm Making and National Lawmaking in the Globalization of Corporate Insolvency Regimes." *American Journal of Sociology* 112(4): 1135–1202.

Hamber, Brandon, and Richard A. Wilson. 2002. "Symbolic Closure through Memory, Reparation and Revenge in Post-Conflict Societies." *Journal of Human Rights* 1(1): 35–53.

Hammar, Tomas. 1990. *Democracy and the Nation State: Aliens, Denizens and Citizens in a World of International Migration*. Aldershot, UK: Avebury.

Hamilton, Nora, and Norma Stoltz Chinchilla. 1991. "Central American Migration: A Framework for Analysis." *Latin American Research Review* 26(1): 75–110.

———. 2001. *Seeking Community in a Global City: Guatemalans and Salvadorans in Los Angeles*. Philadelphia: Temple University Press.

Hammond, Laura. 1999. "Examining the Discourse of Repatriation: Towards a More Proactive Theory of Return Migration." In *The End of the Refugee Cycle*, edited by R. Black and K. Koser, 227–244. New York: Berghahn.

Han, Sora. 2012. "The Long Shadow of Racial Profiling." *British Journal of American Legal Studies*, 1(1): 77–108.

———. 2015. *Letters of the Law: Race and the Fantasy of Colorblindness in American Law*. Stanford, CA: Stanford University Press.

Haney-López, Ian. 1996. *White by Law: The Legal Construction of Race*. New York: New York University Press.

Haraway, Donna. 1988. "Situated Knowledges: The Science Question in Feminism and the Privilege of Partial Perspective." *Feminist Studies* 14(3): 575–599.

Harris, Elizabeth Kay. 1993. "Economic Refugees: Unprotected in the United States by Virtue of an Inaccurate Label." *American University Journal of International Law and Policy* 9(1): 269–307.

Harvey, David. 2005. *A Brief History of Neoliberalism*. Oxford: Oxford University Press.

Hayden, Bridget A. 2003. *Salvadorans in Costa Rica: Displaced Lives*. Tucson: University of Arizona Press.

Hayduk, Ron. 2009. "Radical Responses to Neoliberalism: Immigrant Rights in the Global Era." *Dialectical Anthropology* 33: 157–173.

Hayes-Conroy, Jessica, and Allison Hayes-Conroy. 2010. "Visceral Geographies: Mattering, Relating, and Defying." *Geography Compass* 4(9): 1273–1283.

Hayner, Priscilla B. 1994. "Fifteen Truth Commissions—1974 to 1994: A Comparative Study." *Human Rights Quarterly* 16(4): 597–655.

Heiskanen, Benita. 2009. "A Day without Immigrants." *European Journal of American Studies*. Special Issue, Document 3. Available at http://ejas.revues.org/7717. Accessed July 23, 2012.

Hernández-López, Ernesto. 2010. "Guantanamo as a Legal Black Hole: A Base for Expanding Space, Markets, and Culture." *University of San Francisco Law Review* 45: 141–213.

Heyman, Josiah. 1999. "United States Surveillance over Mexican Lives at the Border: Snapshots of an Emerging Regime." *Human Organization* 58(4): 430–438.

Higham, John. 2002. *Strangers in the Land: Patterns of American Nativism, 1860–1925*. New Brunswick, NJ: Rutgers University Press.

Hing, Bill Ong. 2006. *Deporting Our Souls*. Cambridge: Cambridge University Press.

Hirsch, Susan F. 1998. *Pronouncing and Persevering: Gender and the Discourses of Disputing in an African Islamic Court*. Chicago: University of Chicago Press.

Hondagneu-Sotelo, Pierrette, and Ernestine Ávila. 1997. "'I'm Here, but I'm There': The Meanings of Latina Transnational Motherhood." *Gender and Society* 11(5): 548–571.

Horton, Sarah. 2008. "Consuming Childhood: 'Lost' and 'Ideal' Childhoods as a Motivation for Migration." *Anthropological Quarterly* 81(4): 925–943.

Hull, Elizabeth. 1985. *Without Justice for All: The Constitutional Rights of Aliens*. Westport, CT: Greenwood.

Hume, Mo. 2008. "The Myths of Violence: Gender, Conflict, and Community in El Salvador." *Latin American Perspectives* 35(5): 59–76.

Hyndman, Jennifer, and Alison Mountz. 2008. "Another Brick in the Wall? Neo-Refoulement and the Externalization of Asylum by Australia and Europe." *Government and Opposition* 43(2): 249–269.

Inda, Jonathan Xavier. 2006. *Targeting Immigrants: Government, Technology, and Ethics*. Malden, MA: Blackwell.

Jansen, Stef, and Staffan Löfving, eds. 2009. *Struggle for Home: Violence, Hope, and the Movement of People*. New York: Berghahn.

Jaycox, Lisa H., Bradley D. Stein, Sheryl H. Kataoka, Marleen Wong, Arlene Fink, Pia Escudero, and Catalina Zaragoza. 2002. "Violence Exposure, Posttraumatic Stress Disorder, and Depressive Symptoms among Recent Immigrant Schoolchildren." *Journal of the American Academy of Child and Adolescent Psychiatry* 41(9): 1104–1110.

Jefferies, Julián. 2014. "The Production of 'Illegal' Subjects in Massachusetts and High School Enrollment for Undocumented Youth." *Latino Studies* 12: 65–87.

Jenkins, Janis H. 1996. "The Impress of Extremity: Women's Experience of Trauma and Political Violence." In *Gender and Health: An International Perspective*, edited by Carolyn F. Sargent and Caroline B. Brettell, 278–291. Upper Saddle River, NJ: Prentice Hall.

———. 1998. "The Medical Anthropology of Political Violence: A Cultural and Feminist Agenda." *Medical Anthropology Quarterly* 12(1): 122–131.

Jiménez, Hortencia. 2011. "Factors Influencing the Re-Emergence of Immigrant Rights Coalitions in the United States." *Journal of Immigrant and Refugee Studies* 9(3): 267–290.

Johnson, Kevin R. 1996. "'Aliens' and the U.S. Immigration Laws: The Social and Legal Construction of Nonpersons." *University of Miami Inter-American Law Review* 28(2): 263–292.

Johnson, Kevin R., and Bill Ong Hing. 2007. "The Immigrant Rights Marches of 2006 and the Prospects for a New Civil Rights Movement." *Harvard Civil Rights–Civil Liberties Law Review* 42: 99–138.

Johnson, Reed. "Guided Guerrilla Tours Explore a Unique Side of El Salvador." *Los Angeles Times*. May 8. Available at www.latimes.com/travel/la-trw-et-wartours8may08 -story.html. Accessed February 16, 2016.

Jonas, Susanne, and Catherine Tactaquin. 2004. "Latino Immigrant Rights in the Shadow of the National Security State: Responses to Domestic Preemptive Strikes." *Social Justice* 31(1–2): 67–91.

Kansteiner, Wulf. 2012. "Moral Pitfalls of Memory Studies: The Concept of Political Generations." *Memory Studies* 5: 111–113.

Kanstroom, Daniel. 2000. "Deportation, Social Control, and Punishment: Some Thoughts about Why Hard Laws Make Bad Cases." *Harvard Law Review* 113(8): 1890–1935.

———. 2007. *Deportation Nation: Outsiders in American History*. Cambridge, MA: Harvard University Press.

———. 2012. *Aftermath: Deportation Law and the New American Diaspora*. Oxford: Oxford University Press.

Karakayali, Nedim. 2005. "Duality and Diversity in the Lives of Immigrant Children: Rethinking the 'Problem of the Second Generation' in Light of Immigrant Autobiographies." *Canadian Review of Sociology and Anthropology* 42(3): 325–343.

Kasinitz, Philip, John H. Mollenk, and Mary C. Waters, eds. 2004. *Becoming New Yorkers: Ethnographies of the New Second Generation*. New York: Russell Sage Foundation.

Kaufman, M. 2008. "Detention, Due Process, and the Right to Counsel in Removal Proceedings." *Stanford Journal of Civil Rights and Civil Liberties* 4: 113–147.

Kaye, Mike. 1997. "The Role of Truth Commissions in the Search for Justice, Reconciliation and Democratisation: The Salvadorean and Honduran Cases." *Journal of Latin American Studies* 29: 693–716.

Kearney, Michael. 1995. "The Local and the Global: The Anthropology of Globalization and Transnationalism." *Annual Review of Anthropology* 24: 547–565.

Kerwin, Donald, and Serena Yi-Ying Lin. 2009. *Immigrant Detention: Can ICE Meet Its Legal Imperatives and Case Management Responsibilities?* Washington, DC: Migration Policy Institute.

Kerwin, Donald, and Margaret D. Stock. 2007. "The Role of Immigration in a Coordinated National Security Policy." *Georgetown Immigration Law Journal* 21: 383–430.

Kim, Bryan S. K., Bradley R. Brenner, Chistopher T. H. Liang, and Penelope A. Asay. 2003. "A Qualitative Study of Adaptation Experiences of 1.5-Generation Asian Americans." *Cultural Diversity and Ethnic Minority Psychology* 9(2): 156–170.

Kim, Katherine Cowy, Alfonso Serrano F., and Leda Ramos, eds. 2000. *Izote Vos: A Collection of Salvadoran American Writing and Visual Art*. San Francisco: Pacific News Service.

King, Kendall A., and Gemma Punti. 2012. "On the Margins: Undocumented Students, Narrated Experiences of (Il)legality." *Linguistics and Education*, 23: 235–249.

Kleinman, Arthur, Veena Das, and Margaret M. Lock, eds. 1997. *Social Suffering*. Berkeley: University of California Press.

Kubrin, Charis E. 2014. "Secure or Insecure Communities?" *Criminology and Public Policy* 13(2): 323–338.

Latour, Bruno. 1999. *Pandora's Hope: Essays on the Reality of Science Studies*. Cambridge, MA: Harvard University Press.

Lauria-Santiago, Aldo, and Leigh Binford. 2004. *Landscapes of Struggle: Politics, Society, and Community in El Salvador*. Pittsburgh: University of Pittsburgh Press.

Lederman, Rena. 2006. "The Perils of Working at Home: IRB 'Mission Creep' as Context and Content for an Ethnography of Disciplinary Knowledges." *American Ethnologist* 33(4): 482–491.

Lee, Jennifer, and Frank D. Bean. 2010. *The Diversity Paradox: Immigration and the Color Line in Twenty-first Century America*. New York: Russell Sage Foundation.

Lister, Matthew J. 2007. "Gang-Related Asylum Claims: An Overview and Prescription." *University of Memphis Law Review* 38: 827–852.

Loftus, Elizabeth F. 1993. "The Reality of Repressed Memories." *American Psychologist* 48(5): 518–537.

Löfving, Staffan. 2009. "Liberal Emplacement: Violence, Home and the Transforming Space of Popular Protest in Central America." In *Struggle for Home: Violence, Hope, and the Movement of People*, edited by Stef Jansen and Staffan Löfving, 149–172. New York: Berghahn.

Loyd, Jenna M., and Andrew Burridge 2007. "La Gran Marcha: Anti-Racism and Immigrants Rights in Southern California." ACME: *An International E-Journal for Critical Geographies* 6(1): 1–35.

Lustig, Stuart L., Maryam Kia Keating, Wanda Grant Knight, Paul Geltman, Heidi Ellis, J. David Kinzie, Terence Keane, and Glenn N. Saxe. 2004. "Review of Child and Adolescent Refugee Mental Health." *Journal of the American Academy of Child and Adolescent Psychiatry* 43(1): 24–36.

Lynch, Mona, and Craig Haney. 2011. "Mapping the Racial Bias of the White Male Capital Juror: Jury Composition and the 'Empathic Divide.'" *Law and Society Review* 45(1): 69–102.

Madera, Gabriela, et al., eds. 2008. *Underground Undergrads: UCLA Undocumented Immigrant Students Speak Out*. Los Angeles: UCLA Center for Labor Research and Education.

Magaña, Rocio. Forthcoming. *Bodies on the Line: Migrant Exposure, Death, Abandonment, and Rescue on the Arizona-Mexico Border*. Durham, NC: Duke University Press.

Mahler, Sarah J. 1995. *American Dreaming: Immigrant Life on the Margins*. Princeton: Princeton University Press.

———. 2000. *Migration and Transnational Issues: Recent Trends and Prospects for 2020*. Working Paper #4. Hamburg: Institut für Iberoamerika.

Mannheim, Karl. 1959. "The Problem of Generations." In *Essays on the Sociology of Knowledge*, edited by Paul Kecskemeti, 276–320. London: Routledge and Kegan Paul.

Marcin, Joshua David. 2013. "Migrant Workers' Remittances, Citizenship, and the State: The Case of El Salvador." *Harvard Civil Rights–Civil Liberties Law Review* 48: 531–552.

Marcus, George E., and Michael M. J. Fischer. 1986. *Anthropology as Cultural Critique: An Experimental Moment in the Human Sciences*. Chicago: University of Chicago Press.

Martin, Philip. 1995. "Proposition 187 in California." *International Migration Review* 29(1): 255–263.

Martín-Baró, Ignacio. 1990. "Guerra y trauma psicosocial del niño salvadoreño." *Psicología social de la guerra: Trauma y terapia*, 234–250. San Salvador: UCA Editores.

Massey, Douglas S., Jorge Durand, and Nolan J. Malone. 2002. *Beyond Smoke and Mirrors: Mexican Immigration in an Era of Economic Integration*. New York: Russell Sage Foundation.

Maurer, Bill. 2006. "The Anthropology of Money." *Annual Review of Anthropology* 35: 15–36.

Maynes, Mary Jo, Jennifer L. Pierce, and Barbara Laslett. 2008. *Telling Stories: The Use of Personal Narratives in the Social Sciences and History*. Ithaca, NY: Cornell University Press.

McCarthy, John D., and Mayer N. Zald. 1977. "Resource Mobilization and Social Movements: A Partial Theory." *American Journal of Sociology* 82(6): 1212–1241.

McGuire, Connie. 2011. "Transnationalizing Gangs in the Americas: Advocacy, Expertise, and Policymaking." Doctoral dissertation, University of California, Irvine.

McGuire, Connie, and Susan Bibler Coutin. 2013. "Transnational Alienage and Foreignness: Deportees and Foreign Service Officers in Central America." *Identities* 20(6): 689–704.

Mendoza Aguilar, Gardenia. 2013, March 21. "Salvadoreños denuncian maltrato en México." *La Opinión*. Available at www.laopinion.com/Salvadorenos-denuncian-maltrato -centros-detencion-Mexico&template=print. Accessed April 17, 2015.

Menjívar, Cecilia. 2000. *Fragmented Ties: Salvadoran Immigrant Networks in America*. Berkeley: University of California Press.

———. 2002. "Living in Two Worlds? Guatemalan-Origin Children in the United States and Emerging Transnationalism." *Journal of Ethnic and Migration Studies* 28(3): 531–552.

———. 2006. "Liminal Legality: Salvadoran and Guatemalan Immigrants' Lives in the United States." *American Journal of Sociology* 111(4): 999–1037.

———. 2011a. *Enduring Violence: Ladina Women's Lives in Guatemala.* Berkeley: University of California Press.

———. 2011b. "The Power of the Law: Central Americans' Legality and Everyday Life in Phoenix, Arizona." *Latino Studies* 9(4): 377–395.

Menjívar, Cecilia, and Leisy Abrego. 2012. "Legal Violence: Immigration Law and the Lives of Central American Immigrants." *American Journal of Sociology* 117(5): 1380–1421.

Menjívar, Cecilia, and Daniel Kanstroom, eds. 2013. *Constructing Immigrant "Illegality": Critiques, Experiences, and Responses.* Cambridge: Cambridge University Press.

Merry, Sally Engle. 2000. *Colonizing Hawai'i: The Cultural Power of Law.* Princeton: Princeton University Press.

———. 2004. "Colonial and Postcolonial Law." In *The Blackwell Companion to Law and Society,* edited by Austin Sarat, 569–588. London: Blackwell.

———. 2009. *Human Rights and Gender Violence: Translating International Law into Local Justice.* Chicago: University of Chicago Press.

Mertz, Elizabeth 2007. *The Language of Law School: Learning to "Think Like a Lawyer."* New York: Oxford University Press.

Micieli-Voutsinas, Jacque. 2010. "What the City Re-members: Towards Mapping Visceral Memory Post-9/11." *Cities in Turmoil.* Available from the author.

———. 2013. "'Subaltern' Remembrances: Mapping Affective Approaches to Partition Memory." *Social Transformations* 1(1): 27–58.

———. 2014. "Contrapuntal Memories? Remembering the Holocaust in a Post-9/11 World." *Human Geography* 7(1): 49–68.

Milkman, Ruth. 2011. "Immigrant Workers and the Future of American Labor." *ABA Journal of Labor and Employment Law* 26: 295–308.

Miller, Teresa A. 2002–2003. "Citizenship and Severity: Recent Immigration Reforms and the New Penology." *Georgetown Immigration Law Review* 17: 611–666.

———. 2005. "Blurring the Boundaries between Immigration and Crime Control after September 11th." *Boston College Third World Law Journal* 25: 81–123.

Minow, Martha. 1999. *Between Vengeance and Forgiveness: Facing History after Genocide and Mass Violence.* Boston: Beacon.

Montgomery, Tommie Sue. 1995. *Revolution in El Salvador: From Civil Strife to Civil Peace.* Boulder, CO: Westview.

Moodie, Ellen. 2006. "Microbus Crashes and Coca-Cola Cash: The Value of Death in 'Free-Market' El Salvador." *American Ethnologist* 33(1): 63–80.

———. 2011. *El Salvador in the Aftermath of Peace: Crime, Uncertainty, and the Transition to Democracy.* Philadelphia: University of Pennsylvania Press.

Moore, Andrew. 2007–2008. "Criminal Deportation, Post-Conviction Relief and the Lost Cause of Uniformity." *Georgetown Immigration Law Journal* 22: 665–714.

Morales, Amanda, Socorro Herrera, and Kevin Murry. 2011. "Navigating the Waves of Social and Political Capriciousness: Inspiring Narratives from DREAM-Eligible Immigrant Students." *Journal of Hispanic Higher Education* 10: 266–283.

Morawetz, Nancy. 2000. "Understanding the Impact of the 1996 Deportation Laws and the Limited Scope of Proposed Reforms." *Harvard Law Review* 113(8): 1936–1962.

Morrill, Calvin, Christine Yalda, Madelaine Adelman, Michael Musheno, and Cindy Bejarano. 2000. "Telling Tales in School: Youth Culture and Conflict Narratives." *Law and Society Review* 34(3): 521–565.

Morton, John. 2011, June 17. "Memo from ICE Director John Morton to All Field Officers re 'Exercising Prosecutorial Discretion Consistent with the Civil Immigration Enforcement Priorities of the Agency for the Apprehension, Detention, and Removal of Aliens.'" Available at www.ice.gov/doclib/secure-communities/pdf/prosecutorial-discretion-memo.pdf. Accessed June 26, 2014.

Moss-Racusin, Corinne A., John F. Dovidio, Victoria L. Brescoll, Mark J. Graham, and Jo Handelsman. 2012. "Science Faculty's Subtle Gender Biases Favor Male Students." *Proceedings of the National Academy of Sciences* 109(41): 16474–16479.

Motomura, Hiroshi. 2006. *Americans in Waiting: The Lost Story of Immigration and Citizenship in the United States.* New York: Oxford University Press.

———. 2010. "What Is 'Comprehensive Immigration Reform'? Taking the Long View." *Arkansas Law Review* 63: 225–241.

———. 2014. *Immigration Outside the Law.* New York: Oxford University Press.

Mountz, Alison. 2010. *Seeking Asylum: Human Smuggling and Bureaucracy at the Border.* Minneapolis: University of Minnesota Press.

———. 2011. "The Enforcement Archipelago: Detention, Haunting, and Asylum on Islands." *Political Geography* 30: 118–128.

Mountz, Alison, Richard Wright, Ines Miyares, and Adrian J. Bailey. 2002. "Lives in Limbo: Temporary Protected Status and Immigrant Identities." *Global Networks* 2(4): 335–356.

Nance, Kimberly A. 2006. *Can Literature Promote Justice? Trauma Narrative and Social Action in Latin American "Testimonio."* Nashville, TN: Vanderbilt University Press.

National Immigration Law Center. 2014. "Frequently Asked Questions: Immigration Relief 2014–2015: Immigration Enforcement." Available at http://nilc.org/admin reliefenforcement.html. Accessed May 25, 2015.

Nelson, Diane M. 2009. *Reckoning: The Ends of War in Guatemala.* Durham, NC: Duke University Press.

Nevins, Joseph. 2002. *Operation Gatekeeper and Beyond: The Rise of the "Illegal Alien" and the Making of the U.S.-Mexico Boundary.* New York: Routledge.

Ngai, Mai. 2004. *Impossible Subjects: Illegal Aliens and the Making of Modern America.* Princeton: Princeton University Press.

Nicholls, Walter J. 2013. *The DREAMers: How the Undocumented Youth Movement Transformed the Immigrant Rights Debate.* Stanford, CA: Stanford University Press.

Nuñez, Anne-Marie. 2011. "Counterspaces and Connections in College Transitions: First-Generation Latino Students' Perspectives on Chicano Studies." *Journal of College Student Development* 52(6): 639–655.

Obasogie, Osagie K. 2014. *Blinded by Sight: Seeing Race through the Eyes of the Blind.* Stanford, CA: Stanford University Press.

Okamura, J. Y. 1981. "Situational Ethnicity." *Ethnic and Racial Studies* 4(4): 452–465.

Oliva Alvarado, Karina. 2009. *Transverse: Altar de Tierra, Altar de Sol.* Los Angeles: Izote.

———. 2013. "An Interdisciplinary Reading of Chicana/o and (U.S.) Central American Cross-Cultural Narrations." *Latino Studies* 11(3): 366–387.

Ong, A. 2003. *Buddha Is Hiding: Refugees, Citizenship, the New America.* Vol. 5. Berkeley: University of California Press.

Orange County Register. 2007. "ACLU Sues over Deportation of U.S. Citizen." June 12. Available at www.ocregister.com/articles/aclu-193333-guzman-deportation.html. Accessed October 7, 2014.

Orellana, Marjorie Faulstich. 2001. "The Work Kids Do: Mexican and Central American Immigrant Children's Contributions to Households and Schools in California." *Harvard Educational Review* 71(3): 366–389.

Orellana, Marjorie Faulstich, Barrie Thorne, Anna Chee, and Wan Shun Eva Lam. 2001. "Transnational Childhoods: The Participation of Children in Processes of Family Migration." *Social Problems* 48(4): 572–591.

Ostrow, Leslie A. 2002. "Parent Participation: Salvadoran and Guatemalan Immigrants' Involvement in Their Children's Schools." Doctoral dissertation, Heller School of Social Policy and Management, Brandeis University.

Ousey, Graham C., and Charis E. Kubrin. 2009. "Exploring the Connection between Immigration and Violent Crime Rates in U.S. Cities, 1980–2000." *Social Problems* 56: 447–473.

Padilla, Yajaira M. 2012. *Changing Women, Changing Nation: Female Agency, Nationhood, and Identity in Trans-Salvadoran Narratives.* Albany, NY: SUNY Press.

Paige, S. 2011. "Deportation, Due Process, and Deference: Recent Developments in Immigration Law." *Journal of Politics and Society* 22(2): 149–197.

Pantoja, Adrian D., Cecilia Menjívar, and Lisa Magaña. 2008. "The Spring Marches of 2006: Latinos, Immigration, and Political Mobilization in the 21st Century." *American Behavioral Scientist* 52(4): 499–506.

Pedersen, David. 2002. "The Storm We Call Dollars: Determining Value and Belief in El Salvador and the United States." *Cultural Anthropology* 17(3): 431–459.

Perea, Juan F., ed. 1997. *Immigrants Out! The New Nativism and the Anti-Immigrant Impulse in the United States.* New York: New York University Press.

Pérez Firmat, Gustavo. 1994. *Life on the Hyphen: The Cuban-American Way.* Austin: University of Texas Press.

Perla, Héctor, Jr. 2008. "Si Nicaragua Venció, El Salvador Vencerá: Central American Agency in the Creation of the U.S.–Central American Peace and Solidarity Movement." *Latin American Research Review* 43(2): 136–158.

———. 2014. "U.S. Foreign Policy Provoked Immigration Crisis." *San Francisco Gate.* July 12. Available at http://www.sfgate.com/opinion/article/U-S-foreign-policy -provoked-immigration-crisis-5616041.php. Accessed September 24, 2014.

Perla, Héctor, and Susan Bibler Coutin. 2010. "Legacies and Origins of the U.S.–Central American Sanctuary Movement." *Refuge* 26(1): 7–19.

Peterson, Ruth D., and Lauren J. Krivo. 2010. *Divergent Social Worlds: Neighborhood Crime and the Racial-Spatial Divide.* New York: Russell Sage Foundation.

Peutz, Nathalie, and Nicholas de Genova, eds. 2010. *The Deportation Regime: Sovereignty, Space, and the Freedom of Movement.* Durham, NC: Duke University Press.

Pine, Adrienne. 2008. *Working Hard, Drinking Hard: On Violence and Survival in Honduras*. Berkeley: University of California Press.

Piven, Frances Fox, and Richard Cloward. 1977. *Poor People's Movements: Why They Succeed, How They Fail*. New York: Pantheon.

Polletta, Francesca, and James M. Jasper. 2001. "Collective Identity and Social Movements." *Annual Review of Sociology* 27: 283–305.

Polletta, Francesca, and John Lee. 2006. "Is Telling Stories Good for Democracy? Rhetoric in Public Deliberation after 9/11." *American Sociological Review* 71(5): 699–721.

Popkin, Margaret. 2000. *Peace without Justice: Obstacles to Building the Rule of Law in El Salvador*. University Park: Pennsylvania State University Press.

Portes, Alejandro, and Rubén G. Rumbaut. 2001. *Legacies: The Story of the Immigrant Second Generation*. Berkeley: University of California Press.

———. 2005. "Introduction: The Second Generation and the Children of Immigrants Longitudinal Study." *Ethnic and Racial Studie*, 28(6): 983–999.

———. 2006. *Immigrant America: A Portrait*. Berkeley: University of California Press.

Portes, Alejandro, and Min Zhou. 1993. "The New Second Generation: Segmented Assimilation and Its Variants." *Annals of the American Academy of Political and Social Sciences* 530: 74–96.

Raj, Dhooleka Sarhadi. 2000. "Ignorance, Forgetting, and Family Nostalgia: Partition, the Nation State, and Refugees in Delhi." *Social Analysis* 44(2): 30–55.

Raustiala, Kal. 2009. *Does the Constitution Follow the Flag? The Evolution of Territoriality in American Law*. New York: Oxford University Press.

Richland, Justin B. 2008. *Arguing with Tradition: The Language of Law in Hopi Tribal Court*. Chicago: University of Chicago Press.

Riles, Annelise. 1998. "Infinity within the Brackets." *American Ethnologist* 25(3): 378–398.

———. 2000. *The Network Inside Out*. Ann Arbor: University of Michigan Press.

Rivas, Cecilia M. 2014. *Salvadoran Imaginaries: Mediated Identities and Cultures of Consumption*. New Brunswick, NJ: Rutgers University Press.

Robinson, William I. 2006. "'Aquí estamos y no nos vamos!' Global Capital and Immigrant Rights." *Race and Class* 48(2): 77–91.

Roche, Declan. 2005. "Truth Commission Amnesties and the International Criminal Court." *British Journal of Criminology* 45(4): 565–581.

Rodríguez, Ana Patricia. 2005. "'Departamento 15': Cultural Narratives of Salvadoran Transnational Migration." *Latino Studies* 3(1): 19–41.

———. 2009. *Dividing the Isthmus: Central American Transnational Histories, Literatures and Cultures*. Austin: University of Texas Press.

Rodriguez, Cristina. 2008. "The Citizenship Paradox in a Transnational Age." *Michigan Law Review* 106(6): 1111–1128.

Roque Ramirez, Horacio N. 2003. "'That's My Place!' Negotiating Racial, Sexual, and Gender Politics in San Francisco's Gay Alliance." *Journal of the History of Sexuality* 12(2): 224–258.

Rosaldo, Renato. 1980. *Ilongot Headhunting, 1883–1974: A Study in Society and History*. Stanford, CA: Stanford University Press.

Rosales, F. Arturo. 1997. *Chicano! A History of the Mexican American Civil Rights Movement*. Houston, TX: Arte Publico.

Rosas, Gilberto. 2006. "The Thickening Borderlands: Diffused Exceptionality and 'Immigrant' Social Struggles during the 'War on Terror.'" *Cultural Dynamics* 18(3): 335–349.

Rosenblum, Karen, Ying Zhou, and Karen Gentemann. 2009. "Ambivalence: Exploring the American University Experience of the Children of Immigrants." *Race, Ethnicity and Education* 12(3): 337–348.

Rumbaut, Rubén G. 2002. "Severed or Sustained Attachments? Language, Identity and Imagined Communities in the Post-Immigrant Generation." In *The Changing Face of Home: The Transnational Lives of the Second Generation*, edited by Peggy Levitt and Mary C. Waters, 43–95. New York: Russell Sage Foundation.

Rumbaut, Rubén G., and Alejandro Portes, eds. 2001. *Ethnicities: Children of Immigrants in America*. Berkeley: University of California Press.

Sampson, Robert J., Stephen W. Raudenbush, and Felton Earls. 1997. "Neighborhoods and Violent Crime: A Multilevel Study of Collective Efficacy." *Science* 277(5328): 918–924.

Sánchez, George. J. 1997. "Face the Nation: Race, Immigration, and the Rise of Nativism in Late Twentieth Century America." *International Migration Review* 31(4):1009–1030.

Santacruz Giralt, María. 2005. "Creciendo en El Salvador: Una mirada a la situación de la adolescencia y juventud del país." *Estudios Centroamericanos* 685–686: 1079–1099.

Sarat, Austin. 2014. *Gruesome Spectacles: Botched Executions and America's Death Penalty*. Stanford, CA: Stanford Law Books.

Sarat, Austin, and Thomas R. Kearns, eds. 1995. *Law's Violence*. Ann Arbor: University of Michigan Press.

SCAAN (Stanford Central America Action Network), eds. 1983. *Revolution in Central America*. Boulder, CO: Westview.

Scalia, John, and Marika F. X. Litras. 2002. *Immigration Offenders in the Federal Criminal Justice System, 2000*. Washington, DC: U.S. Department of Justice, Office of Justice Programs.

Scarry, Elaine. 1985. *The Body in Pain: The Making and Unmaking of the World*. New York: Oxford University Press.

Scheper-Hughes, Nancy. 1993. *Death without Weeping: The Violence of Everyday Life in Brazil*. Berkeley: University of California Press.

Schneider, David. 1968. *American Kinship: A Cultural Account*. Englewood Cliffs, NJ: Prentice Hall.

Schwab, Gabriele. 2006. "Writing against Memory and Forgetting." *Literature and Medicine* 25(1): 95–121.

———. 2010. *Haunting Legacies: Violent Histories and Transgenerational Trauma*. New York: Columbia University Press.

Schwarz, Benjamin C. 1991. *American Counterinsurgency Doctrine and El Salvador: The Frustrations of Reform and the Illusions of Nation Building*. Santa Monica, CA: Rand, National Defense Research Institute.

Seattle School of Law. 2008. *Voices from Detention: A Report on Human Rights Violations at the Northwest Detention Center in Tacoma, Washington*. Seattle: Seattle University School of Law International Human Rights Clinic in Collaboration with One America.

Seif, Hinda. 2011. "'Unapologetic and Unafraid': Immigrant Youth Come Out from the Shadows." *New Directions for Child and Adolescent Development* 134: 59–75.

Seron, Carroll, and Susan Silbey. 2004. "Profession, Science and Culture: An Emergent Canon of Law and Society Research." In *The Blackwell Companion to Law and Society*, edited by Austin Sarat, 30–59. Malden, MA: Blackwell.

Shachar, Ayelet. 2007. "The Shifting Border of Immigration Regulation." *Stanford Journal of Civil Rights and Civil Liberties* 3: 165–189.

———. 2009. *The Birthright Lottery: Citizenship and Global Inequality*. Cambridge, MA: Harvard University Press.

Silber, Irena Carlota. 2011. *Everyday Revolutionaries: Gender, Violence, and Disillusionment in Post-war El Salvador*. New Brunswick, NJ: Rutgers University Press.

Silk, James. 1986. *Despite a Generous Spirit: Denying Asylum in the United States*. Vol. 14, no. 10. Washington, DC: U.S. Committee for Refugees.

Simon, Jonathan. 2007. *Governing through Crime: How the War on Crime Transformed American Democracy and Created a Culture of Fear*. New York: Oxford University Press.

Siu, Lok C. D. 2005. *Memories of a Future Home: Diasporic Citizenship of Chinese in Panama*. Stanford, CA: Stanford University Press.

Smith, Andrea, Richard N. Lalonde, and Simone Johnson. 2004. "Serial Migration and Its Implications for the Parent-Child Relationship: A Retrospective Analysis of the Experiences of the Children of Caribbean Immigrants." *Cultural Diversity and Ethnic Minority Psychology* 10(2): 107–122.

Smith, Christian. 1996. *Resisting Reagan: The U.S. Central America Peace Movement*. Chicago: University of Chicago Press.

Smith, Derek. 1989. "A Refugee by Any Other Name: An Examination of the Board of Immigration Appeals' Actions in Asylum Cases." *Virginia Law Review* 75: 681–721.

Smith, Rogers M. 2014. "National Obligations and Noncitizens: Special Rights, Human Rights and Immigration." *Politics and Society* 42: 381–398.

Soto Espinosa, Angélica Jocelyn. 2014, September 15. "Centroamericanas enfrentan más discriminación en México." *Cimacnoticias*. Available at http://www.cimacnoticias .com.mx/node/67578. Accessed April 17, 2015.

Spener, David. 2009. *Clandestine Crossings: Migrants and Coyotes on the Texas-Mexico Border*. Ithaca, NY: Cornell University Press.

Spiro, Peter J. 2006. "Perfecting Political Diaspora." NYU *Law Review* 81: 207–233.

Stevenson, Andrew. 2004. "DREAMing of an Equal Future for Immigrant Children: State Initiatives to Improve Undocumented Students' Access to Postsecondary Education." *Arizona Law Review* 46: 551–580.

Strathern, Marilyn. 1999. *Property, Substance and Effect: Anthropological Essays on Persons and Things*. London: Athone Press.

———. 2004. *Partial Connections*. Walnut Creek, CA: Altamira Press.

Stumpf, Juliet P. 2006. "The Crimmigration Crisis: Immigrants, Crime, and Sovereign Power." *American University Law Review* 56(2): 368–419.

Suárez-Orozco, Carola, Marcelo M. Suárez-Orozco, and Irina Todorova. 2008. *Learning a New Land: Immigrant Students in American Society*. Cambridge, MA: Harvard University Press.

Suárez-Orozco, Marcelo M. 1987. "'Becoming Somebody': Central American Immigrants in U.S. Inner-City Schools." *Anthropology and Education Quarterly* 18(4): 287–299.

Suárez-Orozco, Marcelo M., and Carola Suárez-Orozco. 1995. *Transformations: Immigration, Family Life, and Achievement Motivation among Latino Adolescents.* Stanford, CA: Stanford University Press.

Taylor, Diana. 1997. *Disappearing Acts: Spectacles of Gender and Nationalism in Argentina's "Dirty War."* Durham, NC: Duke University Press.

Taylor, Margaret H. 1994–1995. "Detained Aliens Challenging Conditions of Confinement and the Porous Border of the Plenary Power Doctrine." *Hastings Constitutional Law Quarterly* 22: 1087–1158.

Taylor, Robert W., and Harry E. Vanden. 1982. "Defining Terrorism in El Salvador: 'La Matanza.'" *Annals of the American Academy of Political and Social Science* 463(1): 106–118.

Telles, Edward E. and Vilma Ortiz. 2008. *Generations of Exclusion: Mexican Americans, Assimilation, and Race.* New York: Russell Sage Foundation.

Terrio, Susan. 2015. *Whose Child Am I? Unaccompanied, Undocumented Children in U.S. Immigration Custody.* Berkeley: University of California Press.

Thiranagama, Sharika. 2011. *In My Mother's House: Civil War in Sri Lanka.* Philadelphia: University of Pennsylvania Press.

Thompson, E. P. 1963. *The Making of the English Working Class.* New York: Pantheon.

———. 1975. *Whigs and Hunters: The Origin of the Black Act.* London: Allen Lane.

Thompson, Ginger, and Sarah Cohen. 2014. "More Deportations Follow Minor Crimes, Records Show." *New York Times*, April 6.

Tilly, Charles. 1979. "Social Movements and National Politics." CRSO Working Paper #197. Ann Arbor: University of Michigan, Center for Research on Social Organization.

Tobar, Héctor. 1998. *The Tattooed Soldier.* New York: Penguin.

Trager, Glenn, and Susan Bibler Coutin. N.d. "Gaps between Membership and Belonging: Salvadoran Immigrant Youth and the Possibility of 'Common Law' Citizenship." Unpublished manuscript, in preparation.

Traweek, Sharon. 2009. *Beamtimes and Lifetimes: The World of High Energy Physicists.* Cambridge, MA: Harvard University Press.

Treyger, Elina, Aaron Chalfin, and Charles Loeffler. 2014. "Immigration Enforcement, Policing, and Crime." *Criminology and Public Policy* 13(2): 285–322.

Trubek, D. M. 1990. "Back to the Future: The Short, Happy Life of the Law and Society Movement." *Florida State University Law Review* 18: 1–55.

United Nations Global Forum on Migration and Development. 2010. "Partnerships for Migration and Human Development: Shared Prosperity–Shared Responsibility." Presented at the Fourth Meeting of the Global Forum on Migration and Development (GFMD), November 8–11, Puerto Vallarta, Mexico.

Urciuoli, Bonnie. 1999. "Producing Multiculturalism in Higher Education: Who's Producing What for Whom?" *Qualitative Studies in Education* 12(3): 287–298.

———. 2008. "Skills and Selves in the New Workplace." *American Ethnologist* 35(2): 211–228.

U.S. Department of Homeland Security, Office of Immigration Statistics. 2006. *2004 Yearbook of Immigration Statistics.* Available at www.dhs.gov/xlibrary/assets/statistics /yearbook/2004/Yearbook2004.pdf. Accessed September 17, 2015.

———. 2007. *Yearbook of Immigration Statistics: 2007.* Available at www.dhs.gov/ximgtn /statistics/publications/yearbook.shtm. Accessed March 16, 2009.

———. 2011. *Yearbook of Immigration Statistics: 2010.* Available at www.dhs.gov/files /statistics/publications/YrBk10En.shtm. Accessed July 20, 2011.

U.S. Department of Justice, Bureau of Justice Statistics. 2005. *Federal Justice Statistics, 2005—Statistical Tables.* Available at www.bjs.gov/content/pub/html/fjsst/fjso5st. cfm. Accessed September 18, 2015.

U.S. General Accounting Office. 1999. *Criminal Aliens:* INS' *Efforts to Identify and Remove Imprisoned Aliens Continue to Need Improvement.* February 25. Available at www.gao .gov/assets/110/107752.pdf. Accessed September 18, 2015.

U.S. House of Representatives. 1984. "Temporary Suspension of Deportation of Certain Aliens." Hearing before the Subcommittee on Immigration, Refugees, and International Law of the Committee on the Judiciary, House of Representatives, 98th Congress, Second Session on H.R. 4447. April 12. Washington, DC: U.S. Government Printing Office.

U.S. Immigration and Customs Enforcement. 2013. "ERO Annual Report: FY 2013 ICE Immigration Removals." Available at www.ice.gov/doclib/about/offices/ero/ pdf/2013-ice-immigration-removals.pdf. Accessed January 9, 2014.

Van Hook, Jennifer, Susan L. Brown, and Maxwell Ndigume Kewena. 2004. "A Decomposition of Trends in Poverty among Children of Immigrants." *Demography* 41(4): 649–670.

Varsanyi, Monica W. 2008. "Rescaling the 'Alien,' Rescaling Personhood: Neoliberalism, Immigration, and the State." *Annals of the Association of American Geographers* 98(4): 877–896.

———. 2010. *Taking Local Control: Immigration Policy Activism in U.S. Cities and States.* Stanford, CA: Stanford University Press.

Velloso, João Gustavo Vieira. 2013. "Beyond Criminocentric Dogmatism: Mapping Institutional Forms of Punishment in Contemporary Societies." *Punishment and Society* 15(2): 166–186.

Visweswaran, Kamala. 1994. *Fictions of Feminist Ethnography.* Minneapolis: University of Minnesota Press.

Vogt, Wendy A. 2013. "Crossing Mexico: Structural Violence and the Commodification of Undocumented Central American Migrants." *American Ethnologist* 40(4): 764–780.

Volpp, Leti. 2013. "Imaginings of Space in Immigration Law." *Law, Culture and the Humanities* 9(3):456–474.

Waldinger, Roger, and Cynthia Feliciano. 2004. "Will the New Second Generation Experience 'Downward Assimilation'? Segmented Assimilation Re-Assessed." *Ethnic and Racial Studies* 27(3): 376–402.

Walters, William. 2002. "Deportation, Expulsion, and the International Police of Aliens." *Citizenship Studies* 6(3): 265–292.

———. 2006. "No Border: Games with(out) Frontiers." *Social Justice* 33(1): 21–39.

Welch, Michael. 2002. *Detained: Immigration Laws and the Expanding INS Jail Complex.* Philadelphia: Temple University Press.

Wilkinson, E. 2010. "Examining the Board of Immigration Appeals' Social Visibility Requirements for Victims of Gang Violence Seeking Asylum." *Maine Law Review* 62: 387–419.

Wilkinson, Tracy. 2014. "Desperate to Go North: More Than Rumors Drive Central American Youths." *Los Angeles Times*, July 3, pp. A1, A8.

Williams, Raymond. 1977. *Marxism and Literature.* Vol. 1. Oxford: Oxford University Press.

Wilson, Richard. 2001. *The Politics of Truth and Reconciliation in South Africa: Legitimizing the Post-Apartheid State.* Cambridge: Cambridge University Press.

Wood, Elisabeth Jean. 2003. *Insurgent Collective Action and Civil War in El Salvador.* Cambridge: Cambridge University Press.

Wright, Melissa W. 2006. *Disposable Women and Other Myths of Global Capitalism.* New York: Routledge.

Yasso, Tara J., William A. Smith, Miguel Ceja, and Daniel G. Solorzano. 2009. "Critical Race Theory, Racial Microaggressions, and Campus Racial Climate for Latina/o Undergraduates." *Harvard Educational Review* 79(4): 659–691.

Yngvesson, Barbara. 2010. *Belonging in an Adopted World: Race, Identity, and Transnational Adoption.* Chicago: University of Chicago Press.

Yngvesson, Barbara, and Susan Bibler Coutin. 2006. "Backed by Papers: Undoing Persons, Histories, and Return." *American Ethnologist* 33(2): 177–190.

———. 2008. "Schrödinger's Cat and the Ethnography of Law." *PoLAR: Political and Legal Anthropology Review* 31(1): 61–78.

Zatz, Marjorie S., and Nancy Rodriguez. 2015. *Dreams and Nightmares: Immigration Policy, Youth, and Families.* Oakland: University of California Press.

Zavella, Patricia. 2011. *I'm Neither Here nor There: Mexicans' Quotidian Struggles with Migration and Poverty.* Durham, NC: Duke University Press.

Zilberg, Elana. 2004. "Fools Banished from the Kingdom: Remapping Geographies of Gang Violence between the Americas (Los Angeles and San Salvador)." *American Quarterly* 56(3): 759–779.

———. 2011. *Space of Detention: The Making of a Transnational Gang Crisis between Los Angeles and San Salvador.* Durham, NC: Duke University Press.

Zolberg, Aristide R. 1990. "The Roots of U.S. Refugee Policy." In *Immigration and U.S. Foreign Policy*, edited by Robert W. Tucker, Charles B. Keely, and Linda Wrigley, 99–120. Boulder, CO: Westview.

Zúñiga Núñez, Mario. 2010. "Heridas en la memoria: La guerra civil salvadoreña en el recuerdo de niñez de un pandillero." *Historia Crítica* 40(Jan-April): 60–83.

8–12. *See also* Salvadoran Civil War (1980–1992)

English as a second language. *See* ESL classes

Enríquez, Rocio, *18*

entextualization, 137

Epicentro, 122

ESL classes, 71–72, 74, 146, 178

ethnic categorization, 69–81

ethnic studies movement, 112

ethnography, 12–18, 50, 215–19

exclusion, 7–8, 56, 57, 58, 90, 92, 136, 157, 161, 167, 168, 200, 207–9, 212

families, effects of migration on, 63–69

family visas, 42, 155, 173, 174, 222–23

Farmer, Paul, 218

fear: children's, 67, 81, 148; of deportation, 107, 158, 176, 183; of detention, 157; of prosecution, 6, 41

Firebaugh, Marco, 106

Flores, William, *18*, 19–20

FMLN. *See* Frente Farabundo Martí para Liberación Nacional

Foro de São Paulo, 114

Freedom Rides, 108

Freire, Paulo, 119

Frente Farabundo Martí para Liberación Nacional (FMLN), 15, 22, 28, 51, 112

Fulfillment Fund mentoring program, 74

Funes, Mauricio, 28, 115

gangs: civil war trauma and, 31, 141; effect on neighborhoods, 56, 59–60, 77, 93, 156; membership in, 14, 67, 68, 109, 130, 142, 185–86, 220; Salvadoranness and, 11, 77, 101, 113–14, 126, 147, 187–88; violence of, 59–60; violence prevention program, 186

gap studies, 57, 89, 90–92, 94

Garcia, Maricela, 99

Golash-Boza, Tanya, 148

Gonzalez, Alfonso, 99

Gordon, Avery, 7

Grande, Rutilio, 27

green cards, 21–22, 45, 89, 145, 149–50, 153, 166, 176, 221

Greenhouse, Carol, 217–18

Guerra Vásquez, GusTavo, 122, 228–29

Han, Sora, 70

haunting, defined, 7

Heiskanen, Benita, 99

Hernández-Linares, Leticia, 120

"hibrideidades" (Guerra Vásquez), 122, 229

Homeland (film), 203

Homies Unidos, 13, 135, 186

homophobia, 195

Hondagneu-Sotelo, Pierrette, 148

Human Rights Ombudsry, 28

"hybrideities" (Guerra Vásquez), 122, 228–29

ICE. *See* U.S. Immigration and Customs Enforcement

identity: activism and, 99–100, 122; categories, 79–80; of deportees, 133; language and, 121–22; national, 124; politics, 112; of Salvadoran youth, 11, 79–80, 208; stereotypes, 114

identity documentation, 165–67

IIRIRA. *See* Illegal Immigration Reform and Immigration Responsibility Act (1996)

Illegal Immigration Reform and Immigration Responsibility Act (1996), 41, 43, 71, 102, 134, 139–40, 220

immigrants, Salvadoran: anti-immigrant sentiment, 71–72, 80–81, 102, 177, 205; generations, 7; marginalization of, 9, 17, 69, 90, 125, 212; reinserted subjects, 179–90, 210; rights movement, 99, 101, 105–6, 116, 223–25; scapegoating of, 4–5; segmented assimilation, 133. *See also* asylum seekers; economic immigrants; undocumented immigrants; youth, Salvadoran

Immigration Act (1990), 10, 42, 139

Immigration and Nationality Act (1965), 223

Immigration and Naturalization Service (INS), 137–38

immigration laws and policies: and asylum seekers, 40–49, 132, 134, 136, 137–40, 174–75, 208–9; and criminalization, 180; enforcement of, 10–11, 70, 148–49, 161, 206; securitization of, 7, 141, 153; vagaries of, 173–74; and youth, 25, 160–63

Immigration Reform and Control Act (1986), 21, 42, 45, 46, 70–71, 102, 139–40, 143

origins and, 169; policy implications, 219–24; by Salvadoran youth, 3, 5, 24, 90–91, 101–2, 198–201, 207, 208; temporality and, 211–12; testimonies and, 50, 204, 213, 216; violence and, 25–26
Revolution in Central America (SCAAN), 16
Rivas, Cecilia, 156–57
Rivera, Carolina, 52, 54
Romero, Carlos, 27
Romero, Oscar, 27, 31, 51, 196, 221
Rumbaut, Rubén G., 57–58

Salvadoran Civil War (1980–1992), 1–2, 9, 22, 23, 24–25, 26–33, 51, 193, 206, 211
Salvadoranness, 7, 11, 69–70, 79, 80–82, 101, 153, 190, 213
Salvadoran peace accords, 62
Salvador del Mundo celebration, 114
sanctuary movement, U.S., 2, 16–17, 219, 224–25
SAWS. *See* special agricultural workers
SCAAN. *See* Stanford Central American Action Network
schools. *See* education and schools
Secure Communities program, 43, 180
Sensenbrenner bill, 99
Siu, Lok, 191
slavery, 70
smuggling, 1–2, 22, 33, 35–36, 50, 64, 69, 158
social justice, 2, 71, 99–100, 124, 201, 214
solidarity workers, 1, 16, 42
special agricultural workers (SAWS), 42
Spiro, P. J., 156
Stanford Central American Action Network (SCAAN), 16
state terrorism, 4
Strathern, Marilyn, 12, 215
Students United to Reach Goals in Education (SURGE), 15, 95–96
suffering, social, 24
suicide, 157
SURGE. *See* Students United to Reach Goals in Education
surveillance, 4, 133

Tactaquin, Catherine, 99
Tattooed Soldier, The (Tobar), 55–56
Taylor, Diana, 4

Telles, Edward E., 69
temporality, alternative conceptualizations of, 211
Temporary Protected Status (TPS), 10, 13, 28, 42, 47–48, 102, 136, 139–40, 143, 176–78
territorial personhood, 143–44, 150–51
testimonies, 2, 6; in advocacy work, 15; as dissemination of knowledge, 12–13; in poetry, 120; re/membering and, 3–4, 50, 203, 214, 216; by students, 96, 105
Thiranagama, Sharika, 12
Tobar, Héctor, 55–56
TPS. *See* Temporary Protected Status
Tyler, Stephen, 12

undocumented immigrants, 1; in detention centers, 140, 149, 150, 152, 154, 162; exclusion and, 208, 213–14; higher education and, 87–88, 103–4; increased funding for removal of, 43; marginalization of, 90; stigmatization of, 176; student organizations, 104; violence toward, 23. *See also* DREAM Act; immigrants, Salvadoran
Unión Salvadoreña de Estudiantes Universitarios (USEU), 99, 101, 114–16
United National Global Forum on Migration and Development, 223–24
U.S. Census, 70
U.S. Citizenship and Immigration Services, 175
USEU. *See* Unión Salvadoreña de Estudiantes Universitarios
U.S. Immigration and Customs Enforcement (ICE), 148, 180

violence: accountability for, 220–21; among ethnic groups, 75; dismemberment and, 25–26; of gangs, 59–60; persecution and, 2, 16, 138; re/membering and, 5–6, 210; silence about, 24; social, 5–6, 7, 9–10, 49–50; structural, 218; toward deportees, 11
visas. *See* family visas; work permits
Voss, Kim, 99
voting rights, 110, 209

war on drugs, 140
"What's More American?" (Millet), 163–64